MANAGING RECORDS FOR ISO 9000 COMPLIANCE

Also available from ASQC Quality Press

LearnerFirst™ How to Implement ISO 9000 software
Developed by LearnerFirst, authored by Dr. Lawrence Wilson

ISO 9000: Preparing for Registration
James L. Lamprecht

ISO 9000 and the Service Sector: A Critical Interpretation of the 1994 Revisions
James L. Lamprecht

ANSI/ASQC Q9000-1994 Series Standards: Electronic Version for Windows
Developed by the Harrington Group

To request a complimentary catalog of publications, call 800-248-1946.

MANAGING RECORDS FOR ISO 9000 COMPLIANCE

EUGENIA K. BRUMM

ASQC Quality Press
Milwaukee, Wisconsin

Managing Records for ISO 9000 Compliance
Eugenia K. Brumm

Library of Congress Cataloging-in-Publication Data

Brumm, Eugenia K., 1943–
    Managing records for ISO 9000 compliance / Eugenia K. Brumm.
        p. cm.
    Includes bibliographical references and index.
    ISBN 0-87389-312-3 (alk. paper)
        1. ISO 9000 Series Standards—Documentation. 2. Records—
Management. I. Title.
    TS156.6.B78   1995   94-46885
    651.5'042—dc20   CIP

10 9 8 7 6 5 4 3 2 1

ISBN 0-87389-312-3

Acquisitions Editor: Susan Westergard
Project Editor: Kelley Cardinal

ASQC Mission: To facilitate continuous improvement and increase customer satisfaction by identifying, communicating, and promoting the use of quality principles, concepts, and technologies; and thereby be recognized throughout the world as the leading authority on, and champion for, quality.

For a free copy of the ASQC Quality Press Publications Catalog, including ASQC membership information, call 800-248-1946.

Printed on acid-free recycled paper

ASQC
Quality Press
611 East Wisconsin Avenue
Milwaukee, Wisconsin 53202

To my parents,
who have supported me in all of my ventures,
and to the memory of
Jim Goodwin

Contents

Figures and Tables

Figures

xvii

Tables

Preface

During my 16 years of experience in records management, in both a hands-on and an advisory capacity, I have learned that the records of most organizations are completely disorganized. Records usually are neglected, trivialized, and ill-managed. It seems that an external event is required to underscore the importance of records to an organization's well-being and survival. For the most part, unfortunately, many organizations establish records management programs only after costly litigation or the destruction of vital operating records, both of which could have been prevented had records management programs been in place.

In a quality environment, operating without a records management program can result in loss of business, erosion of client confidence, and citations for noncompliance. Operations can be stopped unless there is appropriate control over the records that document the processes and activities affecting quality.

Organizations today are finding that successful assessment for ISO 9000 compliance often depends on how well their records are managed and whether or not components of records management are included in their quality operations. Assessment by registrars is expensive, and, with 60 percent of companies failing to win immediate recommendation for registration, costs can soar. Areas of greatest failure tend to center around records and document control activities. Because records are cited in most of the paragraphs of the ISO 9000 series, they obviously are important.

It is often frustrating for organizations to know how to comply with the records requirements of the ISO 9000 series, because, for the uninitiated, the requirements are complex and time-consuming. This is especially true in those organizations that do not have a professional records manager and have no components of records management in place. The result can be confusion and panic.

Intended Audience

This book was written primarily to help quality managers, quality engineers, quality auditors, ISO 9000 coordinators, and others who are responsible for and involved with ISO 9000 compliance activities. Most of these individuals do not have the resources or internal expertise to undertake the extensive research needed to determine their recordkeeping requirements. Yet, they must comply with the ISO 9000 requirements if they want to be successfully registered and avoid adverse consequences. While organizations should create and maintain records because they need them for internal operations, the ISO standards require specific types of records for specific reasons, and they enumerate certain components of records management that must be in place.

This book should also appeal to records managers who currently operate records management programs in their organizations, and who would like to learn the requirements of the standards so that they can extend their expertise into the quality records arena. Because of the similarity between the components that are delineated in the ISO 9000 series and those components of records management that conventionally are practiced, many records managers are fully able to fulfill the records requirements of the standards. The quality terminology, however, may be foreign to many records managers. The text is presented in nontechnical layman's language, with detailed explanations, tables, and matrices. It is intended for those who would like to learn how to develop records management programs for quality records.

Scope

This book provides most organizations with the information they need to

- Determine their quality recordkeeping requirements

- Develop and implement successful strategies for satisfying the records requirements of ISO 9000

It clarifies the records and document control requirements of the standards and explains each section of the standards that specifically calls for the creation and maintenance of records and information that pertain to quality.

Two mistakes are usually made when the standards are deciphered for records requirements.

1. Readers search for the word *record* or its variants, and create a system around the activities that are delineated

2. Individuals will focus on only those sections of the standards that have the word *records* in the titles, such as "Quality Records," "Inspection and Testing Records," and the like.

It is important to understand that the standards, by their very nature, are distilled—condensed—in their wording. In this book, emphasis is placed on fleshing out the meaning of the condensed wording in the standards. Another common mistake is to confuse records management with document control. This book will define the differences and explain how the two operate in tandem.

This book provides advice on what kinds of records to create, how to organize them, how to maintain them, and how to use information technologies to minimize resource requirements. It also explains how to develop a retention schedule and a vital records program, two complex and time-consuming components of records management that are specifically mentioned in the standards. In addition, I have made suggestions about the kinds of information and data that are to be collected on each record type. Appendix G includes examples of quality records from some organizations that have successfully been registered under ISO 9000.

This book is not an overview or a text of records management. It is geared specifically to the records requirements that appear in the ISO 9000 series. Although many training seminars and conferences currently are being offered on the ISO 9000 series, none focuses exclusively on the records requirements of the standards, other than my own seminars. Furthermore, to the best of my knowledge, no book exists that deals with this topic in depth.

Throughout the course of this book, I have gone beyond the mechanics and have included explanations of the rationale for records within a quality context. Whenever possible, generalizations are supported with examples taken from the published literature and from personal experiences.

Objectives

The overall objective is to reveal to the reader a systematic, programmatic method of satisfying records requirements of the ISO standards. Frequently, the quality records in organizations that operate without records management programs are in such disarray that it is difficult for quality personnel to know where or how to begin, since records are not their main area of expertise. This book will present an orderly approach to the problem that can be easily followed and implemented. The book has the following objectives:

- Inform the reader about the records requirements in the ISO 9000 standards

- Review and interpret each of the paragraphs of the 1994 version of the ISO 9001/Q9001 standard that implies or specifically states a records requirement

- Present information on what to consider when attempting to satisfy the records requirements of the standards

- Present approaches that can solve the problems normally encountered with records in achieving compliance with the ISO 9000 series

- Explain how to plan, develop, and implement the various components of records management that are called for in the ISO 9000 series

- Educate quality personnel who may not realize that professional expertise already does exist for developing records management programs for quality records

- Provide some insights on the kinds of traps an organization might fall into when developing its records system

- Educate the reader on the various technologies and tools that are available to simplify records management tasks required in the ANSI/ISO/ASQC Q9000 standards
- Provide benchmarking for those organizations that will utilize a professional records manager, by explaining how the records manager should function in the management of quality records

Organization of the Book

The book has 16 chapters as well as appendices. Because American organizations, most likely, will be using the versions of the standards published by the American National Standards Institute and the American Society for Quality Control—ANSI/ASQC Q9000-1 through Q9004-1—the 1994 version of these standards will be referenced throughout rather than the ISO version. Also, because the most complete requirements appear in ANSI/ASQC Q9001-1994, that standard will be used as the reference point, and information will be provided linking the appropriate sections of the *Guidelines*—ANSI/ASQC Q9004-1-1994—to the Q9001 standard.

Chapter 1 provides a brief introduction to the records requirements of the ISO 9000 series and discusses the role of the records manager in the ISO 9000 environment. Chapter 2 emphasizes the important roles that records play in the quality environment, especially in satisfying ISO 9000 requirements. This chapter also provides some definitions and discusses the difference between *implied* and *specified* records in the standards. Chapter 3 provides instructions on where to begin—how to get started—so that the process is orderly and manageable. Chapters 4 through 14 look, in detail, at each section of the standard and explain what the records requirements are and how to fulfill them. Chapter 4 focuses on the development of a quality system and how this translates into records. It includes responsibilities that should be assumed by a records manager in order to facilitate the development process. Chapter 5 discusses the records requirements for design control and review, including verification and changes. In chapter 6, document control is explained, with a set of clear instructions on how to establish and implement a successful document control system. This chapter also includes information on the types of questions auditors frequently pose concerning document control systems.

Chapter 7 covers two topics, purchasing records and material identification and traceability records, with a discussion of their importance and role. Chapter 8, on process control records, reveals the interconnected nature of various types of quality records. Chapter 9 looks at the importance of inspection and testing records. Chapter 10 covers records relating to inspection, measuring, and test equipment, including the critically important records pertaining to calibration and inspection stamps. Chapter 11 addresses nonconforming product records and corrective and preventive action records, as well as the various roles played by records in this activity. Chapter 12 examines the section entitled "Quality Records" and elaborates on the indexing activity and how record format affects many records decisions. Time and resources required are also discussed. Chapter 13 discusses internal audit records, including recommendations for technology assistance. Chapter 14 looks at the importance of training records for all personnel in the quality arena. Again, the interrelationship between records is evident here. Chapter 15 provides an explanation of the soundness of an organization-wide records management program and presents alternatives in reporting structures. Chapter 16 concludes with instructions on developing a retention schedule and a records protection program. Chapters 4 through 14 also include tables that present the responsibilities of the records manager for that quality activity and also pose questions with which organizations can evaluate their records readiness.

Nine appendices are included at the end. Appendix A presents a self-evaluation questionnaire for organizations to use to determine their records readiness. Appendix B provides a list of records-related questions that are commonly posed by auditors. Appendix C includes a list of vendors of electronic document management systems and companies that provide additional services pertaining to electronic document management. Appendix D includes excerpts of articles that describe successful applications of electronic engineering document management systems. Appendix E contains information about the importance of adhering to a records retention schedule. Appendix F excerpts an article describing how Dean Witter Reynolds was able to resume its operations after the World Trade Center bombing in February 1992 because of its records protection program. Appendix G contains examples of quality records from those organizations that have successfully passed through the registration process. Appendix H includes examples of records from a commercial records storage facility. Appendix I provides additional sources—the names and addresses of organizations that have been mentioned in the book as well as the names of publications. The glossary presents a list of records management terms that have been used throughout this book.

Acknowledgments

I would like to thank those individuals who provided me with information and sources to include in this book. I am grateful to ABS Quality Evaluations, especially Bill Sullivan and principal auditor Tom Harris. I am also indebted to the quality managers who provided me with quality records to include, and for their expedient handling of permissions: Jerry Mills of Esco Corporation, Don Jones of EG&G Instruments, and Steve Hughes of FSSL. I am especially grateful to two gentlemen from The Dee Howard Company, who patiently spent hours with me discussing the design review process: Frank Rossi, the quality director, and Lewis E. Blomely, the design quality manager, who also willingly reviewed the chapter on design review.

Finally, I would like to thank the reviewers who provided helpful comments and recommendations, especially Thomas M. Kubiak who saw the project from beginning to end. Special thanks to Ira A. Penn, CRM, CSP, editor of *Records Management Quarterly*, who reviewed the manuscript and enthusiastically supported its publication.

Note About the Standards

This book was written to the 1994 version of the ISO 9000 standards. The issues that were used are the American National Standards, published by ASQC.* Because they are cited heavily throughout this publication, they are referred to only within the body of the text. Footnotes or references are not included at the end of each chapter for each quote taken from the standards themselves. They are referred to by their number in the text, for example, Q9001 and Q9004-1. The following are the standards that are so cited.

ANSI/ASQC Q9000-1-1994, *Quality Management and Quality Assurance Standards—Guidelines for Selection and Use*

ANSI/ASQC Q9001-1994, *Quality Systems—Model for Quality Assurance in Design, Development, Production, Installation, and Servicing*

ANSI/ASQC Q9002-1994, *Quality Systems—Model for Quality Assurance in Production, Installation, and Servicing*

ANSI/ASQC Q9003-1994, *Quality Systems—Model for Quality Assurance in Final Inspection and Test*

ANSI/ASQC Q9004-1-1994, *Quality Management and Quality System Elements—Guidelines*

---

*The standards may be ordered from ASQC by calling 800-248-1946.

CHAPTER 1

The Importance of Records Management Programs in Satisfying ISO 9000 Requirements

Introduction

Techniques, principles, and methods that have long fallen under the purview of records management are being required of organizations wishing to comply with the ANSI/ISO/ASQC Q9000 series of standards. Those organizations that take a fragmented approach toward satisfying the records requirements of the standards are marching down the wrong road. What they need is a compliance blueprint based on solid knowledge of conventional records management practices. When developing a cohesive records plan for the quality arena, the same preparatory steps must be taken and the same information must be gathered as for other administrative functions in the organization. Whether they be consultants or staff, trained, experienced records managers are needed for the task.

Conventional Records Management Components Required in ISO 9000

Activities that comprise the field of records management form the foundation for successful compliance with the records require-

1

ments of the standards. The concise statements in the ANSI/ISO/ ASQC Q9000 series, enumerating the elements pertaining to records, actually comprise major components of a complete records management program, each of which can take several years to develop and implement, depending on the size, age, and complexity of the organization. It stands to reason, therefore, that those organizations that currently have a records management program in place, or those that begin to address records issues before attempting qualification, are infinitely closer to satisfying the requirements, and they can do so less painfully and more successfully.

Grounded in orderly methods and proven approaches, records management provides a recipe for what to do, how to do it, and where to begin. Faced with chaotic conditions in quality records and unaware of how to proceed, an organization can perceive the entire process as formidable and depressing. It need not be so. Section 4.16 of Q9001 specifically includes the following records management components: records creation management, records retention development, vital records security, filing systems management, records centers management, development of organizing schemes, indexing, and knowledge of how and when to dispose of quality records.

> The supplier shall establish and maintain documented procedures for identification, collection, indexing, access, filing, storage, maintenance, and disposition of quality records . . . . All quality records shall be legible and shall be stored and retained in such a way that they are readily retrievable in facilities that provide a suitable environment to prevent damage or deterioration and to prevent loss. Retention times of quality records shall be established and recorded.

Depending on the types of media and technologies that are utilized to organize, store, and retrieve the quality records, by implication, this section also can include knowledge and management of micrographics, optical disk technology, and the integration of information technology tools. Some components that comprise the field of records management, identified in Figure 1.1, reveal that it is wise to take advantage of the professional discipline of records management in developing and implementing those aspects that will result in satisfactory compliance.

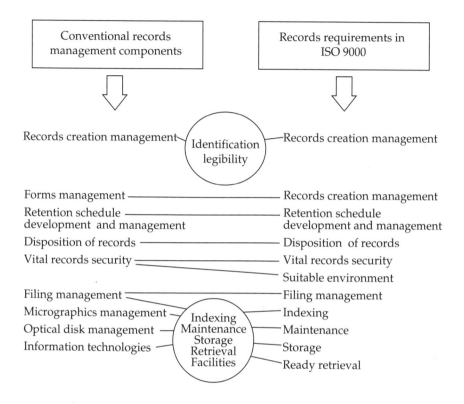

Figure 1.1. Records management compared with ISO records requirements.

Justification for the inclusion of the required ISO records components into one program is apparent, because all quality records have common interests and characteristics, regardless of their different types and, possibly, different media. All quality records are sources of information (whether on a temporary or permanent basis); all quality records document authority and actions that have been taken or are to be taken; all quality records are involved in proving the effectiveness of the quality system; and all quality records are subject to scrutiny during audits. Most questions by auditors revolve around the recorded information *about* activities that took place and are taking place in regard to product and service quality (see appendix B). Various statistics from different

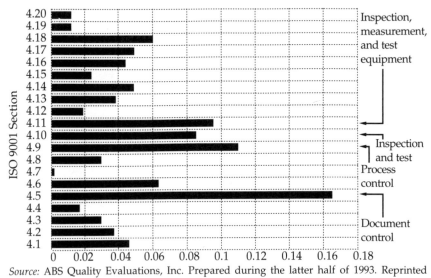

Source: ABS Quality Evaluations, Inc. Prepared during the latter half of 1993. Reprinted with permission.

Figure 1.2. Certification failure by ISO 9000 section.

sources reveal that about 60 percent of companies fail to win immediate recommendation for certification with most problems centering on document control.[1] Figure 1.2 reveals that, of those organizations failing initial assessment, more than 16 percent fail because of poor document control. The remaining failures are related, in part, to documentation in other areas, such as process, inspection, testing, and measurement.[2]

Identifying the failures by ISO standard section number, however, does not reveal the entire picture and can be misleading. Unaccustomed to isolating the specific reason for failure of a section, the examiners have clustered all failures pertaining to a section under that section number. For example, all discrepancies pertaining to purchasing—Section 4.6—are identified as Section 4.6 failures. The failures, however, most often involve records about purchasing activities or procedures that either are nonexistent or are not being controlled properly through document control. Table 1.1 reveals that, even though the failure may be part of

Table 1.1. Examples of Du Pont discrepancies.

1. Revision status of material specifications not described on purchase orders (ISO 9002, clause 4.5.3[b]).

2. Uncontrolled copies of procedure found to be in use (ISO 9002, clause 4.4.1).

3. Data base for limits in computer system does not agree with material specification 220002 (ISO 9002, clause 4.4.1).

4. Procedure T014 for receipt of solvent does not cover sampling. System provides no objective evidence of receipt of lab results prior to unloading (ISO 9002, clause 4.9.1).

5. Contract between Du Pont and Generic Trading Company does not show requirement for supplier to advise Du Pont prior to making changes to specifications as required by Du Pont Raw Material Acceptance Procedures (ISO 9002, clause 4.5.3). Records of visits to and from the Generic Trading Company do not adequately demonstrate effective operation of system (ISO 9002, clause 4.15 and 4.5.2).

6. Procedure regarding bill of lading preparation shown only for export shipments. DOT "shipping name" list had not been issued within document control system (ISO 9002, clauses 4.14.5 and 4.4).

7. There was no documented means of analyzing causes of need to retest lab samples (ISO 9002, clause 4.13[b])

8. No certificate of calibration was available for viscosity tube B49.

9. There was no documented procedure (e.g., QMP-010) to ensure timely corrective action on deficiencies found during internal audits (ISO 9002, clause 4.16).

10. Humidity control equipment in treating room not identified as to calibration status. No records relating to this were readily available [ISO 9002, clauses 4.10 and 4.15).

11. Inspection and test status was unknown on chemical drum #5, batch #5613, in #2 staging area (ISO 9002, clause 4.11).

12. Procedure documenting requirement for inspection of ingredient A and ingredient B and segregation of conforming and nonconforming material in area 7 clean room was unavailable (ISO 9002, clause 4.9.2).

13. System does not ensure that area 8 equipment and instrumentation are maintained in known calibration status. Devices identified as "quality critical" on production line were not part of formal calibration system, and records were unavailable showing status, results, procedures, etc. [ISO 9002, clause 4.10).

Source: George Dzus, "Planning a Successful ISO 9000 Assessment," *Quality Progress* (November 1991), 43–46. Reprinted with permission.

that section, the root causes are the failures in records and procedures.

Organizations have mistakenly named the activity as the problem, when the records pertaining to the activity are the true problem. For this reason, it behooves an organization to take a holistic approach toward its quality records, rather than to establish a network of isolated pockets of records, each one organized, identified, stored, and retrieved in a different manner, and each one managed by default, rather than overtly by an expert.

Records require a specific type of management. It is not sufficient to manage records in the same way as other forms of information, because they are a distinct category of information.[3] The management of records emanates to a degree from the life-cycle theory—that all recorded information has a life, similar to that of a biological organism, in that it is born (is created or received), it lives (is maintained and used), and it dies (is disposed of) (see Figure 1.3). Various components are associated with each of the phases, and functional activities are performed within each component.[4]

There are also interrelationships between the various elements. For example, the files element is interrelated with the development of organizing schemes; intellectual access to the records must correspond to the media and physical housing units that are used (see chapter 12 for discussion). In addition, the files element is interrelated with the records center elements; the amount of space needed for offsite records storage depends on the volume of records in the active files and the frequency with which they become inactive. This latter is also interrelated with retention schedule development; the time frames for active and inactive use are determined by developing a retention schedule. This brief example illustrates the fact that, because records management is an integrated program, it functions best when managed in a holistic way. In a quality environment, the interrelatedness of records and activities is very clear, and this becomes especially evident in the standards. The chapters in this book on individual sections of the standards elaborate this point and identify the codependence of quality activities on records that are required from various sections.

CREATION
forms
reports
drawings
copies
correspondence

DISPOSITION
destroy
discard
archive

DISTRIBUTION
internal
external

MAINTENANCE
storage
retrieval
active records
inactive records

USE
response
reference
decision making

Figure 1.3. Life cycle of records.

Dedicated Management of Quality Records

For administrative efficiency, organizational activities that permeate most or all departments within an organization have evolved into independent functions. The human resources department can serve as a good example of this point. Since each department within a company must deal with personnel issues such as hiring employees, counseling them, and releasing them, it is considered more effective to coordinate the efforts and activities through a single unit such as the human resources department. Its job is to ensure that standardization and similarities in approaches exist in all like activities within each department, and to provide professional expertise on human resources issues.

An analogy exists with records. Since records permeate (and often overwhelm) all departments in an organization, and the same activities must be carried out on all records (for example, retention schedule development), it makes good business sense to coordinate the management of records. This is especially true of quality records that will be the object of microscopic examination. Whether it is fair or not, the soundness and thoroughness of the quality system are judged, in large part, on the structure of the quality records system. The Q9001 standard, Section 4.1.2.3, requires the appointment of a

> member of the supplier's own management who . . . shall have defined authority for: a) ensuring that a quality system is established, implemented, and maintained in accordance with this American National Standard.

This is done to coordinate the disparate efforts and activities in the quality function, so that they all fluidly combine to result in a workable system that complies with the standards.

The same holds true for records management. For example, if each of the quality functions had responsibility for creation, maintenance, identification, retention, storage, and disposition of its own records, much duplication of effort would occur. The result would be either overlap of or gaps in the records and information. Sometimes both can and do occur. In addition, being responsible for the records management activities would require that each quality function become fluent in another professional field. Table 1.2 depicts the overlap in conducting some ISO records activities without a records manager. It is easy to see that each quality-related function is affected. Not only does such an arrangement result in lack of uniformity across all quality records, it diffuses the energies of individuals in those departments whose main purpose is not records management but, rather, operations management. Furthermore, since records experts are not employed in each department, ignorance about records issues is rampant. The following examples illustrate this point.

One company that operates with a paper-based quality records system recently contracted to have some of its records micro-

Table 1.2. Overlap of some records activities without quality records department.

FUNCTIONS	Retention schedules	Vital records	Indexing	Records storage	Dis-position
Contract administration	X	X	X	X	X
Purchasing	X	X	X	X	X
Design engineering	X	X	X	X	X
Each process	X	X	X	X	X
Inspection	X	X	X	X	X
Each testing function	X	X	X	X	X
Maintenance	X	X	X	X	X
Shipping	X	X	X	X	X
Internal auditing	X	X	X	X	X
Human resources	X	X	X	X	X

filmed, simply because it had run out of room to house them.[5] Only the overflow records are being microfilmed, and only one copy of the microfilm reel is being made. The company is not creating any index to images on the reel, and it plans to store the reels in-house, in what has been described as a fireproof file cabinet. A records manager would have made the following decisions in this case.

1. All quality records would have backup. Whether it be in the form of microfilm or hard copy would depend on the cost of the media and the use that is made of the records.

2. If the backup medium is microfilm, the reels would be stored offsite, in an environmentally controlled storage facility. There is no such thing as a fireproof file cabinet. Only fire-retardant file cabinets exist.

3. Some external access scheme would provide access to the records on microfilm. One reel of microfilm can hold approximately 3500–4500 records. Accessing records by viewing each record on the reel sequentially is a nightmare.

4. Microfilm might be suggested as the medium for active use of all quality records, such as is possible with computer-assisted retrieval (CAR) systems. Using a CAR system in this organization would solve all of the problems enumerated so far by providing rapid access to records through a computerized index, eliminating all of the paper records and saving space, and allowing backup reels to be made at very low cost.

The second example involves a large computer company that recently passed ISO registration.[6] As required, it developed a workable document control system but with one major drawback: All of the newly written documents exist in paper, requiring that the entire document control system be handled manually. The quality manager was not aware of electronic technologies that are designed specifically for document control and that greatly simplify the change, review, and distribution process. Both of these examples illustrate the kinds of poor records decisions that can occur when a records manager is not part of the quality function.

The quality records department should function as a hub around which the spokes of various quality records activities revolve, ensuring uniformity in records appearance, identification, organization, and so forth (see Figure 1.4). Such an approach also ensures a central contact for all records-related questions and problems. Organizations that operate without records management programs suffer the consequences. Even without any compliance standards, and regardless of ISO 9000, the lack of records management results in lower productivity, higher costs, and a myriad of other problems, some of them enumerated in Table 1.3. Perhaps no cost is as insidious as the *seek factor*. The seek factor is defined as those resources that an organization consumes looking for information. It includes cost, time, manpower, and qualitative elements such as frustration and loss of credibility and confidence. In one organization, the cost involved in looking for records for one seven-person department was calculated at $64,000 annually.[7] Even though they remain uncalculated in most organizations, such costs are built into operations, and they eat away at productivity and profit.

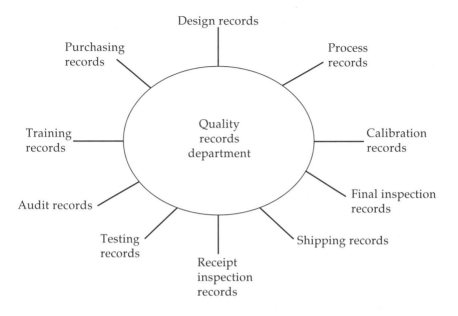

Figure 1.4. Quality records department as hub.

The Multiple Roles of the Quality Records Manager

In satisfying each of the records requirements of ISO 9000, the quality records manager plays multiple roles and has expanded responsibilities. Table 1.4 enumerates the main responsibilities, some of which are different from conventional records management practice. It is the job of the quality records manager to provide records education and training to each quality function, to advise in records design and creation, to ensure that all records requirements in the standards are being addressed, to become knowledgeable about the process and product records, and to make recommendations and institute changes for improving the overall quality records situation. The quality records manager thus functions as an internal consultant, providing advice and assistance to all quality-related units whose records must comply with the standards. The quality records manager should not be a mere custodian, passively collecting records that have already been created and used. Instead, the quality records manager should func-

---

Table 1.3. Results of no records management program in an organization.

- There is no protection of important information.
- The organization risks losing the suit if litigation occurs.
- There is too much delay in finding requested information.
- No distinction is made between active and inactive records.
- Important records are lost, either temporarily or permanently.
- Records are duplicated unnecessarily and maintained in more than one department.
- No policies exist covering the creation, retention, and disposition of records.
- No one knows what the appropriate equipment, supplies, and technologies are.
- No one knows how to evaluate and justify the purchase of new equipment, supplies, and technology for records.
- There is no control over forms, files, procedures, drawings, and so on.
- Too little space is devoted to maintaining and storing records.
- The costs of creating and maintaining records are not known.
- File folders, drawers, and shelves are messy and cluttered.
- Records personnel have no training program, resulting in poor work methods.
- No one understands the function of records, their importance, and the dependence of the organization on records.

---

tion proactively and become a member of the quality management team in the organization, a leader in quality compliance rather than a bystander.

This type of management of quality records emanates from the fact that records management has become increasingly complex, more complex than ever has been anticipated. As a result, it requires professional knowledge, expertise, and conduct. It is based on the supposition that upper management in the organization realizes this fact and does not marginalize its importance by relegating management of records to low-paid clerical talent.

Table 1.4. Responsibilities of the quality records manager in an ISO 9000 organization.

- Managing the quality records department
- Managing the document control center
- Writing records procedures and instructions
- Writing document control procedures and instructions
- Developing an identification scheme for records
- Developing a workable collection program for records
- Designing organizing schemes for records
- Selecting appropriate storage equipment and supplies
- Developing a retention schedule
- Developing a vital records protection program
- Identifying records and document control requirements in standards
- Acquiring and organizing industry specifications and standards as necessary
- Educating employees and managers about records requirements and systems
- Ensuring that the records audit trail is sound
- Monitoring quality records for accuracy and completeness
- Designing forms

The Quality Records Manager as Leader

The main responsibility of the quality records manager in the ISO 9000 environment is to identify and to become familiar with the records requirements in the standards. It is through this that all units documenting quality activities can receive valuable advice and assistance. If the organization has been in operation for a long time, it may believe that it has all of the records necessary for satisfactory complicance. However, part of the value of records professionals is their independence from individual units or operations. Objective evaluation of each category of records that the standards require then becomes possible. Evaluation is valuable for a number of reasons.

1. To verify that a record type exists for each record requirement in the standards

2. To ensure that the record type is appropriately identified

3. To examine if all of the data elements or information items that should be included do, in fact, appear on the record type

4. To ascertain if the records are being used

5. To determine if they are current

6. To learn if multiple versions of the same record type are being used concurrently

7. To ensure that the records are being filled out accurately and completely

8. To identify all locations where the records are being housed

9. To ascertain volume

10. To examine organizing schemes

11. To determine the relative importance of the record to the quality system

12. To unearth any problems that may exist, including retrieval problems

In essence, the quality records manager conducts an initial inventory or assessment of the quality records that do exist, resulting in the design of a foolproof records system that will meet the most stringent audit requirements. Because it is time-consuming, organizations make the mistake of trying to circumvent the inventory. Its value outweighs its cost, however, for it provides the quality department with a complete overview of its records, as well as a picture of how well the quality system functions. An inventory is grounded in the logic that, unless an organization knows what records it has, it cannot make any sound decisions about what it yet needs to do. Its importance cannot be overemphasized, for it is an opportunity to uncover all current quality records problems and to prevent future ones. For this reason, quality departments that are attempting ISO registration and have not yet addressed the issue of conducting an inventory of quality records usually have no idea what records they generate, collect, and retain. A records inventory provides all of the information necessary for the design and implementation of a records program that will lead to successful registration.

Designing (Creating) Quality Records. The initial inventory of quality records results in the preparation of a records improvement plan and also reveals preliminary information about records management components that remain undeveloped—retention schedules, vital records programs, organizing schemes, alternative technologies, and so forth (see chapter 16 for elaboration). The first activity will involve designing (creating) quality records where none exist. This provides the opportunity to develop a standard format and also to institute a records identification scheme that can serve as a model for all quality records.

Frequently, quality records already provide all of the information that is being specified in the standards, but the information may not exist in logical order in one or several records. A common weakness is to split the data elements across several record types, rather than to combine those elements on one record. It then appears that the records lack focus, because they do not provide all of the evidence in one location. This can be true of paper, as well as computer, records. It is easier and cleaner to incorporate all pertinent elements onto one record.

Records should be logical in information capture, professional in appearance, and readily identifiable. Designing records requires knowledge of the quality activity and of the standards themselves, to ensure the inclusion of all data elements. It is important to provide a clear indication of those data elements that are to be entered into each of the record spaces. Vagueness results in inaccurate information or in blank areas. Quality records should never be designed in a vacuum; the design should involve the users of the records, those who enter the information into the records, and other members of the quality team. Not all environments where records must be completed have typewriters, word processors, or computers. There may be instances where information must be entered by hand onto the record. Not only does this affect the design elements, it also requires that the records be readily available in the work area.

At this time, the quality department may elect to redesign its existing records to match the newly created ones and to eliminate those that are no longer pertinent. Combining information from several records that request redundant data not only reduces the number of record types, but also saves time by not requiring repetitive information. For this reason it is highly cost-effective. It is important at this stage to identify bootleg records in the quality operation—those records that are created, at random, by individuals on their computers, word processors, or typewriters. Every attempt should be made to weed them completely from the quality system or to incorporate them as official quality records. Bootleg records are especially troublesome during audits.

Identifying Records. On the basis of the initial assessment, the quality records manager will determine the identification needs of records. Titles and unique identifiers should appear on all quality records. Titles should be meaningful and should reflect the purpose of the record. Alphanumeric or numeric codes serve as unique identifiers for quality records, in addition to a revision number and date. Standardizing identification codes across all types of quality records is good practice. Frequently, the records are referenced in procedures and work instructions by their identifiers, and they are often attached to them as appendices. This is done to correlate the data collected and the record type with the activity described in the procedure.

The Quality Records Manager as Educator and Trainer

One of the most important roles that the quality records manager plays is that of educator and trainer. This holds true across all records activities, but in no place is it more important than in quality records completion and records collection. Each quality worker who is responsible for entering information onto a quality record, paper or electronic, must be fully knowledgeable about the importance of doing so and doing so correctly. Educating workers who complete the records is at the heart of a solid quality records system. If any special methods are developed, workers should be informed. An example might be that all errors are to be corrected with a one-line cross-through, and that these changes are to be initialed. Training should emphasize that the information the employees enter onto the records is as important as the work or activity that they are documenting. The correct completion of the record is a vital part of their job responsibility, and not just its paperwork byproduct. It becomes necessary to educate the managers as well as subordinates, since uncooperative managers can undermine the soundness of a records program.

Devising a workable method for collecting quality records also is an important responsibility of the quality records manager, and training personnel to follow the established collection procedures is key to a successful collection system. The type of system that is developed should be appropriate to the operating environment of the quality organization. In some organizations, a *satellite* method works well. Such a system provides for collection of quality records in the work areas where they are generated and used. If this is the system of choice, a designated records liaison is trained to organize and maintain the area's quality records, checking the records for completeness and appropriate recording techniques as they arrive. Depending on the volume of records, the records liaison function can be part of an individual's job responsibility. The quality records manager, however, must conduct the records training to achieve standardization across all records liaisons.

In some organizations, it is appropriate to send originals of all quality records to the quality records department to ensure a complete file of all pertinent records for decision making and to simplify audits. If this method is chosen, and area managers and employees have frequent need of the quality records, they can maintain copies for administrative need. It must be remembered, however, that these copies are themselves records and have to be organized and maintained as such, requiring training by the quality records manager. Furthermore, once the records have satisfied their retention requirements, it is important to dispose of them at the same time as the originals. If multiple, simultaneous use is required of quality records, the quality records manager may recommend an electronic records system, either a networked computer system or an optical disk system, or both. Regardless of the collection procedure that is developed for quality records, training those who complete and maintain the records is critical to successful implementation.

The Roles of the Quality Records Manager in Retention Schedule Development

Development of retention schedules is a mainstay of records management, and the quality records manager is uniquely qualified to spearhead and facilitate this task. Basing decisions partly on the initial assessment, partly on legal, regulatory, and statutory requirements, and partly on administrative need, the quality records manager can carve out a retention schedule to satisfy the most meticulous registration process. The quality records manager plays multiple roles in conducting this complex activity: leader, educator/trainer, internal consultant, researcher, and even enforcer.

As leader, the quality records manager defines the requisite activities for instituting a quality records retention schedule, spearheads the effort, and oversees the activities. Because departments and employees may be unaccustomed to having their records examined, important aspects of the quality records manager's role, again, are education and training. Explaining to department heads and other personnel the purpose of the activities and emphasizing the benefits that will accrue to each employee are necessary to expedite the task and alleviate fears that the organization is on a witch hunt. It is during this activity that the quality records manager directs purging and destruction of those records that serve no purpose, makes recommendations about scheduling removal of inactive records to offsite storage, and also examines alternative media and equipment for active and inactive records.

Conducting research into the retention times for quality records is a critical aspect of the quality records manager's position. Documenting the rationale behind the times selected and citing pertinent regulations provide the foundation for retention schedule decisions. Devising a plan, disseminating it, and enforcing it are responsibilities that the quality records manager assumes in managing the retention schedule. The schedule ensures that quality records are constantly being removed and destroyed when their retention times have been satisfied, and that, at the same time, those quality records that must be retained are, indeed, retained, and appropriate attention is devoted to them in the process. (See chapter 16 for instructions on how to develop a retention schedule.)

The Interdisciplinary Knowledge of the Quality Records Manager

In satisfying each of the records requirements of ISO 9000, the quality records manager must be able to perform interdisciplinary activities. Ensuring that records are readily retrievable, for example, the quality records manager must function as a diagnostician and problem solver. Making sure that records are retrievable involves knowledge of organizing schemes (including indexing), of equipment and technologies (such as micrographics, optical disks, and computer software), and of a record's use and the users themselves. After addressing the intellectual aspects of retrieval, in order to successfully implement the system, the quality records manager must function as an educator and trainer, to maximize understanding and ease of use. Any new or additional equipment needs place the quality records manager in the role of cost accountant, promoter, and public relations expert. In recommending new technology for records, the quality records manager conducts feasibility studies and makes presentations, oral and written, to senior management.

In developing a vital records security program, the quality records manager plays similar roles. This responsibility requires the quality records manager to explore alternative media and offsite storage facilities, including available disaster recovery services. Again, being knowledgeable about how to protect records from damage or loss, and informing employees and senior management about the selected methods, are educational, consulting, and leadership roles assumed by the quality records manager to ensure maximum effectiveness of the program (see Table 1.5).

Table 1.5. Activities of the quality records manager in developing retention schedules and vital records programs.

Records Management Component	Activities Involved
Retention schedule development	Conducting inventory
	Purging and destroying records
	Examining offsite storage facilities
	Conducting legal research
	Interviewing employees
	Consulting with legal counsel and managers
	Examining and recommending alternative media
	Conducting feasibility analyses
	Preparing the schedule
	Disseminating the schedule
	Adhering to plan
Vital records program	Identifying vital records
	Exploring alternative media
	Examining secure storage facilities
	Contacting disaster recovery services
	Developing a backup plan
	Disseminating the plan
	Educating employees and management
	Conducting trial runs

Conclusion

A professional records manager should be utilized throughout the entire ISO 9000 certification process. Doing so can save organizations countless hours of deciphering the records requirements of the ISO 9000 standards and implementing them. The professional field of records management can aid significantly in implementing ISO 9000 in an organization, make implementation much smoother, and increase the first-pass success rate.

Notes

1. The National ISO 9000 Support Group, *Preliminary Registrar Survey Results*, March 1993 (communication sent to the author).

2. Interleaf, *The Document Guide* (Waltham, Mass.: Interleaf, Inc., 1994), 73.

3. Ira A. Penn, Anne Morddel, Gail Pennix, and Kelvin Smith, *Records Management Handbook* (Brookfield, Vt.: Gower Publishing Co., 1994), 3.

4. Ibid., 9.

5. Author's own experience, December 1993.

6. Author's own experience, December 1993.

7. Author's own experience, spring 1990.

CHAPTER 2

The Role of Records in Compliance

Introduction

Records receive short shrift in most functions in most organizations. They are viewed as a necessary evil by some, as a wholly unnecessary evil by others; and at the very best they are tolerated, albeit grudgingly, with only token resources and personnel devoted to their creation, maintenance, retrieval, and disposition. Their importance is realized only when they cannot be found, when they need to be destroyed or conveniently lost to subvert evidence, or when they are subpoenaed, to be used in pending litigation.

In a quality environment, all activities that affect quality, from the development of a quality plan to the design of the product through the processing of materials that comprise the product to the manufacture or assembly of the completed items and even through shipment, must be recorded. As depicted in Figure 2.1, maintaining records is the only requirement in the standard that must be adhered to in every facet, in every activity. If there is any common thread that runs throughout the ISO 9000 standards, it is the emphasis on recording information that pertains to all aspects of quality. The main reason for this is that *frequently, the only evidence that attests to product quality resides in the information contained on the records.* In many cases, because it is impossible to

23

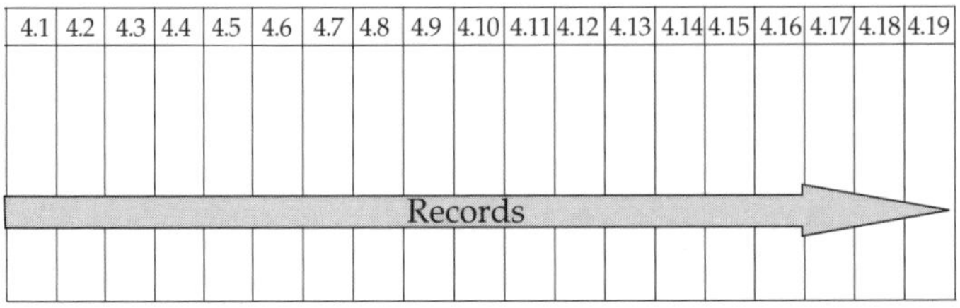

4.1	4.2	4.3	4.4	4.5	4.6	4.7	4.8	4.9	4.10	4.11	4.12	4.13	4.14	4.15	4.16	4.17	4.18	4.19

Records

Figure 2.1. Sections of ISO 9000 standards requiring records.

determine product quality simply by looking at the product, records are required to make determinations about whether or not the product has the level of quality that is required by the customer and that has been promised and intended by the organization. As a result, many decisions regarding the quality of a product are based on data alone—on the records.

The Roles of Records in a Quality Environment

The main roles that records play in a quality environment are as follows:

1. They provide evidence. This is probably their most obvious and strongest role and one that automatically comes to mind. When an airplane crashes, the first thing that the Federal Aviation Administration (FAA) examines, in addition to the black box, is the records, especially the aircraft maintenance records. The investigators want to know about the maintenance activities: What has been done to the aircraft? Who did it? When? Was it signed off? That evidence is considered to be more reliable and trustworthy than human memory, because the records provide or contain information that was recorded at or near the time of the event. For example, when an inspector visually inspects an item, the inspector is supposed to record the results of that inspection at the time of the activity or soon afterwards. The longer the time lag between the activity and recording the information about the activity, the less reliable the information. The reason for this is the fallibility

of human memory. Records are examined whenever anything of consequence malfunctions because they should contain evidence that either exonerates the organization or holds it accountable.

2. They provide confidence. By collecting and recording information about all activities that can affect product quality, the organization provides confidence to clients, customers, and regulatory authorities that it is, indeed, aware of the activities and personnel that affect quality and that it is ensuring that all is being done to create products of consistently high quality. The ongoing creation and maintenance of quality records provides confidence that the organization has produced high quality products in the past and that it is continuing that tradition. Perhaps most important for the continued health of the organization, records instill confidence that the organization will continue to produce high quality products in the future.

3. They demonstrate ability. Consistent recording of information that pertains to product quality and the analysis and use of that information can demonstrate to the external world that the organization has the ability to produce goods of high quality.

Quality records provide strong evidence mainly by inference. This aspect of records should not be underestimated. If records are sloppy, then it will be assumed that the process and the product are sloppy as well. If quality records are in disarray, if they are maintained poorly, if they are difficult or impossible to retrieve, if chaotic conditions surround their creation, maintenance, and use, then by implication, the quality system and the quality of the product is in question. In most cases, this will be true, because records reflect the level and depth of control and order that exists in the quality system. Records are also inferential in the following way: It is assumed that, if certain conditions are in place and information is recorded accurately about those conditions, then the resultant product, made under those conditions, has a certain level of quality. Table 2.1 provides examples of some categories of quality records that are inferential in nature.

Table 2.1. Examples of the inferential nature of quality records.

Category	Inferential Role	ISO Record Type
Personnel	Indicate that personnel were trained in the activities that they are required to perform	Training records
	Indicate that personnel received correct and current instructions to perform their activities	Document control records
Procedures	Reveal that instructions were written by knowledgeable individuals	Document control records
	Provide evidence that instructions have been distributed	Document control records
Manufacturing	Provide evidence that processes are being monitored	Process control records
	Prove that processes are being conducted within specified limits	Process control records

Records can and should be indicative of quality. They provide evidence about personnel, instructions, processes, and product performance. In order for records to serve the roles that they should play in a quality environment, they must be created for the variety of activities that affect and contribute to a high quality product. It is necessary first, to identify those activities and then to identify the types or categories of records that should be created and maintained. Once the types of records are identified, it is important to specify those information elements that must be collected and recorded.

The Characteristics of Records in a Quality Environment

The main function of records is to provide information about what has been done more accurately than is possible with human memory. Records are the necessary means for establishing facts and, as such, can serve as the most powerful tools that management possesses in a quality environment. With facts about actual performance at its disposal, management is in a position to compare the actual with the ideal and can chart its progress toward that ideal.

Records Must Be Accurate. Accuracy is the most important characteristic of quality records. It is the key characteristic that validates and substantiates the entire quality system. Unless the records are accurate, they cannot serve the purposes for which they are maintained, and nothing else is of any consequence.

Accurate records result, in part, from a workforce that is well trained in appropriate recording techniques and understands the critical importance of accuracy of the data on the records. For this reason, information should be recorded by a person who has knowledge of the event, usually the individual who performed the activity. In addition, accuracy depends on properly maintained and calibrated equipment and instruments. The underlying foundation of the calibration concept in a quality environment is to ensure that accurate data are recorded. In order to do so, all instruments, tools, machines, and so forth must be capable of recording the actual conditions under which the goods or materials were processed, manufactured, tested, inspected, and shipped. The basic question becomes one of data integrity: Is the information on the record an accurate description of the event? Is the information on the record what it purports to be?

How Inaccuracies Occur. Regardless of the environment, many things conspire to undermine the accuracy of records. Inaccuracies sometimes occur unintentionally, by accident, and other times they can be carefully planned and contrived. Human error is a major factor in the accidental recording of inaccurate information, and the causes are as numerous as the types of errors that occur. Fatigue, carelessness, and haste are but a few reasons that individuals accidentally check off the wrong box on a form or enter transposed numbers into a computerized system. Regardless of how careful and attentive individuals are, human errors do occur. Numbers are especially troublesome, and errors surrounding their input or recording are easy to make. Transposing numbers is a common problem, as is misreading figures on a gauge or caliper. Automated systems that capture numerical readings, entering them into a computer without human intervention, are more reliable. Information and data, however, that are captured automatically as a byproduct of instrument or process recording, can be inaccurate if the measuring devices are not reading correctly. Tool or instrument failure, thus, can be a cause for inaccurate records.

Another type of human error occurs by signing or dating the wrong line on a work order, and by neglecting to account for an unnecessary activity with N/A (not applicable). On a quality record, completing all blanks or fields is good practice, and employees should be trained to enter N/A adjacent to those items that are not pertinent to the product or order at hand. This practice eliminates the question of whether or not someone neglected to complete a step or to record some data. When N/A is used in such instances, it should always be signed and dated, so that any questions pertaining to its use can be resolved.

The most heinous types of inaccuracies are those caused by intentional deceit. This occurs for a variety of reasons. If an organization places little or no value on data integrity and accurate records, and if it does not allow sufficient time for individuals to record the information when it should be done, records that should have been created at or near the time of the event might not be created until well after the event has occurred. Even though correct information reported on records should be and is claimed to be part of many operating environments, often the emphasis is placed on product manufacture and timely delivery. Employees are pressured to focus on activities that are directly responsible for manufacture or assembly of items and are encouraged, overtly or covertly, to dispense with recording information, including sign-offs, at the time that the event occurs. In such instances, it is difficult, if not impossible, to remember the information with 100 percent accuracy. Records completed under such circumstances are highly suspect and carry little validity.

Situations in which individuals record information after the fact are not rare and carry consequences of varying degree. A common practice in one nursing home was to postpone the completion of required patient-care records until an impending inspection or audit. Employees would then be herded into a "records war room" and were directed to fill out masses of records over a period of days, purposely fabricating the data to pass the inspection.[1] In one such case, an employee who refused to participate was threatened with the loss of her job.

An even worse situation occurs when an organization intentionally falsifies information to prevent the identification of an inferior product. Instead of reworking or scrapping the product, the organization intentionally and falsely represents the product as being of high quality. In such instances, all activities that pertain to process and product must be identified, and the falsified information that has been recorded must coincide across the records. In other words, the audit trail must be completely covered, and that trail must be tight. In cases such as this, the organization deliberately sells a product that it knows will not perform in the manner that is required, by either the customer, the law, or sometimes both.

In addition to undermining the quality of similar products and bringing the credibility of the organization itself into question, deliberate inaccuracies on quality records can have long-term serious ramifications. It is not an exaggeration to state that human lives can even be at stake. Products that are purported to perform in a certain way under given circumstances can malfunction, since weaknesses and defects have not been identified or controlled properly.

The practice of purposely fabricating in-spec data on product quality is a direct result of shortsightedness on the part of the organization. Eager to meet promised shipment dates and quotas, organizations trivialize any activity that does not contribute to product manufacture, and, in fact, refer to such activities as *overhead*. Without accurate data, recorded at or near the time of the event, the organization has no way to identify those products that are either superior or inferior in quality. Without accurate information on records, the organization's ability to replicate the excellent product dies.

The emphasis on accuracy of quality records must originate at the highest levels within the organization and must filter down to each employee involved in quality-related activities. If records are regarded as a nuisance by the chief operating officer or the president, that attitude will be displayed in poorly kept information throughout the quality cycle.

Records Must Be Continuous. A second characteristic of good quality records is that they are continuous. Too often, quality records are viewed only in their limited one-dimensional role as pieces of evidence, as proof that the product has met customer specifications. To be continuous means that the records are kept without any break in the prespecified sequence or time frame during which a set of activities is being conducted. Continuous records kept over a long period of time cause facts to stand out boldly that might have gone unnoticed. Continuous records are especially important in process control. If information about the process is recorded haphazardly, not only can the quality of the end product be compromised, but the organization will be unable to detect weaknesses because of the lack of continuous information about the process.

Continuous records allow root causes to be detected more easily. They reveal, for example, if certain problems occur cyclically, during a certain shift, or during certain times of the month. If breaks in recording are the practice, it is extremely difficult to pinpoint patterns with any degree of confidence.

Records Must Be Used. The third characteristic of quality records is that they must be used. No matter how well and accurately records are kept, they are of little value unless management analyzes and studies them in relation to one another and is able to grasp their significance and act upon them. The most accurate records would become valueless if no use of them was ever made.

Most organizations collect records and never refer to them again. Approximately 90 percent of records are never consulted after their initial use.[2] This is especially true if the organization views the records as requirements, and if they are being created and maintained simply to satisfy externally imposed requirements, whether they be legal, regulatory, or standards compliance.

Most organizations tend to collect more information than they actually need in order to function effectively, and then never utilize the information in any meaningful way. Decision makers commonly complain that they need more information. Yet the fact remains that organizations actually have more information than they need in order to function at maximum effectiveness. They have too much information, maintain too many records for too long a period of time, and never seem to effectively make sense out of the records and information that they collect. Yet they appear to be constantly needing or requesting more information, or complaining about inadequacies in information.[3]

One reason for this is the lack of retrospective behavior and analysis that characterizes organizations in general and that specifically pertains to their records. For the most part, records can be retained in disarray or discarded for as much value as they have in the eyes of most organizations. If the adage, "History repeats itself," is at all true, it pertains as strongly to the chaos, weakness, and decline of organizations as it does to that of nations. The history of an organization is often vividly and accurately described in the records that it has maintained, often as by-products of operating. Studying, analyzing, and utilizing records will not only help organizations avoid repeating mistakes, but will also provide solutions that can lead to success through improved operations and superior products.

In general, organizations neglect to study the valuable information that has been collected as a normal part of their daily operations. For example, administrative records can help the organization improve various aspects of daily functioning, if the information they contain is analyzed and put to work. A good example is the invoice, a common administrative internal and external record, easily understandable by most.

Because invoices must be sent by an organization for every order shipped, they serve as an example of a record that is consistently created and routinely maintained over a period of time. The information that is necessary for the billing process often is not plotted or analyzed statistically over a long period. If it were, such information could not only reveal the anticipated accounting information, that is, customer credit information, but also provide data, for example, on shipping companies—which ones, perhaps, routinely take a longer time to deliver orders, or which ones deliver a greater percentage of damaged goods, or lose items most often. Administrative decisions can be based on such information, maintained consistently, over a period of time.

Providing improved customer service is important. However, if customer service can be improved by using the information that is collected as part of an ongoing activity, the opportunities to gain knowledge about product quality are even greater. With or without external requirements imposed by standards, maintaining records pertaining to process and product for quality control and analysis simply makes good business sense. The ability to operate from a base of facts rather than by rule of thumb is the edge that well-maintained quality records provide. It is important for an organization to know exactly what has happened in each of the steps or phases that contributes to final product. It is important that the information be recorded on an ongoing, continuous basis, rather than randomly, on occasion, in certain situations, or under certain circumstances. Only information from accurate records maintained consistently can reveal the exact workings of operations and can provide organizations with meaningful data upon which they can base their decisions.

Records, Documents, and Document Control

A great deal of confusion exists about the following terms: *record, document, documentation,* and *document control.* Without clearly understanding what each of these terms means, it is not possible to develop strong quality records systems and tight document control systems. To compound the confusion, the ISO standards use the terms interchangeably. Figure 2.2 presents an illustration, intended to clarify the definitions.

The following definitions for the term *record* are equally valid and, in reality, both apply.

1. The Association of Records Managers and Administrators (ARMA), in its glossary, defines a record as "recorded information, regardless of medium or characteristics, made or received by an organization that is useful in the operations of the organization."[4]

2. The *Records Management Handbook* defines a record as "any information captured in reproducible form that is required for conducting business."[5]

These definitions expand upon the traditional idea which views records as existing only in paper. Records may take the form of, for example, books, papers, maps, photographs, magnetic

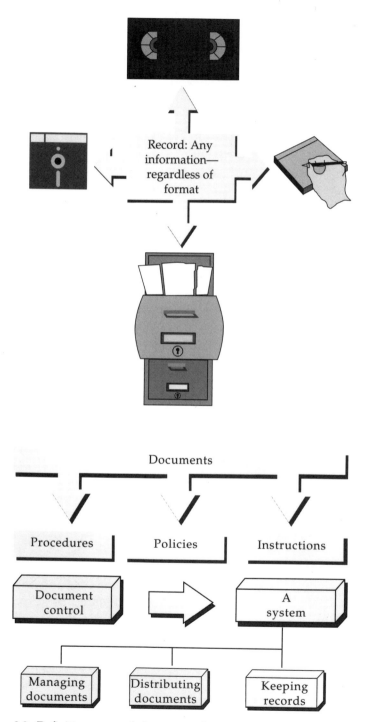

Figure 2.2. Definitions—*record, documents, document control.*

tapes, disks, optical disks, cards, microforms, aperture cards, computer printouts, engineering specifications, catalogs, pamphlets, brochures, advertising copy, galley proofs, and other items. The formats include any and all types, depending upon the nature of the organization or business. Today, most organizations automatically think of paper and micrographics (microfilm, microfiche, computer output microfiche/film [COM]) when they speak of records. Yet, increasingly, electronic records are forming an important part of many organizations. In addition, records are being maintained on optical disk systems to provide quick access to heavily retrieved information.

Documents, on the other hand, as the term is used in this book pertaining to the quality activities delineated in the ISO 9000 standards, denotes procedures, policies, instructions, or other written or graphically depicted methods or ways of conducting oneself or the operations in a given organization. They explain what an organization plans to do and what it intends to do, and they instruct employees on how to perform their tasks. They provide information about how the organization and its employees *should* operate. Documents are part of the larger framework of operating information within an organization. Unlike records, documents exist before the fact—providing guidelines, explanations, and instructions about how to operate. Records contain information about the activity and, thus, do not exist until after the activity has been performed. They come into being *after* the fact. The term *documents* is not synonymous with the term *records* in this book. Examples of quality documents are the quality manual, a procedure for fabricating metal wire product, or instructions for preparing shipping containers. Table 2.2 presents sanitized titles of actual controlled quality system documents.

Documentation, as it is used in the ISO standards, encompasses both records and documents. In some instances the term is used when the standards discuss records requirements, and in other instances it is used when they discuss documented procedures.

Document control is a system of managing documents, distributing documents, and keeping records on the documents that have been created by an organization as part of its overall quality system. Document control and records management are often con-

Table 2.2. Examples of controlled documents.

Marketing procedure—contract filling
Quality assurance records procedure
Operating procedure for the use of receipt inspection summary
Hazardous waste–handling procedure for waste solvents
Procedure for release of products for shipment
Operating procedure for packing strip
Process outline for rolled plate
Raw materials specification—chlorine
Document control procedure
Internal quality audit procedure

fused, because a complex series of records must be maintained about the document control system and these records, like those in other quality functions, are the only way to prove that a tight document control system has been established and is operating.

Use of the Terms in Standards

In the ISO series of standards, the words *recorded* and *documented* or *records* and *documentation* are used interchangeably, thus clouding the issue and contributing to the problem. There is a distinct difference between documents and records in the standards, as well as the activities that control them. Examples of quality records are depicted in Table 2.3. It can be seen that the records contain information about an activity that has already been conducted.

Difficulty arises when the standards discuss controls that should be applied to quality documents under the heading "Quality Records Control" in Section 17.3 of ANSI/ASQC Q9004-1-1994, *Quality Management and Quality System Elements—Guidelines*. The reverse also exists: the standards discuss quality records under the heading "Documentation of the Quality System" in Section 5.3 of ANSI/ASQC Q9004-1-1994. The situation would be much clearer if Section 5.3, "Documentation of the Quality System," actually presented a list of records for the document control system, rather than entered into another category. Records are controlled in a completely different way than documents are. Records control includes the following activities.

Table 2.3. Examples of quality records.

> Supplier corrective action request
> Corrective action request
> Calibration data record
> Nonconformance and disposition report
> Material report
> Project status minutes
> Audit reports
> Deviation request record
> Receipt inspection record
> Vendor inspection record
> Final inspection record
> Visual inspection record

- Controlling the proliferation of records—by instituting procedures to limit the number of copies that are made, by reducing the length of records, and so forth.

- Purging to reduce the number of items that are retained as records. Often nonrecords are retained—for example, outdated notices about the Christmas party, thank-you notes from colleagues. In addition, multiple copies of a record need not be retained and filed.

- Determining the retention times of records—analyzing the records for retention based on legal, fiscal, administrative, and historical needs.

- Deciding between inactive and active records and moving the inactive records to less expensive storage.

- Developing logical and efficient access schemes so that records can be retrieved quickly.

- Disposing of records that have satisfied their retention requirements.

- Ensuring that blank records are available to those who need to use them.

- Protecting records from deterioration and destruction.

Document control is a different function, and it includes the following set of activities:

- Reviewing and approving all quality plans, procedures, and instructions before they are issued.
- Formally distributing documents on a need-to-know basis.
- Creating and maintaining records that reveal which individuals or functions have been issued which documents.
- Retrieving obsolete and superseded documents from individuals and functions.
- Ensuring that revised documents have gone through the same review and approval process that the original documents have.

Records about the document control process can include

- Distribution lists for documents
- Master lists of documents
- Requests for documents
- Periodic reviews of documents
- Document change notices

In Table 2.4, the words *document, documented, documentation,* and *records* are selected from the ISO standards, and a translation is provided, clarifying the actual meaning of the words.

In the chapters of this book that discuss specific records requirements, these terms will also be explained.

The Concepts of Implied and Specified Records

Reading the ISO 9000 standards and deciphering the records requirements is not a straightforward task. It is mistakenly assumed that focusing on sections with titles such as "Records," and "Document and Data Control" and satisfying the requirements therein is sufficient for compliance. But it is important to understand the condensed, distilled nature of the wording in the standards, and it is equally important to understand that familiarity with the entire standard, in all of its sections, is mandatory for gleaning the records requirements.

It is erroneous to believe that the standards specifically state each time records are required, or that they enumerate the types

Table 2.4. Use of terms in ISO standards.

ISO Standard	Section	Words Used	Meaning
9000-1	4.9.1	procedures appropriately documented	documents
		processes implemented as documented	documents
	5.1	preparation and use of documentation	documents and records
		appropriate documentation	documents and records
	5.2	documentation of procedures	documents
	5.3	documentation is important	documents
		procedures are documented	documents
	5.4	combination of documentation and skills	documents
		extent of documentation	documents
		keep documentation to a reasonable level	documents
	8.3	documented evidence	unclear, probably documents and records
		quality system element should be documented	documents
9001	4.1.1	document its policy	documents
	4.1.2.1	defined and documented	documents
	4.1.3	records of such reviews	records
	4.2.1	establish, document and maintain	documents
	4.2.1	structure of the documentation	documents
	4.2.2	documented procedures	documents
	4.2.3	defined and document	documents
	4.2.3	shall be documented	documents
	4.2.3	preparation of quality records	records
	4.2.3	documented procedures	documents
	4.3.2	defined and documented	records
	4.3.4	records of contract review	records
	4.4.1	documented procedures	documents
	4.4.3	necessary information documented	records
	4.4.4	identified, documented	records
	4.4.5	output shall be documented	records
	4.4.5	design output documents	documents and records
	4.4.6	documented reviews	records
	4.4.6	records of such reviews	records
	4.4.7	shall be recorded	records
	4.4.7	design stage documents	records

Table 2.4. Continued.

ISO Standard	Section	Words Used	Meaning
9001	4.4.9	identified, documented	records
	4.5	document and data control (title)	confusing ** documents and records
	4.5.1	documented procedures	documents
	4.5.1	control all documents and data	documents and records**
	4.5.1	documents of external origin	industry standards and specifications, customer specifications, etc.
	4.5.2	documents and data shall be reviewed	documents and records**
	4.5.2	current revision status of documents	documents
	4.5.2	obsolete documents	documents
	4.5.2	appropriate documents	documents
	4.5.2	invalid or obsolete documents	documents
	4.5.2	any obsolete documents	documents
	4.5.3	changes to documents and data	documents and records**
	4.5.3	in the document	documents
	4.6.1	documented procedures	documents
	4.6.2	quality records	records
	4.6.2	records of acceptable subcontractors	records
	4.6.3	purchasing documents	records
	4.6.3	approve purchasing documents	records
	4.6.4.1	in the purchasing documents	records
	4.7	documented procedures	documents
	4.7	shall be recorded	records
	4.8	documented procedures	documents
	4.8	shall be recorded	records
	4.9(a)	documented procedures	documents
	4.9(c)	documented procedures	documents
	4.9	records shall be maintained	records
	4.10.1	documented procedures	documents
	4.10.1	records to be established	records
	4.10.1	plan or documented procedures	recorded in quality plan
	4.10.2.1	documented procedures	documents
	4.10.2.2	recorded evidence	records
	4.10.2.3	identified and recorded	records

** See discussion in chapter 2.

Table 2.4. Continued.

ISO Standard	Section	Words Used	Meaning
9001	4.10.3(a)	documented procedures	documents
	4.10.4	documented procedures	documents
	4.10.4	associated data and documentation	records
	4.10.5	maintain records	records
	4.10.5	records shall show	records
	4.10.5	records shall identify	records
	4.11.1	documented procedures	documents
	4.11.1	shall maintain records	records
	4.11.2(b)	calibration shall be documented	recorded
	4.11.2(d)	identification record	records
	4.11.2(e)	calibration records	records
	4.11.2(f)	assess and document	records
	4.12	documented procedures	documents
	4.13.1	documented procedures	documents
	4.13.1	documentation, evaluation	records
	4.13.2	documented procedures	documents
	4.13.2	shall be recorded	records
	4.14.1	documented procedures	documents
	4.14.1	record any changes	records
	4.14.2(b)	recording the results	records
	4.15.1	documented procedures	documents
	4.16	documented procedures	documents
	4.16	quality records	records
	4.16	data	records
	4.17	documented procedures	documents
	4.17	shall be recorded	records
	4.17	record the implementation	records
	4.18	documented procedures	documents
	4.18	records of training	records
	4.19	documented procedures	documents
	4.20.2	documented procedures	documents
9004-1	4.2	document its quality policy	documents
	4.3.1	should document objectives	documents
	5.2.5	documented operational procedures	documents
	5.2.5	documented procedures	documents
	5.2.6	documented procedures	documents
	5.3	documentation (in title)	unclear
	5.3.1	documented in a systematic manner	documents
	5.3.1	limit documentation	documents (?)
	5.3.1	all quality documents	records and documents

Table 2.4. Continued.

ISO Standard	Section	Words Used	Meaning
9004-1	5.3.2	quality system documentation (title)	probably documents
	5.3.2.1	main document	document
	5.3.2.3	documented procedures	documents
	5.3.2.4	documented quality system procedures	documents
	5.3.2.4	document procedures	documents
	5.3.3	documented quality plans	documents
	5.3.3(d)	specific documented procedures	documents
	5.3.3(f)	a documented procedure	document
	5.3.3	documented operational control	unclear
	5.3.4	quality records	records
	5.4.2(c)	documented procedures	documents
	5.4.3(f)	documentation, reports, recordkeeping	records and documents
	5.4.3	documented to include	document
	5.4.4	recorded and submitted	records
	5.4.5	assessed and documented	records
	7.1	documented requirements	unclear
	8.4.1	a formal, documented	records
	8.6	documented in specifications	design records— documents and records
	8.6	total document package	all design records and documents
	8.8	documented procedures	documents
	8.8	use of documents	some records, some documents
	9.1	documented procedures	documents
	9.1(a)	purchase documents	documents
	9.1(h)	quality records	records
	9.2	purchase documents	records and documents
	9.2	documented procedures	documents
	9.2	purchasing documents	records and documents
	9.4	process control records	records
	9.8	quality records	records
	9.8	records of lot identification	records
	10.1.1	documented procedures	documents
	10.1.4	documented test and inspection procedures	documents
	11.2.3	documented procedures	documents

Table 2.4. Continued.

ISO Standard	Section	Words Used	Meaning
9004-1	11.2.3	should be recorded	records
	11.4(e)	appropriate documentation	probably records
	11.5	documentation should be controlled	records and documents
	11.6	should be documented	recorded
	11.7	inspection records	records
	12.3	data and documentation	records
	13.1	documented procedures	documents
	13.2(d)	documentary evidence	records and documents
	13.2(e)	should be documented	records and documents
	14.1	documented procedures	documents
	14.5	should be documented	recorded
	15.2	recording and monitoring	records
	15.5	quality records	records
	15.5	establishing a file	records
	15.8	should be recorded in work instructions, etc.	should be included in documents
	16.2	procedures established, documented	documents
	16.3	should be documented	documents
	16.4.3	documented procedures	documents
	17.1	documented procedures	documents
	17.1	access of records	records
	17.1	various types of documents	documents
	17.2	sufficient records	records
	17.2	types of quality records	records
	17.3	documentation be available	records
	17.3	subcontractor documentation	records
	17.3	all documentation	records
	17.3	disposing of documentation	records
	17.3	documents requiring control	documents
	18.1.1	documented procedures	documents
	18.1.1	records of training	records
	18.1.4	the documentation provided	documents
	18.2	document qualifications	records
	19(b)	documenting the test results	records
	20.1	documented procedures	documents

of records and/or the information or data that must be collected. Throughout the standards is the concept of *implied records*—areas or sections indicating that the organization must provide proof, or must document the activity. Table 2.5 presents an enumeration of each case in which a record is required, whether it be specified or implied. In no cases were documents implied in the standards.

It is good practice to pose the following questions when reading the requirements: How can this be proven? How and by what means can this be documented? In other words, it is important to read the standards critically and questioningly, with an eye toward identifying how the organization can satisfy the particular section. Often, the answer will revolve around records.

An example of an implied record can be seen in Section 4.13.2 in Q9001, "Nonconforming Product Review and Disposition," which reads

> Repaired and/or reworked product shall be reinspected in accordance with the quality plan and/or documented procedures.

This statement does not explicitly require that a record be created about the activity, but how does an organization prove that it has reinspected the reworked product, if not by creating and maintaining records of having conducted the activity? Furthermore, the standards do not enumerate the data elements or pieces of information that should be collected and recorded. Again, using this statement as an example, some elements that should be recorded include

- Date
- Name of individual(s) who performed the inspection
- Identification of the product or material
- Results of the inspection

Familiarity with all sections of the entire set of standards is mandatory for gleaning records requirements that will result in satisfactory compliance.

Conclusion

Unfortunately, very little thought is often given to quality records. Except in those industries that have been complying with regu-

Table 2.5. ANSI/ASQC Q9001-1994 documents and records requirements.

Section	Documents Required	Records Implied	Records Specified
4.1.1	X		
4.1.2.1	X		
4.1.2.2	X	X	
4.1.2.3		X	
4.1.3			X
4.2.1	X		
4.2.2	X		
4.2.3	X		
4.3.1	X		
4.3.2(a)		X	
4.3.2(b)		X	
4.3.3	X		
4.3.4		X	X
4.4.1	X		
4.4.2	X	X	
4.4.3	X	X	
4.4.4	X	X	X
4.4.5	X	X	X
4.4.6		X	X
4.4.7		X	X
4.4.7		X	
4.4.7		X	
4.4.7		X	
4.4.7		X	
4.4.8		X	
4.4.9	X		X
4.5.1	X		
4.5.2		X	X
4.5.2(c)		X	
4.5.3		X	
4.6.1	X		
4.6.2(a)		X	
4.6.2(b)	X	X	X
4.6.2(c)			X
4.6.3		X	X
4.6.4.1		X	
4.7	X		X
4.8	X		X
4.9(a)	X		
4.9(d)		X	

Table 2.5. Continued.

Section	Documents Required	Records Implied	Records Specified
4.9(e)		X	
4.9(f)	X		
4.9(g)		X	
4.9	X		X
4.10.1	X	X	
4.10.2.1	X	X	
4.10.2.2		X	
4.10.2.3			X
4.10.3(a)	X	X	
4.10.4	X	X	
4.10.5			X
4.11.1	X		X
4.11.2(a)	X		
4.11.2(b)	X		X
4.11.2(c)	X		
4.11.2(d)			X
4.11.2(f)			X
4.12	X	X	
4.13.1	X	X	X
4.13.2	X	X	X
4.14.1	X	X	X
4.14.2	X		
4.14.2(b)			X
4.14.2(c)		X	
4.14.2(d)		X	
4.14.3(a)		X	
4.14.3(b)		X	
4.14.3(c)		X	
4.14.3(d)		X	
4.15.1	X		
4.15.3		X	
4.16	X		X
4.17	X	X	X
4.18	X		X
4.19	X	X	
4.20.2	X		

latory authorities, such as the pharmaceutical and nuclear industries, most organizations have no rationale for the records that they are creating and maintaining. The ISO 9000 standards require that written procedures be in place, that they be properly controlled, and that records capture pertinent information about activities that affect product quality. The burden remains with the organization to define the activities, to ensure that the procedures are complete, and to maintain records that can prove compliance with the standards.

Notes

1. Interview with the former employee of a nursing home, 1991.

2. Mary F. Robek, Gerald F. Brown, and Wilmer O. Maedke, *Information and Records Management*, 3rd ed. (Mission Hills, Calif.: Glencoe Publishing Co., 1987), 29.

3. Martha S. Feldman and James G. March, "Information in Organizations as Signal and Symbol," *Administrative Science Quarterly*, 26 (June 1981), 174.

4. Association of Records Managers and Administrators (ARMA International), *Glossary of Records Management Terms* (Prairie Village, Kans.: Association of Records Managers and Administrators, 1989), 16.

5. Ira A. Penn, Anne Morddel, Gail Pennix, and Kelvin Smith, *Records Management Handbook* (Brookfield, Vt.: Gower Publishing Co., 1994), 3.

CHAPTER 3

How to Get Started

Introduction

As this book points out, records must be created and maintained for all activities that can affect quality. The first step is to become familiar with the standards and determine which activities, equipment, and personnel affect quality in your organization. The next step is to define the records that need to be maintained about the activities, equipment, and personnel. Figure 3.1 depicts the steps that provide organizations with a plan of attack when they begin to address the records portions of the ISO standards. By methodically going through the standards and ANSI/ASQC Q9004-1-1994, you can identify the specific elements that pertain to your organization's business. Different records are required of different business types. A computer manufacturer requires different records than a pharmaceutical company does, for example. Before developing new records for a quality-related function, it is important to identify the records that already exist for the activities that are enumerated in the standards. Conducting a current status inventory of record types provides information about what already exists. This type of inventory is different than the conventional records inventory that is conducted when an organization develops a records management program. The purpose of the conventional records inventory is to identify the records that already

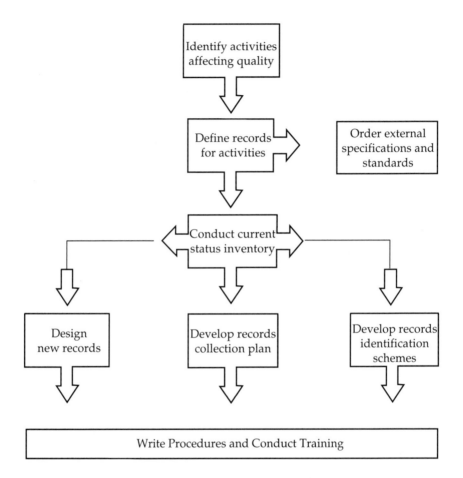

Figure 3.1. Beginning the records process for ISO standards.

exist, without imposing any predetermined criteria about what should exist.

The current status inventory is conducted against a checklist of record types that have been prepared by going through the standards. The purpose of the current status inventory is to identify the record types that already exist as well as those that must be developed. It provides an opportunity to examine the current records to determine if they include the data elements that must be collected and if they satisfy the requirements for clear identification. Furthermore, the inventory reveals where the records are generated, where they are used, and where they are housed. This information is valuable for several reasons. It reveals

- Gaps in records
- Overlaps in records
- The housing conditions—where the records are kept
- Bootleg records
- Problems with format
- Missing data elements that need to be included
- Information about how the records are organized
- Information that will be useful in developing collection schemes for records

This type of inventory, however, does not preclude a complete records inventory for the purpose of developing a retention schedule and a vital records protection program. That type of inventory is discussed in chapter 16. In general, Table 3.1 is an example of the kind of list that can be developed. The activities were gleaned from the ISO standards and are presented with the records that exist for those activities.

As mentioned in chapter 1, many required quality records may already exist in the quality functions, but they are not designed to satisfy specific standards. As a result, they may lack data elements and appropriate identification, and they may not comply with the myriad records management requirements in the standards. Most likely, some records will exist, but many more will have to be created or revised in order to meet requirements. In examining existing records and in developing those that do not exist, the information contained in this chapter and in appendix G can serve as a guideline. Appendix G includes examples of actual quality records being used by organizations that have successfully passed through the registration process

Creating New Quality Records and Forms

Entire books exist that disccuss the design, analysis, stocking, and distribution of forms (see the selected bibliography at the end of

Table 3.1. Quality activities and records.

Activity	Types of Records
Contract review	Contract review records
Design control	Personnel/training/qualification records
	Document control records
	Internal specifications
Design input	Review of design input requirements
	Selection of input requirements
Design output	Identification of critical elements
	Acceptance criteria records
	Compliance with regulatory requirements
	External standards and specifications
Design verification	Design review
	Records of qualification tests
	Records of demonstrations
	Records of alternative calculations
Design validation	Records of product conformance to user needs— inspections, evaluations, and so on.
Design changes	Reviews of changes
	Approvals of changes
	Distribution of changes
Document control	Distribution lists
	Temporary change records
	Records of revisions
	Periodic review records
	Master lists
Purchasing	Records comparing pruchased product with specified requirements and results (can include capability and performance)
	Records of product ordered
	Order review and approval records to ensure inclusion of required elements
	Verification of supplied product
	Storage and maintenance records of supplied product
	Records of unsuitable (lost or damaged) supplied product
	Identification and traceability of supplied product
Process control	Document control records
	Training records of personnel
	Qualification records
	Process monitoring records
	Standards of workmanship
	External specifications and standards

Table 3.1. Continued.

Activity	Types of Records
Special processes	Qualification of process records
	Qualification of equipment records
	Qualification of personnel records
Receipt inspection	Incoming material inspection records (may include testing records)
Nonconformance review	Identification of nonconforming product
	Disposition of nonconforming product
	Traceability of nonconforming product
	Corrective action records
In-process inspection	Process monitoring records
	Process ccontrol records
	In-process inspection records—results of each inspection
	Inspection personnel records—training and qualification records
	Records of inspection stamps
	Document control records
In-process testing	Results of each test type
	Records of release to next phase or step
Final inspection	Records of each type of final inspection, (visual, measurement, and so on)
	Records of inspection stamps
Final testing	Records of each test type
	Records of release after final inspection and testing
Inspection, measuring, and test equipment	Calibration records
Auditing—internal	Audit schedule
	Participants
	Audit reports
	List of audits conducted
	Corrective actions taken
Auditing—external	Results of previous audits
	Corrective actions taken
Training	Records for all personnel affecting quality

this book). That information will not be repeated here. Rather, this section highlights aspects of forms and records creation that pertain specifically to quality-related records and the ISO standards. It is important to design quality records from the following four perspectives.

1. The person who will be entering the information on the record

2. The conditions under which the information will be recorded

3. The manner in which information will be recorded, that is, with a ballpoint pen, typed, or on computer

4. The order in which the activities take place, the results of which are being recorded on the form

These four criteria will dictate which design elements to consider.

As an example, if the information is to be recorded by shop workers who extrude metal product using a graphite lubricant, the record must be designed so that

- It can accommodate handwriting in the spaces provided. The spaces should be larger than might be expected if the record were to be completed by a quality engineer on a computer.

- It is durable and can withstand a manufacturing floor environment. The composition and weight of the paper should be considered. If the record is going to be generated and used in an environment that may deteriorate it, the physical characteristics of the record become considerations as well. Is the environment hot? Is it humid? Do external elements attack the records?

Often records provide information that must be completed by more than one individual, along a series of work steps. When this is the case, the requested information should be placed on the form in order of processing. Records processing denotes the series of activities or steps required to complete the record and to act upon it. The information elements, in other words, should be logically ordered on the form, progressing from top to bottom in the natural order with which the record is processed. All related information should be together. Figure 3.2 presents an example of how information should be arranged on a record. If it must be exposed to hostile environments or situations it may be necessary to encase the record in a protective plastic holder or sleeve. This is especially true of paper *travelers* that accompany materials or

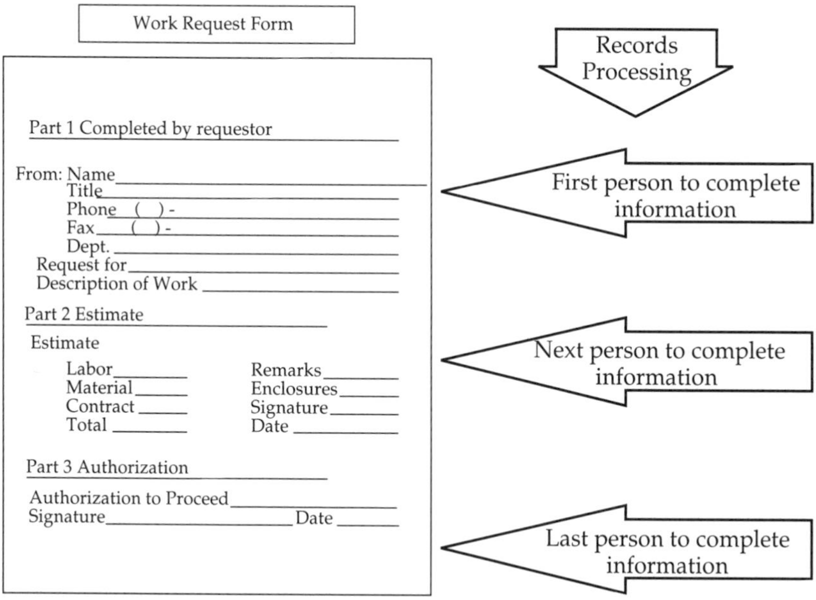

```
┌─────────────────────────────┐
│      Work Request Form      │
└─────────────────────────────┘

Part 1 Completed by requestor

From: Name_____
      Title_____
      Phone  (   ) -_____
      Fax____(   ) -_____
      Dept. _____
      Request for_____
      Description of Work _____

Part 2 Estimate

  Estimate
      Labor_____   Remarks_____
      Material_____  Enclosures_____
      Contract_____  Signature_____
      Total _____  Date _____

Part 3 Authorization

  Authorization to Proceed_____
  Signature_____Date _____
```

Records Processing

First person to complete information

Next person to complete information

Last person to complete information

Figure 3.2. Logical ordering of information on a record.

products through the process. Frequently, not only do the travelers pass through processes that are hostile to paper, but they may also be exposed to weather elements before the product is shipped. In addition to a protective plastic sleeve, travelers may need to be attached to the shipment lot or order with some sort of device such as a chain through the plastic holder. Without such devices, wind can blow travelers away from the shipment that they identify. Rain, snow, and strong sunlight will fade the information on the travelers. Any one of these situations destroys material credibility and traceability, and the traveler fails to fulfill its original function—that is, to verify that the process was completed, to identify the workers involved in each activity, and to document the dates that each activity was performed.

Identifying Quality Records and Forms

The standards include requirements concerning the identification of quality records. Section 4.16 of Q9001 states that "The supplier shall establish and maintain documented procedures for identification . . . of quality records." Section 17.3 of Q9004-1—*Guidelines* requires that "All documentation should be . . . readily identifiable." To satisfy the requirements, quality records should be identified with two pieces of information.

1. A clear and meaningful title

2. A form number, unique to a specific record, accompanied by a revision date and/or number

Forms are tools that can serve many purposes. Among other things, they can be used to authorize, notify, report, request, or record an action.[1] It is important to make the purpose of each form clear to the user. A form title satisfies this requirement by indicating the purpose of the form as well as helping to eliminate errors and confusion. Often, large organizations have forms that are similar in nature and in the data elements that they capture. Without a form title, the wrong form can be used and conversations about using a particular form can be confusing. A form title should be a brief description of the form's purpose. For example "Request for Corrective Action" is a clear title, revealing the purpose this particular form serves.

The form identification number is the single element best suited for identifying a record within the quality system. Assigning a unique number to each form positively identifies it and makes for easier reordering, use, storage, and inventory control. One person in the quality records department should be responsible for assigning form numbers and for keeping track of revision dates. When a form is revised, the revision date should be added to the form number, for example, Form 10886 (Rev. 9/93). This indicates to the user whether the form being used is current or obsolete.

In addition to actually identifying quality records with a title and a unique identification code, the standards require that documented procedures be in place describing the process of records identification. A section of the quality records procedural manual can address the method of assigning titles to forms and the process of developing unique identifiers for quality records. When a form is revised, users should be notified of the form change and told what to do with the older version. The section of the records manual that addresses records identification should include an explanation of the method for notifying users when a record is superseded and directing them what to do with their outdated records.

Routing Instructions

When using a multipart form, preprinted routing instructions at the bottom of the form simplify the transmittal process within the organization. Care should be taken to ensure that all departments and personnel who have need of the record do indeed receive it. Printing costs are lower for routing instructions that include all of the department names on each distribution copy of the record. If only the destination for a particular copy is printed on the bottom of each part, separate print plates must be created for each part of the form, increasing the cost of printing.

Many organizations transmit electronic forms from computer to computer. This eliminates paper copies for distribution and filing. Using electronic forms technology, variable input data are transferred directly into computerized databases for processing by an organization's software applications programs. Designs are provided in a series of templates, or instructions are given so that a template can be created with the necessary attributes. The user is then prompted for the data elements that have to be entered.

Collecting Quality Records

Early in the development of the records system, procedures must be established and written for collecting quality records. The requirement in Section 4.16 of Q9001 to collect quality records underscores the need for the hub concept described earlier. Without a function devoted exclusively to collecting quality records, who would be assigned to the task? The written procedure for collecting quality records becomes a controlled document and part of the document control process. The collection methods that are described in the procedure should be discussed before the document is issued with all personnel who will be sending records to the quality records department. This ensures that the quality records

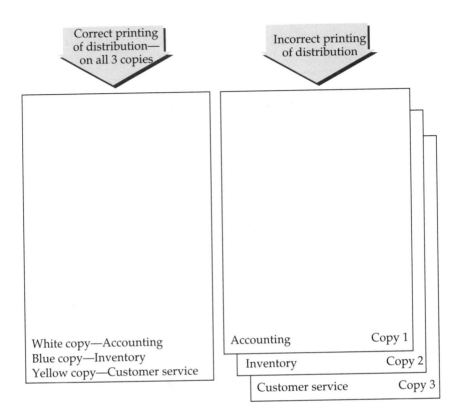

Figure 3.3. How to print distribution on forms.

department clearly understands the situation in each of the units that will be responsible for routing quality records.

Because the quality records department will be relying, to a great degree, on the cooperation and goodwill of the contributing units, the quality records manager should establish good rapport with the personnel in each unit. Before writing a records collection procedure, the quality records manager should visit each unit, meet with the manager, and request a meeting with the employees in that unit. During the meetings, the quality records manager should explain the requirements of the standards and elucidate plans for implementing the collection process. Encouraging discussion, the quality records manager should listen well for potential problems that the unit's manager and employees may foresee. Input from employees in the various areas can be very valuable in suggesting appropriate procedures for collecting the records. Either during the initial meeting or after the procedures have been developed, the quality records manager should emphasize to the unit managers and employees the importance of making sure that the procedures work, stressing that their cooperation is key to the collection of all records. Often, it will be necessary to conduct training sessions so that all those who are responsible for routing records to the quality records department in a timely manner understand what they are required to do and how they should do it. When the collection procedure is distributed as a formal document, the quality records manager should follow up by either writing a memo or meeting with employees to ensure that everyone understands the instructions.

Checklist of Quality Records

One potentially problematic area of the collection process is ascertaining that all of the records that should be collected have arrived. Developing a checklist for those quality records that must be collected is a simple way of avoiding or solving the problem. Depending on the kind of business in which the organization is involved, a checklist can be simple or complex. If the company assembles or manufactures a common product for all customers, one checklist listing the names and/or identification numbers of the records can be developed. If the company makes a variety of product types, each one requiring a different set of records, a quality records checklist should be developed for each type of product. When the records arrive at their destination (this depends on the method chosen—see "Centralized Quality Records" and "Decentralized Quality Records" on pages 58 and 60, respectively), assigned individuals simply check off that the record has arrived.

It is important that the quality records manager be kept apprised of the products being manufactured. The quality records manager can either attend production scheduling meetings or be notified in writing of the schedule. The forewarning enables the quality records staff to prepare checklists for orders or products before the records arrive. A checklist for each order, batch, or product must be developed if the system is to be successful.

The best approach is to develop an electronic checklist. Working with a spreadsheet program or even a simple table format, the quality records manager can design checklists that can be copied as needed, and can be modified for the various configurations of the product. Using checklists for collecting quality records eliminates guesswork and provides assurance that all records have been received.

If a decentralized quality records system is developed, it is the responsibility of the quality records manager to institute standardized methods as well as access schemes for the records that are to be maintained in the various departments. Decentralizing the records means that each department that creates quality records also is responsible for collecting and maintaining those records. There are advantages and disadvantages to both centralized and decentralized systems for quality records.

Centralized Quality Records

When quality records are centralized, responsibility and authority for all aspects of managing quality records and conducting records management activities are concentrated in one department. The advantages to centralized quality records are that

- All of the records expertise resides in one area.
- There is one central contact for any records-related problem or question.
- A consistent approach is taken across all types of quality records.
- A uniform method of access can be developed across all types of quality records. This results in improved retrieval of records.
- Records storage equipment is better utilized.
- Records management tools and technologies can be implemented for all quality records. It is easier to justify the purchase of new technologies if they will be used for a larger volume and variety of record types.

- Because it is known that all records *should* reside in one location, it is easier to determine when some have not been received.

- Quality records personnel can be trained to check over the records as they arrive for completeness and for appropriate recording techniques. Any problem can be identified and corrected before a great deal of time elapses and before any audits are conducted.

Because the main responsibility of the quality records department is the management of quality-related records and not the management of a processing or production activity, complete attention can be devoted to the efficient management of records, resulting in improved organization, storage, and retrieval of quality records. For example, the manager who is responsible for the press forge area is an expert in the press forge process and not in records management activities. Records are secondary to his or her main area of expertise and responsibility.

The disadvantages of centralized quality records are that

- All of the records must be housed in one facility or location which is managed by the quality records department. This is not the case if quality records are electronic and exist on an automated system or if the records are stored on optical disk. In an electronic environment, the quality records manager has the responsibility for developing the format of the records and ensuring that all necessary data elements are included. Providing retrieval is not an issue, because end users usually retrieve the records themselves. The same holds true for records that have been entered into an optical disk system. Indexing, however, for records stored on optical disk should be designed by the quality records manager.

If the records are mainly paper and they must be physically housed, retrieval becomes an issue. In such cases, limited access to quality records is usually instituted, with requests being placed to quality records personnel. This ensures that users cannot walk away with records that prove the quality system is in order. Everything should be done to minimize turnaround time in such a situation. There is no need to make users wait for requested records if the organizing schemes have been properly designed and the appropriate equipment is being utilized. There is nothing that undermines the credibility of a centralized quality records department more than making users wait for records that are not readily retrievable.

- In very large organizations, physically centralizing the records may not be feasible. In such organizations, however, it is highly likely that many records will exist in electronic format—on computerized systems. Theoretically, therefore, the volume of paper-based quality records can be smaller than that of many medium-sized organizations.

- Records that are usually retrieved by only one department will be located away from the main user group. The problem of access can be solved, however, by sending the originals to the quality records department and retaining a working copy of the record.

Decentralized Quality Records

If quality records remain in the areas where they are generated or used, they are said to be decentralized. Advantages to decentralized quality records are that

- Records are physically located in the department or area where they are used or where they originate.

- The department or area can access the records without an intermediary or without making requests for retrieval.

- Departments do not have to route the records to a central source.

Disadvantages to decentralized quality records are that

- There is duplication of all elements required to develop and manage the records—personnel, equipment, supplies, and space.

- Not all departments responsible for maintaining quality records will have records expertise.

- Quality records are dispersed throughout the organization. Coordinating the various elements across departments is difficult. Auditing the records and the associated required activities become especially problematic.

- Responsibility is dispersed.

- The quality of records work usually is impaired because there are no full-time records personnel devoted to the records.

- A certain amount of duplication of records will, of necessity, occur, since various departments will need copies of the records housed in another department.

- Controls are weakened.

- Implementing a retention schedule becomes increasingly difficult, since each department must be held responsible for ensuring adherence to the schedule.

Decentralized Records with Centralized Control

Even if the records themselves are decentralized, control should remain centralized in the quality records department. All departments are then responsible to the quality records manager for their quality records and must coordinate activities with the quality records manager. If this is the selected model, the quality records manager is responsible for development and implementation of all facets of records management as specified in the standards, but the activities are conducted through records liaisons in each of the departments. One major drawback to this approach is that the records liaisons already have full-time jobs in their respective departments. There is usually little time during the work day for the liaison to perform the records activities necessary to keep the quality records system intact and functioning according to requirements. Furthermore, the allegiance of the records liaison is to the department manager and not to the quality records manager. The liaison's salary or wage is on the department manager's budget. Performance evaluations for the liaison are conducted by the department manager and not by the quality records manager. If the department manager feels that the primary work of the liaison is suffering because of records duties, the liaison may not be as diligent in performing the records activities.

Each of the records management components becomes much more difficult to manage in this type of environment. Perhaps what is even more important is the erosion of confidence in the records system. Because responsibilities are dispersed, confidence levels decline. Implementation of the retention schedule, for example, can suffer. The records liaisons must transfer inactive records methodically to remote storage and must ensure that all records on the retention schedule are included. Protection of vital records, as well, can be compromised. The liaisons can be required to segregate the vital records, copy them (either electronically or by photocopying them), and send them to the designated protection facility daily or weekly.

This approach increases the burden on the quality records manager for the continuous training of the records liaisons and the constant monitoring and surveillance of the records being maintained in various departments. In such a situation, it is important that the quality records manager write more procedures and work instructions on the various aspects of managing records, because untrained individuals will be responsible for conducting many of the activities.

External Specifications and Standards

Complying with the ISO requirements for records means more than monitoring the organization's own records and documents. External specifications and standards are part of the operating requirements of most organizations. For example, an organization may use a sampling procedure that has been published by ASQC and is referenced in an internally controlled document. Many such external standards may be utilized. It is necessary, however, to have the external procedure available in the organization and to have it readily retrievable. Part of getting started is identifying those external specifications and standards that must become part of the collection of documents in an organization. These external documents need not be monitored by the document control center, but they do need to be organized.

Information Handling Services (IHS), the world's largest information republisher, provides subscription services to all aspects of technical information. This Englewood, Colorado-based company is known for its extensive collections of industrial manufacturers' catalogs and military standards and federal regulatory documents, as well as for both U.S. and international standards.[2] IHS collects and updates information from more than 63,000 manufacturers' catalogs, 600,000 manufacturers' data sheets, tens of thousands of environmental and safety documents, and an extensive library of international standards documents (see the address for IHS in appendix E). To date, 9.1 million images are stored electronically and distributed to clients, primarily via compact disk—read-only memory (CD-ROM), microfilm, and microfiche. The documents are full-text, fully indexed, cross-referenced to related materials, updated regularly, and reindexed every day. The documents can be segmented and tailored to meet the specific needs of individual organizations. As the standards and specifications are changed, the client organization automatically receives the updated documents. A company like IHS can ensure that the latest revisions of external documents are available and retrievable.

The quality records department should be responsible for organizing the external specifications and standards and for providing access to them. If your company decides not to use a documentation service, you must still index and physically organize the external specifications and standards. An index created on a database allows you to manipulate it according to any indexing parameter. Lists of standards should be generated and provided to each department. It is important to keep abreast of updated, revised standards, as that is one thing that auditors will examine. Typical questions include

- Do you have the American Society for Testing and Materials (ASTM) standard referenced in your tensile test procedure?
- Where is it located? How would you access it?
- How do you ensure that the latest revisions are provided in-house?

Whether you choose to keep track of the external documents or subscribe to a document service, it is necessary to have the documents in your organization. You must make certain that employees can perform all activities that refer to external specifications and standards in the internally produced documents.

Conclusion

Complying with the records requirements of the ISO 9000 standards need not be confusing or frustrating. It can and should be systematic and orderly. Consideration must be given to both internally and externally produced records and documents. Decisions concerning centralized or decentralized records management will affect how the activities are conducted, what kind of expertise is required, and the resources that must be allocated.

Notes

1. Marj Green, ed., *The Business Forms Handbook*, 4th ed. (Alexandria, Va.: National Business Forms Association, 1990), 341.

2. Dan Denkin, "Information Handling Is More Than a Service at IHS," *Document Management & Windows Imaging* 3 (May/June 1993), 35.

CHAPTER 4

Overall Quality System Records

Q9001—Sections 4.1 and 4.2
Q9004-1—Sections 5.3 and 5.5

Contract Review Records
Q9001—Section 4.3
Q9004-1—Section 7.1

Introduction

The ISO standards specify that the organization must "define and document its policy for quality, including objectives for quality and its commitment to quality" (Paragraph 4.1.1, ANSI/ASQC Q9001). Subparagraphs of Sections 4.1 and 4.2 clearly delineate the requirements of and provide specifics about the kinds of documents to create and the types of activities to conduct when implementing and maintaining the documented system. Sections 4.1 and 4.2 of ANSI/ASQC Q9001, as well as Section 5.3 in ANSI/ASQC Q9004-1-1994, provide the essence of the entire quality system and the rationale for establishing the requirements in the standards. Through the documentation, the standards ask the organization to explain that it has made provisions for each section defined in the remainder of the standard. The activities in each of the remaining sections of the standard are either specifically mentioned or alluded to in Sections 4.1, 4.2, and *Guidelines*, 5.3.

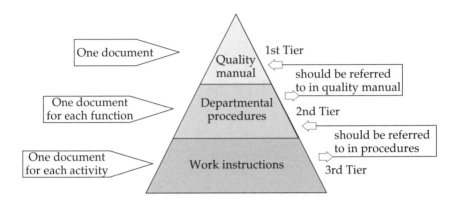

Figure 4.1. The quality document pyramid.

The purpose of Sections 4.1 and 4.2 is to ensure that the organization addresses each facet affecting quality and that everything is put in writing. The requirements for organizations are as follows.

1. Develop an overall quality plan or policy.

2. Delineate the departmental responsibilities through procedures.

3. Communicate this information through specific work instructions to those individuals actually performing the operations.

4. Record that steps 1, 2, and 3 have been done.

5. Review the procedure to ensure that it works.

Documented Quality System

Records reveal that all aspects of a documented quality system are in place. Records are an integral part of the documented system and provide evidence to demonstrate conformance to specified requirements and the effective operation of the quality system. The three-tier approach to documenting the quality system, shown in Figure 4.1, is often used to depict the different types of documents that an organization must produce in order to address the

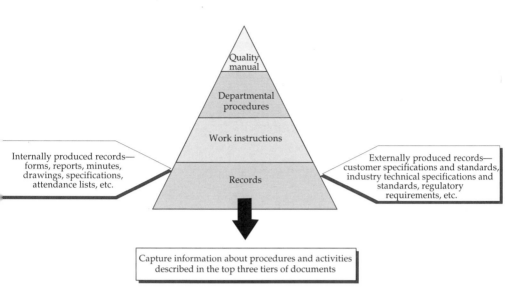

Figure 4.2. Tier 4—quality records.

required aspects of the standards. What is missing in this depiction is Tier 4, shown in Figure 4.2—*the records that provide data and information on the work that has been performed* throughout the entire quality loop.

The quality manual states the policy and objectives for each of the pertinent ISO paragraphs.[1] In other words, it covers the entire spectrum of activities identified in the standards, but in a general way. The quality manual should not include details of departmental procedures or work instructions. As the pyramid model depicts, the documents become more specific, more detailed as they move from the top to the bottom of the pyramid. Quality records form the base of the pyramid. If no records were kept of any of the work performed, there would be no quality system. The foundation then, in the four-tier pyramid, is the thoroughness of the quality records system, supporting and providing validity to the three levels of quality documentation and serving as the base on which the entire quality system rests.

The logic of having a quality manual is that it gathers the company's philosophy and planning for quality in one document.

Predecessors of the organized manual are a wide assortment of memoranda, instructions, marked prints, and other bits of information, all having multiple origins.[2] Because the fragmented approach results in the inability to locate all authoritative information bearing on the company's quality plan, it is often difficult for the organization and those external to it to have a clear picture of how the organization optimizes its performance.

Relationship to Document Control

The organization that complies with ISO 9000 will have prepared numerous procedures and instructions, but only one quality manual. Each of these items—the quality manual as well as the procedures and instructions—is referred to as a document, because they literally document the quality system. At the very outset of compliance activities, document control procedures must be applied to the three tiers of quality documentation. Creating and distributing a quality manual, procedures, and work instructions before establishing a document control procedure will result in chaos. It is, of course, very difficult to locate documents after they have been distributed if you do not have any records about who received them.

As explained in chapter 6, many activities, sometimes very detailed, must be conducted to ensure the effectiveness of the document control system. The records maintained about the approval, distribution, and use of the documents validate the documented quality system. It does little good for an organization to have prepared and distributed a solid quality manual and excellent procedures and instructions if it cannot demonstrate that all those who need copies have received them, and that those recipients can be assured of receiving any revisions that may be made. In other words, no documented quality system is valid without records that show where the documents are, that they are being read and understood, and that provisions exist for any changes that may occur.

It is for these reasons that the ISO standards address the issue of control over designs and documents early in the requirements. In discussing the development of a documented quality system,

the *Guidelines* include a paragraph devoted to configuration management—Paragraph 5.2.6.

> The quality system should include documented procedures for configura-
> tion management to the extent appropriate. This discipline is initiated early
> in the design phase and continues through the whole life-cycle of a prod-
> uct. It assists in the operation and control of design, development, pro-
> duction, and use of a product, and gives management visibility of the state
> of documentation and product during its life-time.
>
> Configuration management can include: configuration identification,
> configuration control, configuration status accounting, and configuration
> audit. It relates to several of the activities described in ANSI/ASQC Q9004-
> 1-1994.

The reason this concept is important is that a tight document
control system is based on principles of configuration management. It applies equally to the design control process and to the
document control process. Organizations wishing to prepare a
flawless document control system simply must adhere to the steps
of configuration management. Table 4.1 provides a description of
the elements involved in configuration management.

It is important to institute document control procedures and
to develop the necessary records *before* creating and distributing
procedures and instructions that document the quality system.
The quality documents, then, that comprise the document control
system—and prove that the organization has a documented quality system—are the quality manual, the procedures, and the work
instructions, including machine and other equipment instructions.
The last category, instructions, is the most specific and detailed
and comprises the greatest number of items. The instructions and
procedures that are referred to in Section 4.2 of Q9001 are as follows.

- Each type of inspection performed
- Each type of test conducted
- How the design is monitored
- How production is monitored
- Instructions for each phase or step in the process
- Procedures for servicing the products
- Instructions for servicing the products

Table 4.1.   Elements of configuration management.

Configuration refers to the physical and functional characteristics of a product including both hardware and software. Ideally, design and development concludes with a design that is "frozen." In practice, design changes are often made after production has started. The collection of activities needed to accomplish these changes is called configuration management. Three elements are involved:

1. Configuration identification: This is the process of defining and identifying every element of the product. Some identification may be marked on the product, but mainly the identification and proof of adequacy are achieved through chains of documentation. The documents consist of engineering drawings, specifications, in-process inspection reports, acceptance inspection and test results, special test results, etc.

2. Configuration control: This is a series of actions which manages a design change from the time of the original proposal for change through implementation of approved changes. Configuration control involves the technical evaluation, costing, and determination of which specific products will have the change incorporated. The trend has been toward a more formalized, coordinated approach. The reason is that as products have become more complex, the effect of an engineering change has multiplied in complexity and cost. Companies have made their review structure more elaborate in order to guard against unneeded or unwise changes and against errors in introducing needed changes.

3. Configuration accounting: This is the process of recording the status of proposed changes and the implementation status of approved changes. As changes may continually be made, a large but necessary, formal accounting type system is required. The major role of verifying that the changes have been made and documentation completed is usually performed by the Quality Department.

Source: Frank M. Gryna, "Product Development" and "Customer Service," in *Juran's Quality Control Handbook*, 4th ed., ed. J. M. Juran (New York: McGraw-Hill, 1988), 13.66–13.68, 20.8. Reprinted with permission.

- Procedures for conducting design reviews
- Procedures for identifying nonconforming products
- Procedures for preventing the occurrence of nonconforming products
- Instructions on how to handle nonconforming products
- Procedures for training personnel to perform various quality-related activities

- Procedures for controlling inspection equipment
- Procedures for auditing the quality system

The 1994 version of Q9001, 4.2.1, requires the following:

> The quality manual shall include or make reference to the quality-system procedures and outline the structure of the documentation used in the quality system.

The quality system procedures, such as purchasing procedures, contract review procedures, and also instructions, such as process work instructions, must at least be referenced in the quality manual. In order for an organization to accomplish this, the writing of procedures and work instructions must begin at the same time that the quality manual is being prepared. In addition, document control procedures and a document control system must be in force at the time that the documents are referred to in the manual. Using unique document identifiers, the document control center (see chapter 6) will ensure consistency in the identification of all procedures and instructions. Figure 4.3 depicts the order of activities for preparing a documented quality system.

Concurrent Activities

Write quality manual; refer to documented procedures in manual	Write procedures; refer to work instructions in procedures	Write work instructions; include copies of records and forms to be used	Develop document control system—to identify, control, and distribute quality documents and to maintain records	Design quality records; identify them

Document control must be in existence BEFORE the three tiers of documents are finalized and distributed

Figure 4.3. Preparing a documented quality system.

Types of Records Required

The very beginning of the standards both specify and imply the creation and maintenance of quality records. Paragraph 4.1.1 of Q9001 requires that

> The supplier shall ensure that this policy is understood, implemented, and maintained at all levels of the organization.

The distribution of the quality manual and the records and procedures created by the document control center (see chapter 6) help prove that the policy has, at least, been distributed and is being maintained in various functions within the organization. In order to satisfy the requirement that the policy is understood, the organization has several options.

- It can require that each individual who receives a copy of the manual sign and date a special form indicating that he or she has, indeed, read and understood the manual. The record, then, serves as evidence of compliance.

- It can institute training or explanation sessions for those individuals or functions whose jobs affect quality. Again, records attesting to the training serve as proof of compliance.

- Both approaches can be used in conjunction: a signed "Read and Understood" form from recipients of the quality manual—to be deposited with the document control center, and a training session—for all individuals whose work affects quality—that explains the quality policies and plans of the organization.

In any case, records are to be created and maintained of any such activities. The records of the training sessions are retained in the quality records department, under the document control center. Records of implementation of the quality policies comprise the focus of this book. Where a quality activity requires records and those records are maintained, the records serve as proof of implementation of the documented quality system.

Other types of records required in the documented quality system section of the standards are (1) internal audit records of the quality system and (2) management reviews of the audited quality system. (Internal audit records are discussed in detail in chapter 13.) Paragraph 4.1.3 of Q9001 states,

> The supplier's management with executive responsibility shall review the quality system at defined intervals sufficient to ensure its continuing suitability and effectiveness in satisfying the requirements of this American National Standard and the supplier's stated quality policy and objectives. Records of such reviews shall be maintained.

As with other types of activities conducted for the purpose of evaluation for quality, records maintained of the management review process serve as the only indication that the stated activities actually occurred. These records should be a category all their own, entitled "Management Reviews of Quality System." This category of records may contain information from various sources as well as cross references to other materials or record categories. The data elements to include are the names of individuals conducting the management review, their titles, dates, the sources examined, and a determination of the effectiveness of the system. The *Guidelines* provide advice about what to include in a management review in Section 5.5 (Q9004-1)—"Review and Evaluation of the Quality System." The section recommends examination of internal audit results to evaluate the effectiveness of the system. The *Guidelines* further recommend that all "observations, conclusions, and recommendations reached as a result of review and evaluation should be documented for necessary action." This is an instance of the word *documented* carrying the meaning of *recorded*. Records are to be created to document not only that the management review actually took place but also the conclusions that were reached, any observations that were made, and any recommendations emanating from the reviews.

Quality Documents to Be Written by the Quality Records Manager

The sections of the quality manual that describe activities under the jurisdiction of the quality records manager should be written by that individual. Depending on the structure of the quality manual, the records activities can be included in each section that discusses a specific quality activity—for example, "Nonconforming Product"—or they can be explained in a separate section. It is easier to examine the quality manual for completeness if the sections in it mirror the layout of the ISO standards. In any case, the quality records manager should be responsible for that portion of the manual addressing Section 4.16—"Control of Quality Records." It is important to remember that what is written in the manual is what must be done in the organization. If the quality records manager writes that procedures are in place for identification, collection, indexing, filing, storage, maintenance, and disposition of quality records, auditors will ask to see the procedures. The same holds true for each of the statements in Section 4.16.

Good records management encompasses procedures for the various components and activities of which the function is comprised. Regardless of the ISO standards, procedures should exist in any records management operation delineating the responsibilities of the department and describing how the activities are conducted. Often, all of the procedures that pertain to the records management operation are combined into a records management manual. Such a solution works well in the quality arena, because a records management manual draws together all records-related procedures into one document.

An alternative is to write a separate procedure for each component of the quality records management program. For example, a procedure would be written describing how the records are stored and maintained to minimize deterioration or damage and to prevent their loss. Regardless of which method is chosen—a complete quality records management manual or separate documents for each activity or component—the important point is that written procedures must exist for the following records operations.

- Identifying quality records
- Ensuring that quality records are legible
- Collecting quality records
- Indexing quality records
- Filing quality records

- Storing and maintaining quality records

- Disposing of quality records

- Protecting the records (environmental and security issues)

- Developing a retention schedule

In addition to written procedures, the retention schedule itself must be developed, and it must be presented for examination during an audit (see chapter 16 for instructions on developing a retention schedule). Furthermore, evidence must exist that the retention schedule is being followed. Records that document the destruction of outdated or obsolete records must be created and maintained.

Information delineating the kinds of quality records that are maintained should be included in the quality manual. If the manual mirrors the standard, indication of records can be inserted in the appropriate sections addressing the quality activity. For example, Paragraph 4.18—"Training"—specifies that "appropriate records of training shall be maintained." The section of the quality manual addressing training should include a statement to the effect that training records are maintained.

Compiling a list of all of the records that are being maintained to satisfy the records requirements of ISO 9000 should be the responsibility of the quality records management function. Such a list serves multiple purposes.

- It clarifies to quality records personnel the types of records that fall under their jurisdiction.

- It combines all of the records requirements in a master list.

- It simplifies and streamlines the audit process. This point cannot be underestimated. Presenting an orderly, organized appearance to registrars and auditors serves as evidence that a good quality system exists. It provides assurance that the organization is in control.

In addition to preparing procedures for records management activities, the quality records manager should write the portion of the quality manual that discusses document and data control. Ta-

---

Table 4.2. Responsibilities of the quality records manager in the development of a documented quality system.

- Write the procedures for records operations.
- Contribute to sections of the quality manual that pertain to records and document control.
- Develop the document control system.
- Write the document control procedure.
- Create the document control records.
- Distribute the controlled documents—the quality manual, the procedures, and work instructions.
- Conduct training about the document control system.

---

ble 4.2 provides a list of responsibilities that the quality records manager assumes in developing a documented quality system.

The document control center is the responsibility of the quality records manager. Because he or she has developed the records and activities associated with a document control system, the quality records manager is the most knowledgeable about the procedures that must be written. Document control procedures should always be accompanied by the training of all affected departments. Since the procedures may be foreign to individuals in organizations that have not, until now, had to control their documents, there may be resistance to what can be perceived as unnecessary controls.

Contract Reviews

Contracts from customers must be reviewed to accurately determine what the customer requirements are and to make certain that the organization can meet those requirements. Meeting requirements includes complying not only with technical product specifications, but also with time deadlines and after-product maintenance and service, if so requested. Records of contract review are implied in Section 4.3.2.

> a) the requirements are adequately defined and documented; where no written statement of requirement is available for an order received by verbal means, the supplier shall ensure that the order requirements are agreed before their acceptance.

In this sentence, the word *documented* means *recorded*. Records are specifically required here, and the type of record is specified.

Records consist of defined requirements. These include performance requirements, technical requirements, and requirements on the level of quality of the finished product.[3] These product requirements can accompany requirements about the execution of the contract. Such requirements may include

- A quality plan
- Reliability analysis and test data
- Product design and manufacture in accordance with other industry or government specifications
- Prior customer notification of changes in material or in the method of manufacture
- Purchase from specified suppliers of certain components of the final product
- Formal approval by the customer of specified documentation
- Special warranties, such as reliability improvement[4]

In addition, if the order was received verbally, written confirmation should exist that the requirements are agreed upon by both parties.

> b) any differences between the contract or accepted order requirements and those in the tender are resolved.

Records must exist proving that the differences have been resolved.

> c) the supplier has the capability to meet contract or accepted order requirements.

A record must exist that reveals the supplier's capability. The proof can be in the form of a signature on a document that has been prepared for other activities associated with contract review. Section 4.3.4 clearly states that

> Records of contract reviews shall be maintained.

As with other records requirements, however, there is no indication in this section of the kinds of activities that must be recorded, other than the statement that the requirements of the order must be documented. Records include a copy of the contract itself and any internal information that comments on the ability of the organization to comply with contractual elements. Data elements should include

- Names and titles of individuals who reviewed the contract with dates

- Any comments made by the individuals that bear upon the organization's capability of meeting contractual requirements

Records can include internal specifications, external specifications (military and industrial specifications and standards), operating procedures, and work instructions. Part of contract review should include identifying those internal specifications that affect the product being ordered. Comparison of contract requirements with internal specifications forms the basis for determining whether or not the company can satisfy the contract. If military or industrial specifications or standards are referenced in the contract or in the supplier's documentation, the supplier must make certain that these documents are in-house. Often organizations fail to realize that each standard or specification that is referred to either in the contract or in internal documentation must be readily available for review. It is not possible to determine, for example, if a plate metal product can be inspected according to an ASTM standard if the standard is not in-house. Usually a long list of standards must be ordered and be readily available to personnel engaged in the design, manufacture, testing, and inspection of most products. (See chapter 3 for a discussion of external standards and specifications.) Table 4.3 presents a list of questions that organizations can ask about their current contract review records to determine if they are satisfying the requirements.

Reviewing a contract can affect and be affected by the organization's quality operating procedures and work instructions—Tier 2 and Tier 3 documentation. (See the quality document pyramid in Figure 4.1 on page 66.) Records should indicate the unique identifiers and titles of those procedures and work instructions that will be used by internal operating personnel to satisfy contract requirements. This is done to ensure (1) that the two levels

Table 4.3. Examination of contract review records requirements.

Questions to ask about contract review records

1. Have the requirements been documented? Performance requirements? Technical requirements? Requirements regarding the level of quality of the finished product?

2. Does the customer require approval of operating specifications or procedures? Has approval been received? Has approval been recorded?

3. Do you need to comply with other industry or government specifications? Do you have these in-house? Are they current?

4. Have you recorded any verbal transactions that may have occurred with the customer?

5. Have all differences been resolved? Has the resolution been recorded?

6. Have all affected departments acknowledged their capability of meeting contract requirements? Have they been notified? Have their acknowledgments been recorded?

7. Have you followed your own contract review procedures?

of documentation do exist for the product being specified in the contract, and (2) that the procedures and instructions accurately depict the necessary steps for this specific product's manufacture.

If documents do not exist (as happens in some instances), they will have to be written and included in the document control system. Only after the documents have been written, approved, and distributed can contract review be continued and completed. It can also happen that a different version of existing documents must be prepared that will address elements of product design, manufacture, testing, and so forth that are specific to a particular customer or order. Reviewing the contract, in a case such as this, precipitates the writing of procedures and instructions to govern specific instances. These added procedures and instructions may need to be submitted to the customer for review and approval before the contract can be considered valid. As is true with all such documents, they are considered to be controlled documents, and, as such, they must comply with document control requirements.

In any case, it is a good idea to include on the contract review record identifying elements (titles and numbers) of all documents, standards, and specifications that are either referred to in the contract or will be used to satisfy the contract. Care must be taken to ensure that the correct revision number of the documents is noted. This is done to reveal to auditors, to customers, and to the organization itself that all information that is necessary for fulfilling the contract has been reviewed and all of that information is available in-house. Records for contract review should include the following information.

- Who participated in the contract review
- The defined product
- Definition of the requirements
- How the requirements are disseminated throughout the organization

Conclusion

The overall purpose of records for contract review is to force the organization to examine its internal resources before it commits itself to a customer. They ensure that all elements—personnel, information, technology, procedures, instructions, machinery, equipment—are in order so that the quality of the product is not compromised and the shipment date is met.

Notes

1. James L. Lamprecht, *ISO 9000: Preparing for Registration* (Milwaukee, Wis.: ASQC Quality Press, 1992), 63.

2. J. M. Juran, "Companywide Planning for Quality" in *Juran's Quality Control Handbook*, 4th ed., ed. J. M. Juran (New York: McGraw-Hill, 1988), 6.40.

3. Frank M. Gryna, "Marketing," in *Juran's Quality Control Handbook*, 4th ed., ed. J. M. Juran (New York: McGraw-Hill, 1988), 19.6.

4. Ibid., 19.6.

CHAPTER 5

Design Control and Design Review Records

Q9001—Section 4.4
Q9004-1—Section 8 (all portions)

Introduction

The importance of the design process cannot be overemphasized, because activities conducted during the various design phases affect the performance of the resulting products. Flaws and malfunctions often can be traced directly to an incomplete or weak design control process, as is evident from the studies presented in Table 5.1.

The importance of design control is reflected in the length of the ISO section discussing these activities. It is one of the longest sections, comprising approximately 60 lines in Q9001. Activities are separated into the phases of the design process, from the initial design planning through design changes. It is a multifaceted, complex activity that involves several reviews, from conceptual design to final product design. Despite the number of records that are

---

Table 5.1. Design process causes most product flaws.

1. In a study of seven space programs, 35.2 percent of component failures were due to design or specification error.

2. During a typical period of 11 months at a chemical plant, 42 percent of the rework dollars were traced to research and development.

3. In a study of "quality calamities" by the British Institute of Management, 36 percent were due to lack of proving new designs, materials, or processes, and 16 percent were due to lack of or wrong specifications.

4. In one chemical company, a startling 50 percent of the product shipped was out of specification. Fortunately, the product was fit for use. A review concluded that many of the specifications were obsolete and had to be changed.

5. For mechanical and electronics products of at least moderate complexity, it is the author's opinion that errors during product development cause about 40 percent of the fitness-for-use problems. Where Product Development is responsible for both creating the formulation (design) of the product and also responsible for developing the manufacturing process, as in chemicals, about 50 percent of the problems are due to development.

6. The amount of activity within product development to correct deficiencies in products can be surprisingly high. In one typical year, an electronics organization determined that the cost of design changes was about 67 percent of the operating profit. Some of these changes were initiated by the customer but over 80 percent of the changes were related to design deficiencies.

Source: Frank M. Gryna, "Product Development," in *Juran's Quality Control Handbook,* 4th ed., ed. J. M. Juran (New York: McGraw-Hill, 1988), 13.3. Reprinted with permission.

created and generated during the process, the standards are remiss because they mention records requirements only twice: (1) Paragraph 4.4.6—Design Review; "Records of such reviews shall be maintained" and (2) Paragraph 4.4.7—Design Verification; "The design-verification measures shall be recorded."

Needless to say, implied records prevail in the design control requirements, and, furthermore, so do implied activities. Any organization wishing to maintain control and sanity during the design process must collect, review, and maintain a host of records that are not mentioned in the standards. Regardless of the ISO requirements, it simply does not make good business sense to conduct the design process without recording and, subsequently, analyzing all information that is pertinent to the quality of the product.

The standards require that procedures clearly describe activities pertaining to the design process and that records be maintained indicating that the activities have taken place as they were described. This holds true for all phases of the design process and for all input activities and all personnel involved. Design records serve two purposes: (1) They provide evidence that the activities have occurred as described in the procedures, and (2) They collect data for the organization to use in pre- and post-production analysis. In the fullest sense, design records provide an accumulation of experiences pertaining to the product at hand, and they can serve as a mine of information for current and future designs.

The design sections of the standards demonstrate how important it is to be fully familiar with all of the sections of the standards if you are to comply with the records requirements. The paragraph about configuration management, 5.2.6 in the *Guidelines*, must be brought to bear on design control and review activities. The concepts of configuration identification, configuration control, and configuration accounting can provide outlines of plans for handling the documentation and activities associated with the design processes. The design section also is a good example of the close relationship with records from other areas of the standards. As Figure 5.1 depicts, records from training, contract review, and document control—as well as procedures, both internal and external—are involved in the design process.

Requirements in Section 4.4

Table 5.2 itemizes the requirements that were culled from all paragraphs of Section 4.4, Q9001, and it indicates where records must be created and maintained. As Table 5.2 indicates, records are required in 23 of the 28 steps of the design process. This does not imply that only 23 records must be created and maintained for these activities, as one activity may comprise numerous facets. As an example, design verification can include the following activities, as is mentioned in Q9001, 4.4.7: alternative calculations, tests

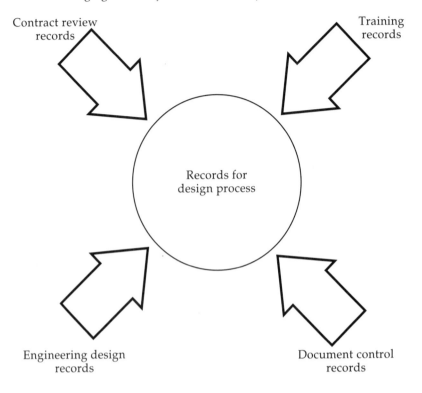

Contract review
records

Training
records

Records for
design process

Engineering design
records

Document control
records

Figure 5.1. Interconnection of records in the design process.

and demonstrations, comparisons with proven designs, and review of the design stage documents before release. The design
verification stage, therefore, can include hundreds of separate records, depending on the complexity of the product. In addition,
multiple design reviews may be conducted at various phases of
the design and development process. The standards assume that
each organization is capable of defining its own review activities,
relative to the product and industry type. The standards do not
detail the phases through which designs progress and the subsequent reviews and activities connected with those phases.

Beginning with the first explicitly stated requirement, that procedures be in place for activities in the design process, through
the last requirement, that all design changes and modifications be
reviewed and approved by authorized personnel, almost all requirements imply that information and data be collected and main-

---

Table 5.2. Itemized requirements of Section 4.4—records requirements indicated.

---

* 1. Procedures must be written for all activities in the design process.

2. Specified requirements must be met.

* 3. Responsibilities must be identified for each design activity.

* 4. Personnel must be qualified to perform the activities.

5. Adequate resources must be available to personnel.

* 6. Organizational interfaces must be identified.

* 7. Technical interfaces must be identified.

* 8. Information that is passed across groups must be documented, transmitted, and reviewed.

9. Design inputs must be identified.

*10. Design inputs must be documented.

*11. Design inputs must be reviewed for adequacy.

*12. Incomplete, ambiguous, or conflicting requirements must be resolved with those who are responsible for imposing the requirements.

*13. Results of contract review activities must be considered at the design input phase.

*14. Formal, documented reviews of the design results must be planned and conducted.

*15. The design review process must include representatives of all functions that are concerned with the design stage being reviewed.

*16. Records must be maintained of the design reviews.

*17. Design output must be documented.

18. Design output must be expressed in terms of requirements that must be verified.

*19. Design output must meet design input requirements.

*20. Design output must contain or refer to acceptance criteria.

*21. Design output must identify characteristics that are crucial to safety and proper functioning.

*22. A review must be conducted of design output documents before release.

*23. Design verification must be performed.

*24. Records must be kept of design verification measures.

*25. Design validation must be performed.

*26. Design changes and modifications must be identified.

*27. Design changes and modifications must be documented.

*28. Design changes and modifications must be reviewed and approved by authorized personnel.

---

* Indicates that records are required.

tained about the activity and personnel involved. Records, as a result, are really more numerous than what may initially appear from
a literal reading of this section. Organizations, once again, are encouraged to ask themselves, "How can we prove that we have
complied with this requirement? How can we prove that we have
conducted this activity?" Records here, as elsewhere, provide the
proof.

*Requirement 1: Procedures must be written for all activities in the
design process.* Organizations are required to establish and maintain "documented procedures to control and verify the design of
the product in order to ensure that the specified requirements are
met" (Paragraph 4.4.1). As is true of other ISO requirements, it is
left to the discretion of the organization to select and implement
those activities that ensure compliance with requirements and
then to be certain that written procedures exist describing those
activities. Organizations, however, are not free to select only those
design activities that they currently have in place if the activities
are inadequate or if gaps exist in the process. Procedures for the
design process can be numerous, and all must be controlled documents (see chapter 6). Again, depending on the nature of the
organization and its products, each design phase can require several documented plans and procedures.

Records

Records pertaining to the general requirements include a list of
documents (plans and procedures) that have been prepared.
Needless to say, the design plans and procedures are controlled
documents, and appropriate records about their creation and distribution must be maintained. Those records that are part of the
document control system—for example, current revision status, a
list of recipients, and so forth—form part of the network of records
pertaining to the general requirements category.

   Because the design process is multistep, it is helpful to create
a flowchart or diagram of the steps or activities that are involved
in a particular organization. Such a diagram can become part of
the records that identify the activities, and it clearly illustrates to

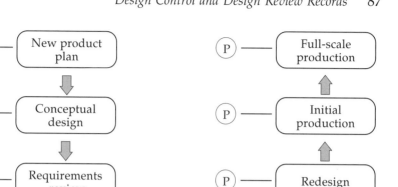

(P)—Indicates procedures are required

Source: Modified from Kaoru Ishikawa. *Introduction to Quality Control.* Tokyo: JUSE Press, Ltd., 1991, p. 340. Reprinted with permission.

Figure 5.2. Example of the generic design process—showing where procedures are required.

the organization itself where written plans and procedures are required.

As shown in Figure 5.2, the design process progresses through many steps, some of which are repeated in circular form, until the item has the performance characteristics desired by the organization and required in the specifications.

Procedures themselves can form part of the required records pertaining to the design process. Organizations that design on a project-by-project basis often have two-tiered design procedures. At the bottom tier are basic operating procedures governing the day-to-day mechanics of operation. Examples include *design approval and release, drawing list control and usage,* and *drawing checkout and revision.* The second tier procedures govern the actual project itself and serve two purposes.

1. To tailor standard procedures to fit the specific requirements of a particular program

2. To plan and direct the activities peculiar to the particular program

The project-specific procedures and plans, the second tier, become records of the project from a management point of view. They reflect not only the initial intent of the project, but, if well maintained, the changes that occurred as the project progressed.

Requirement 2: Specified requirements must be met. The organization proves that it has met specified requirements by adhering to each of the enumerated activities. No specific category of records is required by this statement. Rather, the cumulative records that pertain to all of the activities reveal that the organization has met specified requirements.

Requirement 3: Responsibilities must be identified for each design activity. Identifying who is responsible for each design and development activity can be accomplished by developing functional descriptions of the categories of responsibilities. This is in addition to the standard organizational charts. When working on a project basis, the organization can assign more specific responsibilities within the planning documents, even assigning individual tasks.

Some projects may be large enough to warrant their own organizational charts.

Requirement 4: Personnel must be qualified to perform the activities. The proof that individuals are qualified to perform the activities should be in the form of records. Similar to training records (see chapter 14), personnel qualification records should be maintained separately from the human resources personnel file and used only for purposes of quality assessment. It is easier to identify those who perform the design activities and to retrieve and update their quality-related qualifications if separate files are maintained in the quality records department. Thus, the personnel qualification file should contain only information that pertains to an individual's qualifications for performing some function within the design process.

A quality auditor might ask, "Why is this individual qualified to conduct this design activity?" Qualifications can include either experience or education or both, depending on the level of skill required and the activity in question. For example, some purely technical staff can be qualified because of experience. For designers, on the other hand, education is often the qualifying factor. Extensive experience and an associate's degree may qualify some designers. But in some disciplines, extensive design and analysis experience may be as valuable as a college degree. The individual's record should clearly define the factor that qualifies him or her to perform a particular design activity.

Since responsibility for design and development activities most logically is defined by function, paper-based, manual qualification files should be organized in similar fashion. Under the department or function, the next hierarchical level should be job title. Individual files are the third order in the hierarchy, with one file folder for each person who holds that title in a particular function.

Maintaining this information on a database facilitates the operation, since it permits rapid updating and ready retrieval. If a master database of personnel attributes is maintained in the human resources department, a subset of those individuals who

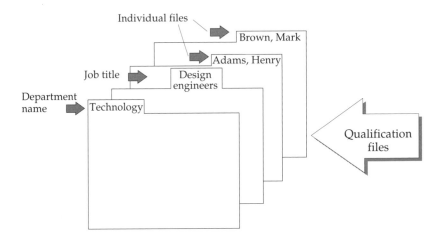

Figure 5.3. How to organize paper files for qualification.

function in the quality units can be retrieved for qualification status.

Requirement 5: Adequate resources must be available to personnel. As discussed in chapter 3, information that is external to the organization must be in-house and organized in a way that provides ready access. Such information is part of the resources requirement that must be made available during the design process. Industry as well as customer specifications and standards form part of the technical data that must be available for reference. In addition, historical reference data pertaining to similar designs that have been developed in the past by the company may be used. Items such as parts catalogs, repair manuals, service bulletins, and drawings—internal as well as from other companies—are included in this resources category. Some organizations provide control and access by organizing such items in a technical library. Procedures similar to those developed for bibliographic control can be instituted to facilitate use by personnel involved in the design process.

Requirement 6: Organizational interfaces must be identified. Requirement 7: Technical interfaces must be identified. Accomplished through procedures and written in text format or, more frequently, depicted graphically, these interfaces should always be defined by department, function, or title, never by individual names. No further records are required other than those maintained for the document control system.

Requirement 8: Information that is passed across groups must be documented, transmitted, and reviewed. Records are required here to reveal the nature of the information that has been communicated across the different groups having input into the design process. Records can consist of memos, E-mail, descriptive documents, and even conversations—by phone or in person. There must be concrete evidence revealing the kind of information that has been exchanged pertaining to the design process. There must be evidence that reviews of interdepartmental information are taking place regularly. Such records should be maintained together with the design history information and organized according to project management rules.

Requirement 9: Design inputs must be identified. Requirement 10: Design inputs must be documented. Requirement 11: Design inputs must be reviewed for adequacy. Although these three requirements appear under the heading "Design Input," an initial review must first be held to define project or design requirements. The main purpose is to ensure that all project requirements are understood and that they are accounted for. Requirements are accounted for by undersanding what they are, where they come from, and how they will be reflected in the design. Technical requirements and project requirements must be accounted for at this stage.

This means documenting the requirements that have been identified and providing evidence that appropriate personnel have reviewed them for adequacy. Records should include the following.

- Technical requirements (often found in the contract)
- Statutory and regulatory requirements
- Project management requirements (examples are schedule, budget, personnel, organization, and responsibilities)

It is important that evidence is available to indicate that these requirements have been reviewed. This includes minutes of any meetings and lists of attendees. Any action items that arise from the meetings should be recorded, together with the names of the individuals responsible for the action items. Action items should be sent to the individuals responsible for carrying them out.

Technical requirements can be broad or extremely detailed, depending on the item. They can include such factors as performance, size, weight, reliability, maintainability, and so forth. The technical requirements should be referred to the document from which they emanate, and this information becomes part of the record.

Applicable statutory and regulatory requirements should be cited as well, and it is mandatory that these be available in the organization for active use. Chapter 3 discusses the importance of collecting, organizing, and retrieving all externally produced standards and requirements.

Project management requirements include such record items as schedules, budgets, personnel, organization, and responsibilities. Schedule requirements are contractual and records of prepared schedules can take several forms from a time line to a detailed milestone schedule. Personnel and budget are decided internally to support the schedule requirements. An organization chart for a project can be developed at this point, even if individual names are not yet available.

Requirement 12: Incomplete, ambiguous, or conflicting requirements must be resolved with those who are responsible for imposing the requirements. Any requirement that cannot be met by the organization must be discussed with the party or group that has imposed it. This includes project requirements, such as schedule deadlines, as well as technical requirements. Evidence in the form of records must exist that proves that communication has occurred between the organization and the party that is imposing the requirement. Letters, faxes, telephone conversation accounts, and E-mail should be retained as proof that discussions have occurred. If any changes in requirements result from the discussions, the changes must be documented and the source of the changed requirements must be cited. Changes must also be communicated to all individuals and departments affected in the supplier organization. Records of the communication must also be created and maintained.

Requirement 13: Results of contract review activities must be considered at the design input phase. If any changes are made during contract review, the affected departments must be notified before the contract is confirmed. Records of these notifications must be maintained. In addition, affected groups must ensure that the company has the capability for fulfilling the contractual requirements. If customer specifications differ from the supplier's general internal specifications for the product, the customer specifications must be prepared and routed for approval. Each department should maintain records of customer specifications for the products for which it is responsible.

Usually a design plan is prepared at this point that incorporates all of the requirements, internal and external, that guide the design process. The design plan, in essence, serves as a blueprint for the design process.

Requirement 14: Formal documented reviews of the design results must be planned and conducted. The design reviews must be formal. Prepared agendas and documents pertinent to the design should be distributed to attendees in advance of the review meeting. These items serve as proof that the design review meetings are planned, and they become part of the records for this activity. Minutes of the design review meetings must be recorded and distributed to attendees afterwards. The minutes and the list of attendees at the meetings become records that the design review meetings have been conducted. Any actions that result from the review meeting must be documented and the responsibilities for those actions clearly delineated. Those responsible for performing the actions must receive copies of the action lists as a record that they have been notified of what they are to do.

Requirement 15: The design review process must include representatives of all functions that are concerned with the design stage being reviewed. Records include a list of attendees at the meetings, their titles, and their department or function name. Information should also include their function's pertinence to the design stage that is being reviewed.

Requirement 16: Records must be maintained of the design reviews. Because several design review meetings are held throughout the design phase—preliminary, intermediate, and final design reviews—records of the review meetings and all attendees as well as action items and responsible parties can be quite voluminous. Minutes should include information on the topics that were discussed at the meeting. It is common for the following topics to be included in design review meetings.

- A discussion of the requirements

- A presentation of various design options, their pros and cons, how they were evaluated, and the reason that the final configuration was chosen

- A description of the chosen design configuration at its current state of development

- A discussion of further design development, including why, how, and when it will be done

- Identification of those design features critical to the success and safety of the design

- An assessment of risk to the project as well as suggestions for minimizing the risk

- A description of the analysis and testing necessary for design qualification

- A time line, showing efforts and intermediate deadlines, as well as a completion date for the design

Design reviews can take place at several phases of the design—concept, prototype, testing, and final design. Design review checklists are used frequently for each product development state. These checklists then become records of the design control process. During design reviews, data on performance and reliability tests should be available as well as information on subcontractors, process capabilities, and manufacturability. Incomplete data should be identified. Test items and conditions that will ensure quality and reliability are also data that become very valuable to the organization.

The *Guidelines,* Q9004-1, in Section 8.4.2 enumerate the following elements to be considered during the design review meetings.

a) Items pertaining to customer needs and satisfaction
   1) comparison of customer needs expressed in the product specification with technical specifications for materials, products, and processes;
   2) validation of the design through prototype tests;
   3) ability to perform under expected conditions of use and environment;
   4) unintended uses and misuses;
   5) safety and environmental compatibility;
   6) compliance with regulatory requirements, national and International Standards, and organization practices;
   7) comparisons with competitive designs;
   8) comparison with similar designs, especially analysis of the history of internal and external problems to avoid repeating problems.
b) Items pertaining to product specification
   1) dependability and serviceability requirements;
   2) permissible tolerances and comparison with process capabilities;
   3) product acceptance criteria;
   4) installability, ease of assembly, storage needs, shelf-life and disposability;
   5) benign failure and fail-safe characteristics;
   6) aesthetic specifications and acceptance criteria;
   7) failure mode and effect analysis, and fault tree analysis;
   8) ability to diagnose and correct problems;
   9) labeling, warnings, identification, traceability requirements, and user instructions;
   10) review and use of standard parts.
c) Items pertaining to process specification
   1) ability to produce product conforming to the design, including special process needs, mechanization, automation, assembly, and installation of components;
   2) capability to inspect and test the design, including special inspection and test requirements;
   3) specification of materials, components, and subassemblies, including approved supplies and subcontractors as well as availability;
   4) packaging, handling, storage, and shelf-life requirements, especially safety factors relating to incoming and outgoing items.

It must be remembered that the *Guidelines* are precisely that—they do not impose requirements; but they do provide guidance about satisfying the specific portions of the three contractual standards. In the *Guidelines,* the supplier is encouraged to consider the elements that have been itemized earlier "as appropriate to the design phase and product." In other words, it is not necessary to review each of the items for every kind of product at every single design review meeting. Some elements are more appropriate at certain phases than at others. The itemized elements, however, do provide good guidance on the types of records that feed into the design review process. Table 5.3 depicts the types of records that can be required for each of the itemized elements, depending on the nature of the product.

Requirement 17: Design output must be documented. Records consist of the design outputs themselves, the technical documents that an organization produces as the result of the design process. They include documents used throughout the process from production through servicing and can include drawings, specifications, instructions, software, and servicing procedures.[1] Many of these technical documents will enter the document control system and will, therefore, have records created for them as part of the document control process. It is necessary to identify any technical documents that are specific to customer or product so that identification and traceability requirements are satisfied.

Requirement 18: Design output must be expressed in terms of requirements that must be verified. Verification of requirements is accomplished through records pertaining to the next four requirements—19 through 22.

Requirement 19: Design output must meet design input requirements. What are the procedures and controls in place during the earlier design phases that reveal that the design output has met the design input requirements? The basis for the comparison should be described. It should be recorded to provide evidence that input requirements have been satisfied.

Requirement 20: Design output must contain or refer to acceptance criteria. The design output documents must include information about the acceptance criteria that they are meeting. The source of all requirements must be cited.

Requirement 21: Design output must identify characteristics that are crucial to safety and proper functioning. Features that are critical to the safe and proper functioning of the design must be identified in the design output documents.

Table 5.3. Records for elements of design reviews.

1. Product brief
2. Technical specifications—materials, products, and processes
3. Prototype tests—results
4. Conditions of use—results
5. Performance under certain environmental conditions—results
6. Unintended uses and misuses—what are they?
7. Compatibility with environment
8. Compatibility with concerns for safety
9. Compliance with regulatory requirements
10. Compliance with standards—national and international
11. Compliance with organization's practices
12. Comparisons made with competitive designs—results.
13. Comparison with similar designs—results.
14. Analysis of internal and external problem history of similar designs—results.
15. Requirements for reliability, serviceability, and maintainability.
16. Permissible tolerances
17. Comparison of tolerances with process capabilities
18. Product acceptance criteria
19. Description of installability
20. Description of ease of assembly
21. Description of storage needs
22. Description of shelf life
23. Description of disposability
24. Benign failure characteristics
25. Fail-safe characteristics
26. Diagnosis of problems; correction of problems
27. Labeling to be used
28. Warnings that have been prepared
29. Identification of products
30. Identification of traceability requirements
31. User instructions
32. Identification of special process needs
33. How assembly will be accomplished
34. How components will be installed
35. How automation is used in making the product
36. How mechanization is used in making the product
37. Organization's capability to inspect the design
38. Organization's capability to test the design
39. Identification of special inspection requirements

Table 5.3. Continued.

40. Identification of special test requirements
41. Material specifications
42. Specifications for components
43. Specifications for subassemblies
44. List of approved subcontractors
45. Identification of approved supplies
46. Availability of approved supplies
47. Identification of packaging requirements
48. Identification of handling requirements
49. Identification of storage requirements
50. Identification of shelf-life requirements
51. Identification of safety factors

Requirement 22: A review must be conducted of design output documents before release. All of the design output documents, such as drawings, specifications, and servicing procedures, must be reviewed before they are released. This is not unusual, because it conforms to the principles of configuration management, and it is the same requirement for all controlled documents that fall within the document control system.

Requirement 23: Design verification must be performed. Requirement 24: Records must be kept of design verification measures. A note in 4.4.7—"Design Verification"—elaborates on some of the activities that can be included in design verification.

> —performing alternative calculations;
> —comparing the new design with a similar proven design, if available;
> —undertaking tests and demonstrations, and
> —reviewing the design-stage documents before release.

If these activities are part of the verification process, records that provide results and attest to the fact that the activities have been conducted become necessary. Records of alternative calculations, records of similar proven designs and comparisons with the new design, records of demonstrations that have been conducted, records of test results, and records that provide evidence that the design stage documents have been reviewed before release all may need to be created and maintained for compliance with the design verification process. The *Guidelines, Q9004-1* elaborate on the activities that appear in Q9001. If testing and demonstrations are conducted using models or prototype tests, the test programs must be clearly defined, and the results must be recorded.

Requirement 25: Design validation must be performed. Design validation is performed to ensure that the product conforms to defined user needs or requirements. The standards specify that multiple validations may be necessary if there are different intended uses of the product. The *Guidelines* point out that periodic evaluations should be conducted at significant stages, and they can take the form of analytical methods, such as failure mode and effect analysis, fault-tree analysis, or risk assessment. Inspection and testing of prototype models or actual production samples can also be done. The records that should be maintained are those that provide the method of evaluation and the actual evaluation results. Section 8.5 of the *Guidelines* suggests conducting the following activities.

a) evaluation of performance, durability, safety, reliability, and maintainability under expected storage and operational conditions.

Records include the results of the evaluations that have been conducted and the conditions under which the evaluations have been conducted.

b) inspections to verify that all design features conform to defined user needs and that all authorized design changes have been accomplished and recorded.

Records include the types of inspections and the results of the inspections. The authorized design changes must be recorded as well, and there must be indication that the changes have been accomplished.

c) validation of computer systems and software.

Records consist of the results of any validation activities that have been conducted on the automated technologies that have been used.

Requirement 26: Design changes and modifications must be identified. Requirement 27: Design changes and modifications must be documented. Requirement 28: Design changes and modifications must be reviewed and approved by authorized personnel. Design changes are at the heart of configuration management, a concept that was discussed in chapter 3. The basic purpose is to control the release of changed documents that define the baseline of the design. Design changes in one aspect may affect the other aspects of the product. Design changes include the drawings themselves and any procedures that pertain to the product or process. All changes should be reviewed, approved, and signed by an authorized individual before they are released. Procedures similar to those instituted for document control should be followed when instituting design change procedures. Obsolete design documents must be removed from work areas and individuals' files. Care should be taken to ensure that the necessary reviews and approvals of design changes have taken place. The entire process should be formalized, and records must be kept of all activities that have taken place during the design change. Records include distribution lists for the drawings or documents, release dates, and master lists (similar to controlled documents), and signature lists—revealing that individuals have received the changes.

The 28 requirements reveal the numerous activities that take place during the design process. They imply that numerous records must be created and maintained for the organization itself to use and analyze as well as to prove that the activities have been conducted. Table 5.4 provides a list of questions that organizations can ask themselves about their design records as they prepare for ISO 9000 compliance.

The Role of the Quality Records Manager

Because of sheer volume alone, maintaining control over design process records is a complex, time-consuming task. Add to this the array of equipment, tools, and technologies available for managing design-related records and it becomes clear why devoted records management expertise in this area is desirable. The technical design process activities require education and experience that is vastly different from that necessary to manage the records pertaining to these activities. By devoting attention to the records,

Table 5.4. Examination of design process records requirements.

Questions to ask about design records

1. Have all of the design plans and procedures been included in the document control system?

2. Are the records that describe the qualifications of all design personnel clear? Are they organized well? Are they easily retrievable?

3. Do you have all of the industry specifications and standards that pertain to the design? Do all design personnel know where they are? Are they organized? Are they easily retrievable? Are they the latest issue?

4. Are the customer's specifications and standards available for reference?

5. Do you have access to similar designs that have been developed by the company in the past?

6. Are you creating and maintaining records on the interdepartmental communication that occurs pertaining to the design? Are you reviewing these records? How are these records organized? Where are they housed?

7. Do you have records revealing review of the technical requirements?

8. Do you have records revealing review of statutory and regulatory requirements?

9. Have you been creating and maintaining minutes of meetings? Do you have lists of the attendees at the meetings?

10. Have you created records of schedules?

11. Do you have records revealing the resolution of conflicting requirements?

12. Have all affected departments been notified of the customer's requirements? Do you have records of this notification?

13. How complete are your records of design review meetings? Do you distribute agendas in advance of the meetings? Do you have lists of attendees? Do you keep minutes? Do you distribute the minutes to attendees afterwards? Do you distribute action items to responsible individuals afterwards?

14. How do you prove that design input requirements have been met? What is your basis for comparison? What are the acceptance criteria? What are the sources of the requirements? Have all of these items been recorded? How and where?

15. Do you have records that identify the characteristics crucial to the safe and proper functioning of the design?

16. Can you prove that all design output documents have been reviewed before they are released?

Table 5.4. Continued.

17. Do you have records that provide results of design verification activities? Do you have records of alternative calculations? Do you have records of tests and demonstrations that have been conducted? Do you have the results? Are the test programs clearly defined?

18. Do you have records of validation activities? Do you have records of performance, durability, safety, reliability, and maintainability evaluations? Do you have records describing the conditions under which these evaluations took place? Have you inspected the design features to verify that they conform to defined user needs? Have all authorized design changes been recorded?

19. Do you have a clear and understandable process for making design changes or modifications? Do you have records revealing that the design changes have been reviewed and that they have been approved? Do you have records that reveal that all obsolete drawings and changes have been removed from individuals' files and work areas? Do you have records that the new ones have been distributed?

20. Do you have a design file of all configurations of the design?

21. Are your designs physically protected, or are they vulnerable to technical, human, or environmental destruction? Do you have backup?

the quality records manager can liberate technical personnel to concentrate on the design activities themselves. Table 5.5 summarizes the responsibilities of the quality records manager in the design control and review process.

Using Micrographics and Automated Technologies to Manage Engineering Drawings

The following has been excerpted and modified from a white paper entitled "Merging Technologies," written by Thomas W. Sims, president of Quintek Electronics. The paper was received by the author in 1993. It is reprinted with permission.

> The advances made in computer-aided design (CAD) technology during the past decade have provided the engineering community with a low-cost and extremely effective design tool. The capability of creating and modifying complex drawings electronically has revolutionized the design and drafting industry. In addition, the emergence of other new technologies such as optical disk, local area networks, and raster graphics workstations

Table 5.5. Responsibilities of the quality records manager in the design control and design review process.

1. Develop a records system for all records pertaining to design processes. This should include

    Definition of the types of records to create and maintain

    Selection of the appropriate tools and technologies to use—which media and formats.

    Selection of equipment and housing for the records

    Development of a collection system for the records

    Design of an effective retrieval system

    Design of organizing schemes

    Determination of retention requirements

    Development of checklists to ensure the completeness of required records

    Development of a records protection program—especially for designs, drawings, and test results

2. Ensure principles of configuration management are followed in all design-related activities. Monitor design change process.

3. Ensure that records from other areas are available for activities in the design process—contract review records, records of qualified personnel, and so forth.

4. Conduct training about design records for affected departments and personnel.

has provided the capability of controlling, storing, maintaining, and distributing drawings in digital format. To many companies, these new technologies and different data formats can be very confusing. Data control managers are faced with making key decisions affecting two of the company's most valuable assets, its documentation and its documentation control system. Most companies are looking for a way to merge their existing documentation data base with the new technologies in order to improve overall efficiency.

Paper Drawings

Engineering drawings on paper may be adequate for companies that have very few drawings, that require minimal access by employees, and that have a low volume of distribution. The disadvantages to paper become obvious as the amount of paper begins to grow. This can happen sooner than expected, especially when a large number of D- and E-sized sheets must be managed. The basic drawing management functions—accessing originals, making copies, distributing drawings, archiving, revising drawings, and so forth—can become extremely cumbersome during peak work hours. Inefficiencies created by the drawing control system can easily ripple through the entire company.

Digital Databases

The digital database provides storage of drawing data in raster or vector format. A network of terminals and workstations is typically tied to the storage subsystem, allowing retrieval, viewing, editing, and storing of image data. Print servers can also be connected to the network, allowing output to paper for working prints as well as the generation of aperture cards for external distribution. A complete digital documentation system requires a substantial investment initially, but it can pay for itself many times over by increasing overall efficiency in the long term, especially when large numbers of drawing are involved. The following system components are required.

- Optical storage subsystem
- Central or distributed processing software and hardware
- Raster or CAD workstations for all employees who require frequent access to the database
- Print servers and plotters
- A local area network to tie the system components together

Aperture Cards

Aperture cards require low upfront cost and provide several advantages over the paper database. Aperture cards are small, consistent in size and shape, and marked or punched with the drawing title and other pertinent information. These features simplify all drawing management functions, including storage, manual access, automated access, card duplication, and drawing distribution. Other benefits include the following.

- Paper copies can be generated from aperture cards in volume, using standard reader and printer equipment.

- The small size of the card makes it practical for an entire database to be duplicated and stored offsite in order to ensure the safety of the designs.

- Past revision levels can be stored and accessed to support outdated equipment in the field.

- Different drawings can be distributed to different locations.

- The images on microfilm will not degrade over time if it is used and stored in a reasonable environment.

- The aperture card can be used in a court of law as an admissible form of evidence.

One company, Quintek, manufactures a system that generates an aperture card directly from the digital file (raster or vector) using a low-power laser to image the film and a heat process to develop it. Check prints or design review drawings can be produced on aperture card first, then converted to C-sized paper prints. Released cards can be copied to paper format and distributed. A list of vendors of automated systems that handle engineering design changes and drawing revisions, including redlining, are included in appendix C.

Conclusion

The design control and design review processes clearly distinguish Q9001 as the most rigorous of the compliance standards. Neither Q9002 nor Q9003 include requirements pertaining to design control and review. Because the entire design process can be complex, so can the records. Records are often numerous and include not only information captured after the fact, but also the designs themselves, the calculations, time lines, and various graphic depictions of the design, and the planning and review activities. Organizations are encouraged to be systematic and orderly in activities pertaining to the design process and to incorporate existing technologies to streamline the process.

Notes

1. Robert W. Peach, ed. *The ISO Handbook,* 2nd ed. (Fairfax, Va: CEEM Information Services, 1994), 55.

CHAPTER 6

Document Control

Q9001—Section 4.5
Q9004-1—Sections 5.3, 8.8, 11.5, and 17.3

Introduction

Document control is a system of managing, distributing, and keeping records on the documents that have been created by an organization as part of its overall quality system. Confusion about document control can arise when a clear distinction is not made between activities pertaining to the creation and revision of a document and the records about the document—records of approval, authority, distribution, revision, retirement of the document, and so forth. Unfortunately, a clear distinction is not made in the ISO standards or in articles discussing document control. This book clarifies the distinction (see chapter 2) and presents the main elements that must be included in a document control system.

A tight document control system is based on principles of configuration management (described in chapter 4) as specified in Q9004-1 (*Guidelines*), 5.2.6. If the organization adheres to the elements that configuration management comprises and institutes activities and records commensurate with the elements, a compliant document control system will result. The interplay of a large number of documents that fall within the category of controlled documents and the number of activities that the control system comprises can easily lead to chaos, confusion, and disintegration of control. Emphasis on order, organization, and the logical conduct of activities leads to a smoothly operating document control system.

The main weakness in most document control systems centers around records: poorly created records, insufficient records, outdated records, and inaccurate records. Ironically, the ISO standards do not even mention the word *records* in Section 4.5. Yet a good document control system is based on a thoughtful, clear, and organized records system. Without the records maintained *about* the document control system, there would be no system.

Section 17.3 of Q9004-1 (*Guidelines*) does provide examples of the types of documents requiring control.

drawings,
specifications,
inspection procedures and instructions,
test procedures,
work instructions,
operation sheets,
quality manual,
quality plans,
operational procedures, and
quality-system procedures.

The procedures explained in this chapter can be incorporated into either a paper-based system or an electronic document management system. Emphasis should be placed on the procedures that exist and the tightness of those procedures, rather than on the media or format of the documents and records. The requirements to control the issuance and revisions of documents remain the same in both manual (paper-based) and electronic systems. Only the format of the document changes, and the manner in which the requirements are satisfied is different.

Reasons for Document Control

A document control system is required in a quality environment to ensure that

- All documents have been written by individuals who are knowledgeable about the activity that is being described.

- The documents have been reviewed by others in the organization who are also familiar with the described activity. Review ensures that all quality aspects of the activity have been addressed and that the document is accurate and complete.

- All individuals or workstations performing the activity have, indeed, received a copy of the procedures pertinent to their function.

- Individuals responsible for performing the activity have read and understood the procedures.

- Any changes made to the controlled documents go through the same route of creation, approval, and distribution as the originals.

- All obsolete or outdated procedures are removed from the workstations or individuals.

- Only valid procedures are being employed.

The basic purpose of a document control system is to prevent individuals and units within the organization from using inaccurate or outdated instructions and procedures that can adversely affect the quality of the product. These premises serve as the underlying foundation for the concept of *control* of documents. Violation of any one of them can result in inferior product quality. If, simply to expedite document preparation, anyone in the organization were permitted to write procedures or instructions, documents might be incorrect or incomplete. Inaccurate procedures or instructions can result in inferior products or in products that deviate from customer specifications. Thus control is imposed at the very origin of the document—on the individual who writes the procedures as well as on those who approve them.

In addition, document dissemination is limited to those predesignated individuals who must use the document. Section 4.5.2 of Q9001 specifies that documents should be controlled to ensure that

a) the pertinent issues of appropriate documents are available at all locations where operations essential to the effective functioning of the quality system are performed.

For example, it is highly unlikely that metallurgical laboratory personnel would need to receive instructions on how to inspect plate metal product. Sending documents to illogical sources like this can result in obsolete documents finding their way to the workstations where the activity is actually conducted. This can create confusion when a worker refers to a document for instructions not realizing that it has been superseded by a revision, and thus performs the activity incorrectly. Therefore, control over distribution, based on a need-to-know criterion, is justified.

Just as important, if not more so, are the records of those individuals and workstations designated as document recipients. At the heart of a document control system is the knowledge of who has which document—knowledge that can critically affect product quality. The reason is that changes occur to the document because of altered specifications, new customer requirements, or internal company modifications. Section 4.5.2 of Q9001 stipulates that control over documents should ensure that

b) invalid and/or obsolete documents are promptly removed from all points of issue or use, or otherwise assured against unintended use.

Unless the individuals or workstations can be identified, changes to the document, and even future revisions, cannot be delivered with any assurance or ease. Retrieving the outdated or obsolete versions of documents and replacing them with current ones directly affects product outcome.

The Elements Required in a Document Control System

Good records are absolutely critical to a smoothly operating document control system. Many quality records prove that certain procedures have been followed and that pertinent documents have been prepared and distributed to the proper individuals. The following elements must be included in any document control system if it is to satisfy the requirements of ISO 9000.

- Documents must be written by knowledgeable individuals.

- Documents must be approved before being distributed.

- Recipients must be selected by knowlegeable individuals within the organization.

- The names of individuals and workstations receiving documents must be recorded.

- Documents that are being used must be current.

- Documents must be received by individuals and customers (when this is required).

- Superseded and obsolete documents must be retrieved from in-house recipients, and customers must be notified of changes.

- Changes to documents must be reviewed and approved by the same functions or organizations that performed the original or previous review.

- Records of revisions must be maintained.

- Periodic document reviews must be conducted to ensure their current validity.

- Changes must be accounted for.

- A master list of documents must be maintained.

- Written procedures must exist that describe the document control system.

The document control section in the Q9001 standard is deceivingly short, but the activities required to institute and maintain document control procedures are cumbersome, detailed, and complex. The most important aspect of the entire document control activity is the records—the meticulous creation and maintenance of excellent records. Because many organizations are vulnerable in their document control procedures as well as in their record-keeping, it is a well-known fact that auditors will focus on this aspect of the quality system to find weaknesses. Because record-keeping can be difficult, if auditors cannot find noncompliance elsewhere, they usually will cite poor records in the document control system. It is the Achilles' heel in many organizations. As chapter 1 reveals, poor document control accounts for the greatest percentage of failures in those organizations desiring to be registered under the ISO 9000 standards.

The Hub Concept

Although many organizations operate by allowing individual departments to issue controlled documents, it is recommended that a *hub concept* be utilized. Borrowed from the airline and express mail industries, the hub concept promotes both the centralized handling of original documents—including records about the documents—and also the monitoring of information necessary for each controlled document. Centralized administration provides standardization, increases administrative efficiency, and ensures adequate control.

Under the hub concept, a document control center develops and operates a company-wide standard to systematically identify, distribute, issue, review, and revise all quality documents. The document control policies and procedures developed by the document control center are reviewed and approved by each department in the organization that is affected. Written procedures describing the document control system must be prepared, circulated for approval, and distributed to all affected departments. The document control procedural manual, in fact, is a controlled document and is subject to the rules that govern all controlled documents. The document control center reports to the quality records manager and can be managed by a paraprofessional at the supervisory level. Table 6.1 presents the responsibilities of the quality records manager in the document control process.

The document control center is responsible for administering the program that has been established to control documents. This includes maintaining the records necessary to support a document control system. The records should be available for inspection by the customer, by quality assurance representatives, by auditors, and by those departments participating in the document control procedures.

The document control center should be responsible for the following tasks.

Table 6.1. Responsibilites of the quality records manager in a document control system.

1. Develop a document control system to incorporate the elements specified in ISO 9000.
2. Manage the document control center.
3. Design all records pertinent to the document control system.
4. Develop an error-proof distribution method for controlled documents.
5. Ensure that all documents are reviewed and approved prior to release.
6. Develop and ensure compliance with an identification scheme for all controlled documents.
7. Ensure that revised documents pass through the same route of review and approval as original issue documents.
8. Ensure that all superseded documents are retrieved from individuals and workstations.
9. Develop and keep current a master list of all controlled documents.
10. Ensure that temporary document changes are handled according to established procedure.
11. Ensure that documents are revised after a certain number of temporary changes have been made to the document.
12. Develop backup procedures for all controlled documents to ensure that they are protected.
13. Develop a system to prevent the unauthorized reproduction of controlled, released documents.
14. Develop a periodic review program for all controlled documents to ensure the current validity of contents.
15. Educate all departments on the document control procedures that affect them to ensure their understanding and compliance.
16. Develop a method for ensuring that recipients have read and understood the documents that they have received.

- Developing a document control system to satisfy compliance with ISO 9000 requirements
- Preparing a document control manual
- Establishing release records for the documents and maintaining them
- Keeping accurate and complete records about the documents under its jurisdiction
- Providing document review procedures and approval requirements

- Maintaining historical records on documents
- Applying the same release system to all documents, regardless of type
- Preventing unauthorized changes to documents
- Retrieving superseded or obsolete documents
- Distributing documents
- Issuing unique identifiers to documents
- Preparing a master list of documents and keeping it current
- Administering an annual review program for controlled documents
- Ensuring consistency in the elements required to identify documents

Organizations currently operating document control systems may refer to Table 6.2 to determine how well their systems operate.

Developing a Document Control System

Preparation of Documents

The department issuing the document is responsible for preparing the original document according to its own established procedures. The issuing department has the necessary expertise in the subject. Procedures for testing corrosion of metal products, for example, should be prepared by individuals whose expertise lies in that area. The document control center does not write or revise documents.

Identification of Documents

The document control center should develop a method for assigning unique identification codes to documents. Before initiating a document, the issuing department should notify the document control center to avoid duplication and to establish consistency. An identification code should be placed on the approval page as well as on each page of the document. It is a good idea to des-

Table 6.2. Examination of document control requirements.

Questions to ask about a document control system

1. Do you have a written document control procedure?
2. Is your document control procedure a controlled document?
3. Are documents reviewed and approved before they are distributed?
4. Are pertinent documents approved by customer(s) before they are distributed?
5. Do you have a list of all documents that are valid and operative?
6. How can you prove that documents are distributed to those who should have them before operations are conducted?
7. Can you demonstrate which individuals or workstations should have copies of each document?
8. Do you have a system for revising documents?
9. Do the revisions pass through the same route of review and approval that the original issue documents do?
10. How do you prevent the use of superseded or obsolete documents?
11. Do you permit ad hoc, handwritten changes to documents that have already been officially distributed?
12. Are the current documents available at all of the workstations or operations where they are needed?
13. How do you prevent the unauthorized distribution of documents?
14. Are the documents appropriately identified?
15. Do you have backups of all current, valid documents?
16. Are documents reviewed periodically to ensure that they are still valid?
17. How do you handle changes to documents that must be effected immediately?
18. How many changes can be made to a document before it must be officially reissued as a new revision?
19. Have you instituted any way to check documents before they are released for distribution?
20. How do you ensure that all those who should receive a document have received it?
21. How do you ensure that previous versions of the document have been retrieved before the current revision is distributed?

ignate a specific format for the identification code, one that bears meaning and that can be used for all types of controlled documents. For example,

QRD-DCP-001—Quality Records Department—
Document Control Procedure

In this example, the first element is an abbreviation of the department that wrote the procedure. The second element is an abbreviation of the title of the document. The numbers simply designate it as the first document control procedure that was written. The department may issue several document control procedures, one for each aspect of the program. If another one is prepared, it will be designated with −002.

In addition, a specific location on each page should be designated for the placement of identifying document data, one element of which is a unique identification code. Many organizations place the document identifier in the upper right corner, or create a header or a footer on each page in which all identifying information appears.

The Responsibilities of the Issuing Department

Before a first-issue document is released for distribution, certain procedures should be followed. The issuing department should

- Ensure that the document number has been obtained from or coordinated with the document control center
- Identify the authorities that must approve the release of the document
- Prepare the document
- Prepare the approval page or cover page according to procedures specified by the document control center manual
- Circulate the original of the document to those whose approvals are required.

The manager of the issuing department is responsible for

- Reviewing the document for accuracy, content, and format.
- Either specifying the recipients of the document or indicating that the recipients specified by the individual who wrote the document are correct. (The issuing department is responsible for specifying individuals, departments, and workstations to which the document will be distributed.)
- Ensuring that the approved original document, together with completed paperwork, is routed to the document control center for release and distribution.

Approvals

The department issuing the document should provide proof to the document control center that approvals have been secured before the document control center releases the document for distribution. The centralized hub concept works especially well at this point. Whether it be in an electronic or a manual environment, a centralized checkpoint for approvals prevents the dissemination of unauthorized documents. Proof may be in the form of the signatures of personnel authorized to approve the document, as well as the dates on which they signed it.

Each organization should establish its own approval authorizations for different document categories, and this information should be disseminated to the departments that issue quality-related documents. The following examples are guidelines for establishing an effective approval process for document control.

- Quality assurance operating procedures and instructions often are reviewed by engineering departments and then approved by quality assurance.

- Specifications and process outlines can be reviewed and approved by engineering, production, and quality assurance.

- Production operating procedures or work instructions often are reviewed and approved by engineering and quality assurance.

- Laboratory procedures often are reviewed and approved by engineering and quality assurance.

- Marketing procedures can be reviewed and approved by engineering, production, and quality assurance.

The Approval Page

A document cover page or approval page can be used to record all approval signatures and dates. Thus, all elements identifying the document appear in one place. Identifying information should include

- Company name

- Type of document (if applicable)—for example, "Operating Procedure"
- Title of document—for example, "Qualification of Fabrication Furnaces"
- Revision number
- Effectivity date

Below the identifying elements appear the signatures.

- Signature of the person who wrote the document, together with his or her title and the date of signature
- Approval signatures, titles, and dates

The signatures should appear above the typed name and title. (See appendix G for an example of a cover page for an engineering procedure from Dee Howard Company.) The document control center is responsible for establishing a format for the cover page and for subsequent pages, so that control information appears on each page of the document.

Revision Numbers

Each document must bear a revision number. The first issue of a document may be designated as *Revision O*, with each succeeding revision bearing a sequential revision number. The revision number appears on each page of the document in a prespecified location, as well as on the cover page.

The Effectivity Date and Release of the Document

After the issuing department has secured all necessary approvals, the document control center reviews the approved document and assigns an effectivity date. The effectivity date is the date that the document is officially released for use by the document control center. A document is considered released after the original has been reviewed by the document control center and has been found to comply with procedures specified in the document control center procedures manual. Documents should never be issued unless they go through the document control center hub. This restriction prevents the inadvertent use of invalid or obsolete documents.

The release system provides records verifying that correct procedures have been adhered to prior to a document's release. The responsibility for maintaining release records for documents lies with the document control center under the direction of the quality records manager. To ensure tightness in the system, only the document control center should be allowed to prepare or revise release records.

The Distribution List

At the heart of a controlled document system is an accurate distribution list—the names of those departments, individuals, workstations, and, in some instances, customers who must receive the document. The department issuing the document provides the document control center with a completed *request for distribution*— a form that lists the recipients of the original issue document. The manager of the department issuing the document completes and signs the request for distribution. The request for distribution includes recipients within the organization as well as those outside the company—its customers. (It must be remembered that not all controlled documents must be submitted to customers.) Figure 6.1 provides an example of such a form.

For a revised document, the previous distribution list should be reviewed to ensure that there are no changes to the recipients of the previous revision. The document control center should send the distribution list to the manager of the issuing department for review before the document is reissued. The issuing department's manager indicates any changes to the distribution list and officially conveys these changes, in writing, to the document control center. The document control center, however, should be the only department authorized to make any changes to the distribution lists. If any changes to the distribution list are deemed necessary at any time, the document control center should be notified and provided with the current information.

Distribution of Documents

After approvals have been secured, the department issuing the document should route it to the document control center, along

---

REQUEST FOR DISTRIBUTION

Document number _____ Revision number _____

Title _____

Customer approval required? Yes ☐   No ☐

Names of customers requiring approval:

_____   _____

_____   _____

INTERNAL DISTRIBUTION

Recipient   Department   Number of copies

_____   _____   _____

_____   _____   _____

_____   _____   _____

_____   _____   _____

_____   _____   _____

_____   _____   _____

I have checked the attached document and verify that it is accurate both in content and format. I request that it be distributed to the recipients indicated.

_____   _____

Department manager   Date

Figure 6.1. Example of a request-for-distribution form.

with the completed request for distribution. At this point, the document control center checks the title page and headings of the document for accuracy. If any errors are found, regardless of their nature, the issuing department is responsible for correcting the errors. The document control center cannot alter any information on an approved document. Rather, the document is routed back to the manager of the issuing department, with a request for corrections. To prevent any confusion, requests for corrections on approved documents should be made in writing. Developing a simple form, such as that depicted in Figure 6.2, facilitates this process.

Responsibilities of the Document Control Center

Internal Distribution. After reviewing the original document and the request for distribution, the document control center should

- Check the document for complete identification on each page.
- Check the document for complete information on the approval page, ensuring that all items of information specified are included. The approval page is always considered to be page 1 of the document. Each page of the document should include the page number and the total number of pages in that particular document, for example,

   Page 15 of 45

- Check that, in addition to the page number, the document and revision numbers also appear on each page, for example,

   Page 2 of 8

   QAR-DCP-001

   Rev. 1

- Prepare a file folder for that document, placing identifying information on the file folder label, for example,

---

DOCUMENT CONTROL
REQUEST FOR CORRECTIVE ACTION

Document number _____   Revision number   _____

Title _____

The following problem with this document has been identified. It is herewith attached and sent to you for correction.

DESCRIPTION OF PROBLEM

_____

_____

_____

_____

_____

_____   _____

Document control signature   Date

CORRECTIVE ACTION: Please specify the corrective action that will be taken to remedy this problem.

_____

_____

_____   _____

Department manager   Date

[Please return completed form to the document control center]

Figure 6.2. Example of a request for corrective action form for controlled documents.

QAR-DCP-001 (document identifier)

Hiring Procedures (abbreviated title)

- Prepare a distribution list for that document.
- Create the necessary number of copies.
- Assemble the documents to be distributed.
- Deliver the documents.
- Require the recipients or designated alternates to sign and date the *distribution list form* (see Figure 6.3 for an example of such a form).
- Retrieve any previous revisions of the document from the recipient prior to distribution of the current revision. The new revision should not be relinquished until the previous revision is retrieved.

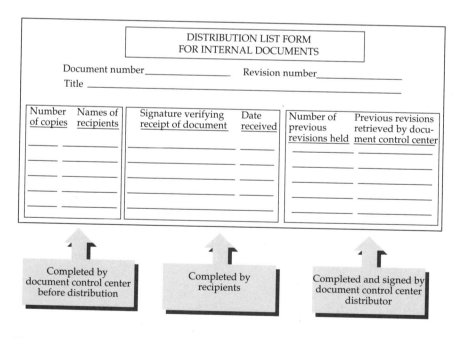

Figure 6.3. Example of a distribution list form.

- File the distribution list form of the document with the original document.
- Pull the previous version of the document from the active document file and retire it to the superseded file.

External Distribution. When the recipient of a document is a customer of the organization, different procedures must be followed. Depending on customer preference, electronic or paper documents will be distributed. When documents are electronically distributed externally, the document control center should

- Prepare a transmittal form, specifying the date and enumerating the documents that are being sent.
- Keep a record in the customer file of the transmittal form.
- Notify appropriate departments within the organization that electronic transmittal has taken place.

Distribution of Documents Requiring Customer Approval. Some documents require customer approval prior to implementation. If this is the case, the department initiating the document indicates this on the request for distribution form, where the customer is specified as a recipient. A document that requires customer approval before implementation cannot be distributed internally until approval is received. If an individual in the organization requires a copy of an unapproved customer document, the document should include a note indicating that it is as yet unapproved. This procedure also holds true for internally distributed documents. Designating the unapproved document as a "work copy only" is one way of handling such a requirement. The document can be made inaccessible to individuals within the organization in the same manner as those documents that are going through the review and approval process. The document control center is responsible for creating and maintaining records on customer approvals, indicating that they have been received and showing the dates they were received.

Using Databases for Recordkeeping in Document Control

A database should be used to record all data elements pertaining to the document: the document's name, its revision status, the date of issuance, and all recipients. The database should also include customer names and the date that approval has been received for each document requiring customer approval. The customer information should include all necessary document information as well: the document title, document number, revision number, the writer, the department, the date transmitted (or sent), and the date and mode of approval. An effectivity date is then assigned by the document control center, and the same procedures are followed for internal distribution that have been described earlier in this chapter.

It often is necessary to establish a follow-up system for those documents that require customer approval. This ensures that necessary procedures and work instructions can be distributed prior to material processing. Some documents require approval by some customers but can be used to perform operations for other customers without their approval. In such cases, it should be noted on the document that customer approval is required, but the specific customer's name should be added after the notation. For example, the information on the first page of the document can read "Customer Approval Required—Alliance Only." If several customers require approval, it should be so noted, with the actual names of the customers specified on the document. When approvals are received, the dates should be recorded on the document, adjacent to the customers' names.

Requests for Additional Documents

After a document has been released by the document control center, there may be requests for additional copies. Such requests should be made in writing, either electronically or on a paper form, such as a request for distribution. Verbal requests for copies should not be accepted or processed.

Revisions

All changes to documents that affect quality or are part of the quality system are monitored by the document control center. Section 4.5.3 of Q9001 requires the following:

Changes to documents and data shall be reviewed and approved by the same functions/organizations that performed the original review and approval, unless specifically designated otherwise.

Only the department that issued the document originally should be allowed to make any changes to that document. Revisions to documents must be formally processed, and they require approval by the same functional organizations as the original issue, or by others authorized by the original signers on their behalf. The following procedures should be employed in making revisions.

- The originating department notifies the document control center that it wishes to make a revision.

- The original document should not be changed, but, instead, a working copy should be made for purposes of revision. The document writer works with the copy. The document control center can provide the writer with a designated working copy.

- The person wishing to make the change completes a form describing the changes and their location. A *record of revisions* form can accompany the revised original when it is being routed or circulated for approval signatures. (See appendix G for an example of a revision log from The Dee Howard Company.) This form, which accompanies the revised original, becomes a record and is deposited with the document control center. If the revisions are to be sent to a customer, the record of revisions can be printed and will accompany the revised document as it is sent to the customer.

- The section that has been revised in the document should also be marked by some sort of distinguishing characteristic such as a different typeface or a marginal indicator, to highlight the section that has been changed. Section 4.5.3 of Q9001 states,

  Where practicable, the nature of the change shall be identified in the document or the appropriate attachments.

- It is important to note the revision status on each page of the revised document. The revision number forms part of the identifying information that appears on each page and should be accompanied by a date.

- The revised document is circulated to authorized personnel for full approval processing. Revisions to documents require approvals by the same departments and levels of management as the original issue document.

- After approvals have been secured, the issuing department notifies the document control center and requests that the document be checked and released.

- At this point, the document control center follows the procedures described earlier in this chapter prior to distribution and for distribution.

- Unless individuals have left their positions, the people who received the original also receive the revision.

All records pertaining to the previous revision must be updated by the document control center. The document should be removed from the active documents file, placed in a *superseded* file, and preserved for historical purposes. It is not uncommon for auditors to ask how the superseded documents and records are handled.

When several customers require approval of a specific document before its use, and approval has not been received from all of the customers, two revisions can be considered valid—one revision for some customers and another for others. The earlier version is considered valid to use for some customers' products until they approve the newer version.

Appendixes and Addenda

Appendixes and addenda to documents should be considered as major changes. If such changes are required, the document should be revised.

Temporary Document Change Notices

A system must be devised that can accommodate changes to documents that must be effected immediately. Organizations often accomplish this with a *temporary document change notice*. This notice is completed by the individual who wishes to effect the change, and it includes all pertinent information about the document: title, number, and revision number. It also should include a description of the change itself. It should be signed by the initiator and the same individuals (or their designated alternates) who signed the original document. The change to the document cannot become effective before the last dated signature on the change form.

It is a good idea to limit both the number of change notices that can be issued for a particular document and the amount of time that the change notices can remain valid. After a certain number of changes to a document, the change should be incorporated into the document, thus creating a new revision. This is done to avoid confusion on the part of the document's readers.

Document Control Center Responsibilities. The document control center is responsible for releasing and distributing a temporary document change notice, and the release and distribution should be handled in the same manner as that of a complete document. The document control center prepares a distribution list for the temporary document change, duplicates the document, and requires signatures from recipients of the temporary document change notice. When the change has been incorporated into the document, thus creating a new revision, the document control center distributes the revision and retrieves both the previous revision and the temporary document change from the recipients. Distributed copies of both of these items should be destroyed by document control center personnel.

Annual Review of Documents

All documents should be reviewed annually by the issuing department, according to a schedule determined by the quality records department. During this review, each document should be examined for current validity, and, if no changes are required, the document may stand as written. At this time, the issuing department should also review the distribution list to ascertain the current validity of each document that it issues. Any necessary additions or deletions can be made at this time. The issuing department officially notifies the document control center of distribution changes by completing a request for distribution form with all necessary changes. The document control center is required to maintain the obsolete distribution list as well as the updated one. In order to prove that the annual review has taken place, the document control center should request information, in writing, from the issuing department that it has reviewed both documents and distribution lists. A form can be developed to accomplish this proof. The form is then signed by the issuing department and is returned to the document control center.

A rotating annual review schedule for documents should be prepared by the document control center, and this schedule should be sent to all affected departments. Developing a tickler file will facilitate the management of the annual review process and can be used to notify the document control center (1) that a certain category of documents is approaching the annual review date, and whether or not (2) the issuing department has completed its annual review on time.

Master List of Documents

The document control center should maintain a master list of all controlled documents. Section 4.5.2 of Q9001 states,

> A master list or equivalent document-control procedure identifying the current revision status of documents shall be established and be readily available to preclude the use of invalid and/or obsolete documents.

Utilizing a database, this list can be reconfigured to provide valuable information concerning document distribution. The document control center should publish periodically a list of controlled documents by recipients, enumerating those documents that are currently valid and operative and should be in that individual's or department's possession. Each individual who receives a copy of the list should check the documents in his or her possession against the list to ensure that the documents are current and valid and that the document control center distribution records are accurate. The individual should return a signed *verification form* to

VERIFICATION FORM
FOR CONTROLLED DOCUMENTS

To _____ Date sent _____

Title _____ Department _____

Please check the attached list of documents against those that you have in your possession. Complete this form and return it to the document control center.

Documents in my possession match the list: Yes ☐   No ☐

If your answer is NO, please indicate the discrepancies below.

Document number	Document title	Problem
_____	_____	_____
_____	_____	_____
_____	_____	_____
_____	_____	_____
_____	_____	_____
_____	_____	_____

_____   _____
Signature   Date

Figure 6.4. Example of a verification form.

the document control center. See Figure 6.4 for an example of such a form. If updated or additional documents are necessary, or if there are discrepancies in the document control center records, the individual should notify the document control center.

The Organization of Documents in Document Control Center Files

Document control files should be physically separated into active, superseded, and obsolete sections. The active section includes the originals of all documents that are active and operative. The superseded section contains originals of those documents that have since been superseded by revisions. The obsolete section contains documents that are not operative in any form or revision—those documents that have been removed from circulation. It is a good idea to microfilm and index the superseded and obsolete documents for historical purposes. If this is done, and two copies are made of the microfilm, one for in-house use and one for an offsite storage facility, then the superseded and obsolete documents in the file should be destroyed by document control center personnel according to procedure.

The Active Documents File. Originals of active documents should be organized physically in some order that is meaningful for the organization and appropriate to the document types. A section should be established for each document type—for example, "Operating Procedures," "Final Inspection," and so forth. Within each section, the documents can be arranged in order based on the identification code for each document. A separate file folder is prepared for each document, with identifying information on the label: document number, document title, and revision number. Using color-coded labels for different document types aids in filing and retrieval, as does the file folder tab placement. Each file folder should contain the original of the document and all information and records pertaining to that document. This includes, but is not limited to, requests for distribution for the document, the document's distribution list form, and an annual review of documents form.

The Superseded and Obsolete Documents Files. When a document has been replaced by a revised version, the entire file folder should be removed from the active documents section in the files and placed in the superseded documents file. The folder and all of the contents should be stamped with the word *Superseded* by the document control center personnel. The same procedure should be followed for obsolete documents, with the file folder and all supporting records being stamped *Obsolete*. Section 4.5.2 of Q9001 specifies

> any obsolete documents retained for legal and/or knowledge-preservation purposes [should be] suitably identified.

The distribution lists for both superseded and obsolete documents should be retained as part of the document file because questions often arise as to who received copies of certain documents issued in the past.

The Effect on Document Control of a Change in Personnel

In order to keep document control records current and accurate, and in order to ensure the correct and complete distribution of documents, a procedure should be instituted that notifies the document control center of personnel transfers, resignations, and additions in departments where controlled documents are involved. If an employee leaves a department, either because of transfer or resignation, the documents in his or her possession should be given to the document control center, and document control center personnel should be notified of the change. A database that includes all pertinent document information can expedite personnel changes that affect document receipt. In order for such a system to be effective, however, a mechanism must be in place to notify the document control center so that names of individuals can be added and deleted and, in the case of transfers, department names can be changed. Otherwise, the accuracy of document distribution and receipt records cannot be ensured, and documents cannot be distributed to the proper personnel.

Using Electronic Document Management Systems

In today's organization, it makes little sense to institute a document control system from scratch by employing manual, paper-based methods. Organizations that are weighed down with three-ring binders and the need to physically deliver paper documents find it increasingly difficult and costly to maintain such paper-based document control systems. This becomes evident as changes to documents begin to escalate. Electronic document management systems provide built-in security and control, electronic routing, rapid signature approvals, and monitoring of access to documents in the system. Appendix C contains a list of vendors providing such systems for engineering and document control.

Organizations that currently do not have a document control system in place are encouraged to design one utilizing the available electronic tools, collectively referred to as electronic engineering document management (EDM) systems. EDM systems streamline document revision through computerized editing, markup, and redlining and distribute the latest revision of a digitized document to all parts of an organization.[1] EDM systems should be able to

- Manage a wide variety of document formats, such as scanned paper drawings, CAD files, illustrations, text documents, and technical manuals.
- Provide indexing and search and retrieval capabilities.
- Offer access for groups and individual users according to specific document types.
- Link documents.
- Prevent the accidental updating of a document simultaneously by more than one person.
- Control revisions and changes. Systems should enable access by default to the most recent revision. After a document is changed, the system should automatically increment the revision. It should be able to remove previous versions from the active documents file and store them elsewhere for historical purposes.
- Create an audit trail. An important aspect is that they should automatically capture all actions taken on the document and all access to the document, as well as provide an audit trail that captures the history of the change.

- Manage markup. It should enable reviewers to create notations and to suggest changes without altering the original document.

- Control document release.

One example of such a system, CIMLINC, used at General Electric (GE) Gas Turbines in Greenville, South Carolina, was described in an article in *Document Management* in 1992.[2] At this facility, GE maintains between 25,000 and 30,000 documents, each one having multiple distribution copies and some having multiple revisions. Using the LINKAGE product from CIMLINC, the manufacturing, quality assurance, and systems groups scan their paper documents into LINKAGE forms. New documents are created in LINKAGE. The documents then pass through five levels prior to distribution.

1. In engineering—under development

2. QC unchecked—awaiting quality review

3. QC unapproved—checked, but needs work—not approved

4. QC checked—OK, awaiting release

5. Released

"QC checked" applies the approver's scanned, cursive signature to the form. Sign-offs and approvals are obtained electronically by passing draft versions of the documents across the network. LINKAGE keeps track of a document's status automatically, recording dates, times, and names of those participating in the development and approval process. Historical document files (superseded versions) are locked and cannot be edited, written over, or erased. If an approved or released procedure is copied for modification, the scanned signature stays behind, permitting use but clearly designating the variant as unchecked by the quality assurance department. Utilizing such a system will save thousands of hours of clerical effort just in tracking the genealogy of documents.

Organizations preparing for ISO registration should consider the cost of developing and then maintaining a paper-based, manual, document control system and weigh that against the benefits that they can reap from establishing one that will reduce the need for ring binders and their costly, cumbersome control.

Conclusion

Document control is a major weakness in many organizations. The pitfalls center around a poor understanding of the records involved: what kinds of records to create, how to maintain them, how to ensure currency, and how to verify that all information across the record types is compatible. Focusing on the development of a clear, logical, and orderly records system for document control will protect organizations from vulnerability in this area.

Notes

1. Les Cowan, "Engineering Document Management Systems Come of Age," *Document Image Automation* 11 (March/April 1991), 60–67.

2. W. Lee Hales, "ISO 9000: The CIM Connection," *Document Management* 2 (November/December 1992), 17–22.

CHAPTER 7

Purchasing Records

Q9001—Sections 4.6 and 4.7
Q 9004-1—Section 9.0 (all portions)

Material Identification and Traceability Records

Q9001—Section 4.8
Q 9004-1—Sections 9.8, 11.2.2, and 11.2.3

Introduction

According to a recently completed study, Section 4.6 of the Q9001 standard, "Purchasing," is responsible for more than 6 percent of the instances in which organizations fail to achieve registration (see chapter 1). Most of the problems center around weak or non-existent documents and records. Since this portion of the standards is a major cause of failure, it is discussed in detail.

How Purchasing Activity Relates to Product Quality

To be succinct, the output of one organization becomes the input of another. If a company begins its operations with inferior materials or components, it is nearly impossible to achieve high quality in the finished product. Good quality raw materials are the basis for a good quality finished product. Raw materials become part of the company's final product, and, as such, directly affect the quality of that final product. The rationale for quality standards in the purchasing arena is therefore evident. The purchasing system and its documents must clearly define the procedures for all of the activities that affect product quality, and records must capture the information about what has been done to satisfy and comply with those procedures. The purchasing system thus becomes an integral part of the quality loop.

As with all other elements of the standards that affect quality, the key phrase in this section is "planned and controlled," as stated in Q9004-1. Purchasing activities must not be haphazard or chaotic, as happens in many organizations. There should be clearly defined steps to follow, ensuring consistency in ordering and resulting in consistency of the quality of raw materials. The planning phase begins with the careful preparation of purchasing procedures, including

- The evaluation and selection of acceptable subcontractors
- A description of quality system controls
- The review and approval of purchasing documents to ensure that the specified requirements are adequate
- The verification of purchased product
- The control of product supplied by customers
- The storage of purchased product
- The maintenance of purchased product

The quality activity involves (1) selecting subcontractors who can supply the materials, components, and assemblies that become part of the company's product, (2) clearly and accurately defining the requirements for the materials that have been ordered, and (3) verifying that the received materials conform to the requirements. The basic requirement, as stated in Q9001, is that

> The supplier shall establish and maintain documented procedures to ensure that purchased product conforms to specified requirements.

As is true with most requirements in the ISO 9000 series, it is good business practice to operate according to this standard, regardless of whether or not the ISO standards serve as the organization's general guidelines.

The Role of Records

Records serve as evidence that planning and controls are in place. Unfortunately, implied records prevail in this section. The only requirement for records is stated in Q9001, Paragraph 4.6.2, c: "establish and maintain quality records of acceptable subcontractors." Complying with the purchasing requirements of the standards, however, necessitates more records than are specified in this statement.

Beginning with purchasing procedures, records of the controlled documents provide proof that individuals who should be working according to given procedures have received them. Furthermore, records reveal that the procedures have been followed and, perhaps most important, that the system is working according to plan. The purchasing system, as it relates to the quality program, begins with the selection of qualified suppliers. The method used to determine suppliers' qualifications must be recorded. Records about the selected suppliers should be maintained, providing clear reasons for their selection. As is enumerated in Q9004-1, Paragraph 9.3, various reasons can serve as the basis for selection; or a combination of the following methods can be utilized.

   a) on-site evaluation of subcontractor's capability and/or quality system;
   b) evaluation of product samples;
   c) past history with similar products;
   d) test results of similar products;
   e) published experience of other users.

Selection of qualified suppliers, therefore, must be based on information, and the organization should create and maintain records that provide data on which method or methods have been used as the basis for selection. Depending on the selection criteria, the following records can be required.

- *Records of the onsite assessment and evaluation of a supplier's capability and/or quality system.* Such records can be voluminous in both kind and number. Assessment and evaluation amounts to supplier audits, which can be time-consuming and result in audit records that examine most or all aspects of the supplier's quality system. Records can encompass each of the activities covered in the ISO series of standards and involve the soundness of the entire quality system.

- *Records of product sample evaluations.* When an organization evaluates product or material samples from a supplier, records of that evaluation must be created and maintained. The records, of course, will depend on the type of evaluation conducted. For example, if chemical analysis is required to determine the composition of a raw material, the records of evaluation will comprise the results of the analysis, including the elements tested for and the percentages of those elements in the materials. It is understood that part of the activity will be a comparison with the organization's internal specifications for chemical composition—with upper and lower limits. The records, then, should also include an indication that the comparison was made, and by whom.

- *Records of past history with similar products.* An organization may elect to use a particular supplier by relying on the reputation of the supplier for providing high quality materials or components. If this is the method chosen, records can include the organization's past experiences with that particular supplier, such as chemical analysis, as described in the preceding paragraph. The organization can also rely on another, similar, organization's records of past history with the supplier. If the latter approach is taken, it must be noted that it is possible to rely on the records of another organization's experiences *only* if that organization is reliable and responsible *and* if the quality system in that other organization equals its own.

- *Records of test results of similar products.* As explained in chapter 2, many quality decisions are based on records through inference, that is, it is assumed that, if the records are controlled and orderly, then the quality system also is controlled and orderly, and the product that emanates from that quality system is above reproach. The rationale for this category of purchasing records is also inferential, that is, if similar supplies from the vendor have been tested and the test results comply with the organization's specifications, then it is assumed that other supplies from the same vendor also will meet the requirements of the purchasing organization.

Regardless of the method used to select qualified suppliers, it is important to (1) document the methods that the organization will use to write procedures, (2) create and maintain records proving that the described methods have followed the procedures, and (3) record the results of the selection criteria. The quality records manager can be extremely helpful in ensuring that quality system controls are effective. Some of the responsibilities that the quality records manager should assume in purchasing and in material identification and traceability activities are presented in Table 7.1. The purchasing organization must be able to prove, through records, that the methods being utilized result in the receipt of consistently high-grade materials from the supplying organization.

Purchase Orders

Part of the controls involve clearly and accurately describing the items or materials that are being ordered from the subcontractor. If the subcontractor produces many similar materials, it is imperative that there be no confusion as to which materials are being ordered. What are referred to as *purchasing documents* in the ISO standard include all types of records, specifications, drawings, and even conversations that elucidate and describe the ordered materials, with the purpose of ensuring that no misunderstanding exists. Of course, it is always possible to return the wrong materials, but this can affect contract deadlines and risk displeasing customers. Complying with requested deadlines is part of the contract review process and agreed-upon deadlines should be adhered to as part of the quality process.

Table 7.1. Responsibilities of the quality records manager in purchasing and material identification and traceability.

1. Define records requirements for purchasing activities.
2. Develop records (forms) to ensure that all appropriate information is being recorded.
3. Ensure that purchasing documents fall under the jurisdiction of the document control center.
4. Create and maintain records about qualified subcontractors.
5. Develop a records system for the onsite assessment of a subcontractor's quality system.
6. Collect, organize, and maintain records of product sample evaluation of subcontractors' materials.
7. Collect, organize, and maintain records of subcontractors' past history with similar supplies.
8. Be able to match the list of qualified subcontractors with the results of prior evaluations of those subcontractors.
9. Be able to retrieve receipt inspection and test results of materials from qualified subcontractors.
10. Ensure that all external industry and military specifications and standards cited in the purchase order are in-house, organized, and readily retrievable.
11. Develop a records system for organizing and retrieving all written agreements with subcontractors.
12. Develop quality performance history files on all subcontractors.
13. Develop a records system for any customer-supplied product.
14. Develop a workable identification system that will provide confidence in material traceability.
15. Include places for recording identification on all product and process records.
16. Conduct training on the importance of recording identification codes for processes and products that have been developed.
17. Ensure that all records pertaining to traceability are being correctly completed.
18. Ensure that the audit trail of material traceability is working.

Both Q9001 and Q9004-1 are very specific about the types of documents that should be considered part of the purchasing description. The first sentence of Q9001, 4.6.3 provides an example of the misuse of the word *documents*.

> Purchasing documents shall contain data clearly describing the product ordered.

What the standard is requiring here is *records*. Organizations that read the word *documents* and believe it means *procedures* will be confused and misled at this point. As discussed in chapter 2, using the word *documents* to mean *procedures* as well as *records* leads to misunderstandings and confusion for the user. Although it is very unusual for the ISO standards, this section actually enumerates data elements that should be included as part of the records that are maintained. The data elements to be recorded are presented in Q9001, 4.6.3.

> a) The type, class, grade, or other precise identification;
> b) The title or other positive identification, and applicable issues of specifications, drawings, process requirements, inspection instructions, and other relevant technical data, including requirements for approval or qualification of product, procedures, process equipment, and personnel;
> c) The title, number, and issue of the quality-system standard to be applied.

The *Guidelines*, Q9004-1 reiterate some data elements specified in Q9001.

> Purchasing documents should contain data clearly describing the product ordered. Typical elements are as follows:
> a) precise identification of type, class, and grade;
> b) inspection instructions and applicable issue of specifications;
> c) quality-system standard to be applied.

All externally purchased materials should have a specification. The purchase order for the raw materials should either list the specification or refer to the specification or purchase contract containing the specification. This should include effective dates and/ or other identifiers of the purchase contract. If applicable, the purchase order should include the title, number, and issue of the quality system standard to be applied to the ordered materials.

The purchasing organization should ensure that the subcontractor organization possesses the quality system standard that must be applied to the ordered materials. If that standard is prepared by the purchasing organization, it must be a controlled document and must be issued to the subcontractor according to the procedures established by the document control center and described in chapter 6.

The standard also can be an industry standard, and, if this is the case, it is the supplier's responsibility to ensure that it is adhered to. Clearly and accurately describing the purchased product may require referring to internal and external standards that apply to the supplied materials. As described in chapter 3, the purchasing organization is required to possess any industry or military standards that it utilizes in its quality system. If such standards are referred to in the purchase order documents, it is assumed that the latest issue of external standards is available for use by those preparing the purchase order. It is also possible that the purchase order must refer to internally prepared documents. If such is the case, those documents must be provided to the subcontractor well in advance of the purchase, to ensure that the subcontractor can indeed comply with the requirements of the procedures.

Review and Approval of Purchasing Documents

All documents and records that the purchase order comprises must be checked for completeness and accuracy before they are released to the subcontractor. Q9001, 4.6.3. states,

> The supplier shall review and approve purchasing documents for adequacy of the specified requirements prior to release.

Again, this is to ensure that all information necessary to thoroughly describe the ordered materials has been gathered and is being provided to the subcontractor. An independent party, one not responsible for preparing the purchase order, should check and approve the purchase order for adequacy. A checklist, similar to the one that was recommended for ensuring the collection of quality records in the quality records department, can expedite the process. In order to ensure accuracy, it is important to have a subject specialist check the purchase order documents. It is also important to remember that checking the purchase order documents for accuracy and completeness in no way absolves the organization from dismissing the requirement for design/drawing verification specified in Section 4.4, "Design Control." These two activities are separate and are required for different reasons. Both must be conducted in order to comply with the requirements of the standards.

Verification of Supplied Product

Depending on the criteria and information provided to the subcontractor, the purchasing organization should expect records from the subcontractor documenting and verifying the data elements, specifications, drawings, and so forth that have been complied with in supplying the material. The subcontractor should confirm, for example, that the raw material is of the grade ordered and that it has complied with the defined quality system standard. Specific names, numbers, individuals, tests, and so forth are to be provided to the purchasing organization. This is done to clearly identify the ordered material and distinguish it from similar materials that the purchasing organization may be using from that subcontractor. This prevents the wrong materials from being used in the process or product.

Section 4.6.4 of Q9001 is not a mandated requirement. It permits the purchasing organization to verify the purchased product at the subcontractor's premises. If this is the chosen arrangement, then the standards state in 4.6.4.1, Q9001,

> the supplier shall specify verification arrangements and the method of product release in the purchasing documents.

The *Guidelines*, Q9004-1, Paragraph 9.5, elaborate on this aspect.

> A clear agreement should be developed with the subcontractor on the methods by which conformance to requirements will be verified. Such agreements may also include the exchange of inspection and test data with the aim of furthering quality improvements.

The standards are vague in their requirements concerning the specifics of verifying purchased product and especially regarding records. It is important to remember that (1) verification should be conducted against specified requirements, and (2) records of verification activities must be created and maintained. Records serve to reveal that the activity did occur, and they report the results of verification—the acceptance or rejection of the purchased product. This section of the standard allows the purchasing organization to verify the purchased product, while Section 4.10—"Inspection and Testing"—actually *requires* verification of purchased product. In other words, the incoming materials used in product assembly and manufacture *must* be examined in some fashion—either through the incoming inspection process or through an alternative method of verification that will yield acceptable information about the supplies.

Regardless of the method selected, the records must include the following information.

- A description or identification of the purchased material(s)
- The specified requirements against which the material was verified (the requirements against which the material was verified must be available within the organization)
- The verification process that was used (visual examination, testing, and so on)
- Names and dates
- The results of verification

Control of Customer-Supplied Product

Section 4.7 includes both document and records requirements. The first sentence of this paragraph states the following requirement.

> The supplier shall establish and maintain documented procedures for the control of verification, storage, and maintenance of customer-supplied product provided for incorporation into the supplies or for related activities.

In other words, the procedures must clearly explain the organization's plan for verifying that customer-supplied product conforms to specified requirements. What methods or approaches will be used? If the purchased product must be stored or maintained for any time prior to incorporation into the product, procedures must also exist explaining the method(s) of storage and upkeep that will be utilized to prevent deterioration or destruction of the purchased material.

Section 4.7 next states,

> Any such product that is lost, damaged, or is otherwise unsuitable for use shall be recorded and reported to the customer.

That is, records must be maintained providing information on any customer-supplied product that is lost, damaged, or unsuitable for use. Clearly identifying unfit material prevents inadvertent use in the process or in the product. According to Section 4.7, the only records that must be maintained regarding customer-supplied product pertain to lost or damaged material. Logically, however, if the supplier is verifying customer-supplied product, records of those activities must be created and maintained. The same holds true for the storage and maintenance of customer-supplied product.

Product Identification and Traceability

Section 4.8 requires both procedures (documents) and records where they are appropriate and pertinent to the process and products. Product identification and material traceability are inextricably intertwined. Without adequate and intelligent identification of batches and individual products, tracing the materials of which the batches and product are comprised is not possible. A certain amount of thought must go into developing a workable product identification system that will permit easy tracing of the materials and components of the product. In order to satisfy the traceability requirements, the system must allow for the development of unique codes for each batch as well as for each product item. Organizations should be utilizing some system of identification for their own internal control, because product and batch identification permits easy detection of the root causes of defective batches and products. For example, if particular products have been determined to be defective, identification provides the key to (1) pinpointing the conditions under which that product was manufactured or assembled, (2) tracing the materials or components of the product to ascertain if they might have been tainted, and (3) identifying the individuals who worked on the product, and so forth. It thus becomes possible to more accurately assess the conditions or actions that resulted in defective product. In addition, unique identification permits easy location of all items that were produced or assembled under the same conditions or that consist of the same materials or components. It is easier to determine other items that also might be defective.

Traceability is needed principally to

- Ensure that only materials and components of adequate quality enter the final product—sterile drug materials or adequate metallurgical composition and heat treatment in structural components, for example.

- Provide obvious identification to avoid confusion between products that otherwise look alike.

- Permit precise recall of a suspected product.

- Localize the causes of failure and take remedial action at a minimal cost.[1]

Records for Material Traceability

Section 4.8, Q9001 contains the following requirements for product identification and traceability.

> Where appropriate, the supplier shall establish and maintain documented procedures for identifying the product by suitable means from receipt and during all stages of production, delivery, and installation. Where and to the extent that traceability is a specified requirement, the supplier shall establish and maintain documented procedures for unique identification of individual product or batches. This identification shall be recorded.

The standards do not require product identification and material traceability in every situation, but only in those where it is appropriate, that is, where it makes sense and is necessary. In organizations where product identification and material traceability are important, procedures should be in place describing how identification of the product is handled, and the same holds true for

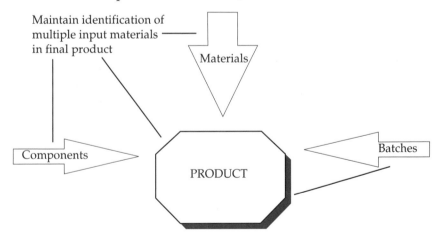

Figure 7.1. Multiple components comprising a single product.

traceability. Material traceability and product identification are two separate activities, but they are intertwined, and, furthermore, traceability is completely dependent on developing a workable identification system and on maintaining accurate product or lot identification.

Two main types of traceability situations can occur. Figure 7.1 depicts the multiple components, batches, or materials making up a single product. In this case, each component or lot of material must be uniquely identified, and the records that are created about the manufactured or assembled product should include the identification codes or names of the input materials. This can be a simple identification, such as the one depicted in Figure 7.1, or it can be more complex. Raw materials can lose their chemical or physical identity as they are combined with each other or as they are processed. In such an environment, control over identification becomes even more important. Batch 1 may be mixed with other materials, lose its properties, and become Batch 1a (see Figure 7.2). It may be combined further, lose the properties it had as Batch 1a and become Batch 1ab. Regardless of the number of times this procedure is repeated, it must be possible to identify and trace the

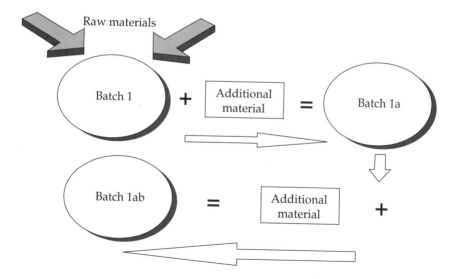

Figure 7.2. Material traceability—combining of batches.

material back to its original identification code—Batch 1. It also must be possible to identify each subsequent processing step as well as the batches of materials that were added at each step.

Figure 7.3 presents another type of material traceability problem: the creation of multiple products from one source or one item. The identification of the one item must be maintained throughout its breakup into individual units. In other words, it must be possible to identify all of the individual products as emanating from the one item. For example, an ingot can be used to fabricate different types of metal products for different customers. Each product item from the ingot should have a unique identifier, but should be identified so as to trace its source—the ingot. The identification of the ingot should not be lost in the manufacture of individual products for different customers.

There are also situations that combine the traceability activities depicted in Figures 7.1 and 7.2, as is shown in Figure 7.4. Difficulties can arise in material traceability if identification codes are not developed that will accommodate this situation. Identification

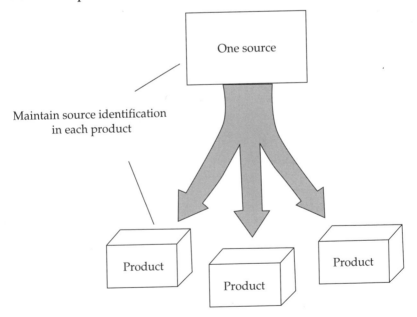

Figure 7.3. Multiple products from one source.

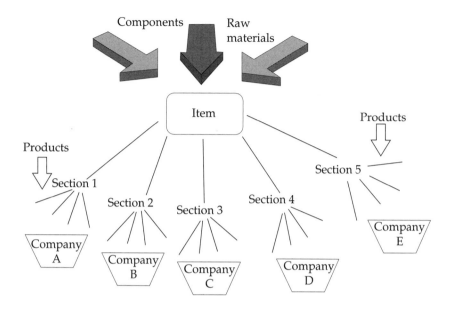

Figure 7.4. Multiple batches combining to result in multiple products.

and traceability can be managed by developing a two-phase tracking system. One both begins and ends at *Item* and the second ends at *Products*. Step 1—*Item* file consists of records that clearly trace the materials and components composing the item. The *Item* identification is unique. Step 2—Each section emanating from the item then bears its own identifying code, one that includes the identification of the item within it. Products bear unique identifiers, relating them to the section of the item. In a case such as this, it is not necessary to trace the end product identification back to the raw materials that compose the item in one unbroken step. End products need be traced back only to the item stage. Item records then provide the tracing of the input materials.

For example, raw materials and scrap materials that make up an ingot will be identified in the ingot file. Since the ingot may be used to fabricate different products for different customers, each end product must bear a unique identifier that includes the ingot identification. Testing and sampling of the ingot will reveal the chemical and metallurgical composition of the metal at that stage. The ingot file will include all relevant inspection results as well as identification of the raw materials and scrap materials that it comprises. The end product files include the ingot identification. If the input materials need to be known, the ingot file can be examined and thus complete traceability is provided—in two phases.

It is important that the quality records manager create records to facilitate the recording of the identifiers. If electronic records are being utilized, field definition will affect, and be affected by, the type of identifiers that are used. Not allowing enough spaces in the field is a common problem in initialing software instructions.

Problems can be avoided by developing clear procedures and instructions that describe how materials will be identified. It is often necessary for the quality records manager to institute mini-training sessions, explaining the procedures and instructing users how records should be completed. Materials and end products must be identified on each record that provides information about them. In-process as well as final product inspection and testing records must bear the identification of the items. The items themselves should be clearly and legibly identified. Often a list of items shipped must be included in the shipment package. The list should bear the identification of the items, and this must coincide with what has been inspected and with what has been released for shipment.

Types of Records

The volume of records required to identify and trace materials can become formidable. Depending upon the type of materials that must be identified and traced, lot numbers, serial numbers, item numbers, and even dates can be used as identifiers. The complexity of the products will determine the number of records that are required; the more complex the products, the more records will be required. All of the processing data and product test data must be recorded, and each record must bear the identification of the material. As the product is prepared for shipment, the packaging containers should be identified with the material or product iden-

Table 7.2. Examination of purchasing records requirements and product identification and traceability records requirements.

Questions to ask about purchasing records and product identification and traceability records

1. Do you have the latest revisions of material specifications to cite in the purchase order documents?
2. Depending on the method selected for subcontractor's qualification, do you have the following records?
   a. Records of on-site assessment of subcontractor's capability.
   b. Records of evaluation of product samples from subcontractor.
   c. Records of past history of subcontractor with similar supplies.
   d. Records of test results of similar supplies provided by subcontractor.
3. Do you have a list of qualified subcontractors? Are the reasons for qualification stated clearly?
4. Do you have records indicating that your purchasing "documents" are reviewed for adequacy of the specified requirements before they are released?
5. Do you have records furnished by the subcontractor verifying that everything has been complied with in supplying the material?
6. If you are performing verification of customer-supplied product, do you have records of the verification activities?
7. If customer-supplied product is unsuitable for use, do you have records indicating that the customer has been notified of this?
8. Do you have identification codes or numbers on all of the records that capture information about process and product?
9. Do your process and product records provide a tight audit trail for material traceability requirements?
10. Are the purchasing records and the product identification and material traceability records logically organized and readily retrievable?

tification code. Remember that the purpose of the records is to record the history of the input materials, the process conditions, and the inspection and test results. For those organizations that need to know how their records fare, Table 7.2 presents a list of questions pertaining to the records for material traceability and purchasing. Attaining complete traceability for complex products (made of many materials and components and employing numerous processes) can be a formidable job involving extensive paperwork, records, bonded stockrooms, physical markings on the products, and so forth.[2] This is actually done for many products in the drug, aerospace, and nuclear industries.

Conclusion

Purchasing records reveal information about the materials and components that compose the final product. As such, they are the first category of records in the process/production stream that describes the quality of materials. Thus they become an important part of the quality activities pertaining to the acceptability of the final product by the customer. Accurate records about material identification and traceability are critical. They form the basis for decisions regarding nonconforming product (see chapter 11) and provide valuable information that can be used to detect the root causes of defective batches and products. Organizations should maintain records of both activities for their own internal control.

Notes

1. Frank M. Gryna, "Manufacturing Planning," in *Juran's Quality Control Handbook*, 4th ed., ed. J. M. Juran (New York: McGraw-Hill, 1988), 16.39.

2. Ibid., 16.40.

CHAPTER 8

Process Control Records

Q9001—Section 4.9
Q9004-1—Sections 10 and 11

Introduction

Kaoru Ishikawa defines a *process* in the following way: "A collection of causes producing a certain result."[1] It includes not only manufacturing processes but also a way of doing a particular job—work performed in various ways, the overall work of quality assurance, sales, purchasing, or servicing. He further explains that controlling a process means getting it to deliver its maximum capability in the controlled state.[2]

> Control consists of making comparisons with control standards or control limits on control charts, seeking assignable causes in the process or work if the standards are violated or points fall outside the limits, and taking action on the process.[3]

Process Control and Its Relationship to Product Quality

The quality of the raw materials or components and the process conditions affect the properties and performance of the final prod-

155

uct. The most economical quality control is achieved by building the right conditions into processes before commencing full-scale manufacture.[4] To state this simply, the processing of materials builds into the final product its determining characteristics and properties. If metal is beta-quenched or not, if it is annealed or not, affects its metallurgical properties, and such processes will cause the metal to behave differently during its life span. Following through, such processes alter the molecular structure of metal and affect the tensile properties, and, thus, the performance of the metal. The same holds true for most processes. The conditions under which the activities take place build characteristics into the final product that affect and determine the performance of the product.

Activities That Are Involved

The chain of process control activities comprises all activities wherein the materials and components are handled, sampled, tested, worked on, and analyzed. The actual work or process itself is involved, as are the personnel who perform the various functions, the equipment on which the materials are processed, and the conditions under which they are processed.

The Role of Records

The concept of *controlled conditions* is important to understand in relation to records for process control. Q9001 provides aspects of controlled conditions that should be satisfied in Section 4.9.

Controlled conditions shall include the following:
a) documented procedures defining the manner of production, installation, and servicing, where the absence of such procedures could adversely affect quality;
b) use of suitable production, installation, and servicing equipment, and a suitable working environment;
c) compliance with reference standards/codes, quality plans, and/or documented procedures;
d) monitoring and control of suitable process parameters and product characteristics;
e) the approval of processes and equipment, as appropriate;

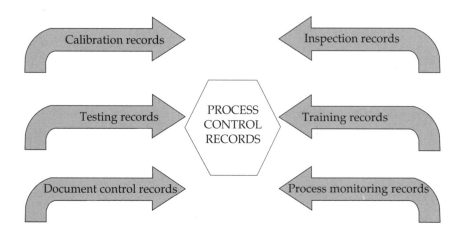

Figure 8.1. Records from other sections of ISO 9000 standards that are necessary for process control.

f) criteria for workmanship, which shall be stipulated in the clearest practical manner (e.g., written standards, representative samples, or illustrations);

g) suitable maintenance of equipment to ensure continuing process capability.

As the standards point out, controlled process conditions are inextricably intertwined with calibration, inspection, testing, training, and document control. As a result, as Figure 8.1 depicts, records from these various quality-related activities come into play in satisfying the process control requirements of the ISO standards. Unless the indicators attached to machinery, equipment, and testing tools are reading accurately, there is no control, because there is no method of determining if the material has met specifications. Training activities also affect how the process functions. Furthermore, document control and the activities associated with writing and distributing documents affect whether or not workers have the appropriate information in their work instructions.

Records serve three roles in the process activities.

1. They ensure that all activities, equipment, and personnel are being monitored.

2. They serve as evidence that appropriate control is being exercised over the process.

3. They provide proof, in the form of data, that all aspects affecting the process were in control when the product was being manufactured.

Types of Process Control Records

The types of records that satisfy the process control requirements of the ISO standards emanate from the activities that prove that controlled conditions are in place. Section 4.9, Q9001 begins with the following statement.

> The supplier shall identify and plan the production, installation, and servicing processes which directly affect quality and shall ensure that these processes are carried out under controlled conditions.

Implied records prevail in Section 4.9. Written plans and procedures must be in place that identify those steps in the process that directly affect quality. Such plans and procedures fall under the category of controlled documents. Records that are created and maintained by the document control center (see chapter 6) as part of its function can prove that the plans and procedures are in existence, that they have been appropriately distributed, and that they were in place before the processes were carried out.

Subparagraph "a" also requires documented procedures to define the manner of production, installation, and servicing. Once again, records pertaining to document control activities enter into the picture. Control over the activities associated with writing documents affects their content and accuracy, while control over distribution ensures that work instructions are disseminated to operators in a timely fashion. The paragraph entitled "Planning for Process Control," 10.1, Q9004-1, *Guidelines*, states,

> The operation of processes should be specified to the necessary extent by documented work instructions.

Subparagraph "b" of Section 4.9 stipulates the use of suitable equipment and a suitable working environment. Compliance involves several activities that can result in records. Equipment control is a main aspect of process control. Equipment includes machinery and any other apparatus such as dies, molds, tools, and so forth. Controlling equipment can involve the following activities.

* Design of equipment
* Installation of equipment
* Standards for using equipment
* Process capability studies
* Equipment capability studies
* Preventive maintenance and equipment repair

Records should be created and maintained for each of the activities that is conducted pertinent to equipment control for process or product quality. Records, thus, can encompass each of the enumerated activities pertaining to equipment control. The *Guidelines*, Q9004-1, 11.3, stipulate that

> All equipment, including fixed machinery, jigs, fixtures, tooling, templates, patterns, and gauges, should be proved for accuracy prior to use. Special attention should be paid to computers used in controlling processes, and especially the maintenance of the related software.

Records should be created and maintained for any testing or validation activities pertaining to equipment accuracy, proving suitability prior to use. Subparagraph "b" of Q9001 also specifies a suitable working environment. The *Guidelines*, 10.3, elaborate on this aspect.

> Where environmental conditions, such as temperature, humidity and cleanliness, are important to product quality, appropriate limits should be specified, controlled, and verified.

If it is important to the process and product to control environmental conditions, records must be created and maintained revealing that those conditions are being monitored and controlled. Many industries require control over environmental conditions—the semiconductor, microfilm processing, pharmaceutical, and other industries, for example.

Subparagraph "c" requires compliance with reference standards and codes, quality plans, and/or documented procedures. All reference standards or codes necessary to conduct the processes should be available in the organization (see chapter 3), and every attempt should be made to ensure that employees are made aware of them and are complying with them. Often industry standards and codes are referred to in procedures and work instructions, but employees have no knowledge of their existence or the requirements that they stipulate. Standards may also exist for equipment usage, and, if this is the case, such standards also should be available in the organization (see chapter 3).

Discussion of process control most often evokes images of process control charts. Subparagraph "d" stipulates the monitoring and control of suitable process parameters and product characteristics. Process control charts are one type of important process record that does satisfy a requirement in the standards. They provide evidence that the processes are being monitored and are operating within controlled, prespecified limits. If they reveal that an out-of-control situation has occurred, other types of actions may need to be taken, necessitating the creation of various records. Abnormality reports may need to be filed, describing the nature of the condition, and follow-up activities should be conducted. Records should be maintained revealing that the process has been examined and corrected. Any material that was being processed at the time that out-of-control conditions were detected must be inspected or tested to ensure that it has not been compromised. Records must be created and maintained about the inspection or testing of such material to prove that it does meet specification requirements. Such results form part of an information package pertaining to the detection of the abnormality and provide confidence in the quality system.

The *Guidelines,* Q9004-1, 10.1.3, elaborate on process monitoring.

> Monitoring and control of processes should relate directly to finished product specifications or to an internal requirement, as appropriate .... In all cases, relationships between in-process controls, their specifications, and final product specifications should be developed, communicated to the personnel concerned, and then documented.

The *Guidelines,* therefore, recommend comparing product characteristics, attributes, and test results with specification requirements. In other words, the results of measuring process variables are compared with internal specifications or with finished product specifications. Records would include a listing of those characteristics or attributes that are to be examined, with the results of the product analyses, to reveal that the product does meet specification requirements. By providing comparative results, records reveal that process controls are effective and produce material that conforms to defined specifications.

The last word in the referenced paragraph, *documented,* means that the results should be *recorded.* It might also be necessary to record that the results have been communicated to the personnel who are concerned or affected.

The *Guidelines,* Q9004-1, 10.1.4 provide further advice on monitoring and controlling the process and product.

> All in-process and final verifications should be planned and specified. Documented test and inspection procedures should be maintained for each quality characteristic to be checked. These should include the specific equipment to perform such checks and tests, and the specified requirements and workmanship criteria.

In addition to process control charts, the organization should verify the quality status of material at important points in the production sequence. Sampling plans and procedures, testing, and inspection plans and procedures provide evidence that the in-process and final verifications are planned and have been specified. Items such as plans and procedures belong to the controlled documents category, and records about their creation, approval, and distribution serve an important role in process activities. Brought into this activity as well are the requirements for records resulting from in-process inspection and testing as well as final product inspection and testing (see chapter 9).

Subparagraph "f" states that criteria for workmanship must be stipulated in the clearest practical manner. They can be in the form of written standards, illustrations, or representative samples. The criteria form a type of record, even if they are physical objects such as metal samples. Criteria for workmanship must be clearly identified, controlled, and maintained in such a manner as to prevent damage and deterioration. As with all quality records, they must be readily retrievable for use by those who need to refer to them. If the criteria are illustrations, they may need to be displayed in the work areas where they are needed. They should be identified clearly, be legible, and easy to understand. Special provision must be made for housing and, sometimes, displaying the criteria in the areas where they are needed. Criteria can be considered a vital operating record, and backup copies should be stored offsite for protection (see chapter 16).

Because preventive maintenance of equipment is critical in ensuring process capability, it is emphasized as a separate requirement in subparagraph "g" of Q9001.

> . . . suitable maintenance of equipment to ensure continuing process capability.

The *Guidelines*, 11.3, recommend that

> A program of preventive maintenance should be established to ensure continued process capability.

Records would include identification of equipment and equipment characteristics that contribute to quality, with a plan or schedule of preventive maintenance to be conducted on that equipment. Furthermore, records should be created and maintained revealing that preventive maintenance activities do occur as planned, together with the results of the activities. If the equipment must be repaired, it may be necessary to inspect or test material that was being processed prior to the repair to determine if it meets specification requirements. Records of such examinations must be retained as proof that the material was not adversely affected.

Records for Special Processes

According to the ISO standards, special processes require the prequalification of process capability, qualified operators, and possibly the continuous monitoring of process parameters. A process is prequalified to determine if it is performing the way it was intended and anticipated. Prequalification can involve the following activities, some of which have been discussed earlier in this chapter.

- Selection of equipment
- Installation of equipment

- Spare parts
- Meeting environmental conditions
- Qualification of personnel
- Training of personnel

The first four items have already been discussed, together with their recommended records. The qualification process for personnel can consist of on-the-job training. After mastering the task, the operator is "qualified" by an authorized individual who observes his or her performance. What is important is recording that this procedure has taken place and that the operator is now qualified. Thus, a qualification record is created.

Continuous monitoring and control of process parameters for special processes is best accomplished with automated monitoring. Records would include the results of monitoring to prove that the process parameters are within product specification limits, the process specifications themselves, and the comparison of results with process specifications.

The Physical Formats of Process Records

Process control records can be voluminous as well as varied in type and physical characteristics. Various charts may be created, for example—process control charts, temperature charts, strip thickness charts (for metal products), ultrasonic charts, heat treatment charts, furnace charts, and so forth. Records may be created and maintained on the composition of materials, their mechanical properties, if appropriate, and, if pertinent, their dimensional and visual characteristics.

In an automated environment, much of this data will be captured and recorded as a byproduct of the process. In a mixed or highly manual environment, a variety of records are gathered throughout the process to comply with the requirements. Paper process records pose special problems, since, in many instances, they cannot be filed with the rest of the 8½-inch by 11-inch quality records that are being collected. Charts can be round, ultrasonic test strips can be quite long, and X-rays pose special records problems. The quality records manager should address the variety of physical sizes and shapes early, when designing the quality records system. It is possible that special equipment will need to be ordered or constructed to house the various types of process records. Further responsibilities of the quality records manager in process control are enumerated in Table 8.1.

Furthermore, because such records may be housed in a different physical location from the remainder of the quality records, special emphasis should be placed on the organization of these records. Deciding on access schemes entails keeping in mind that odd-size materials must be intellectually linked to the remainder of the quality records pertaining to a specific product, lot, or shipment. They must be able to be accessed in the same way that other types of quality records are. Whether they are organized according to project number, name, product identification, or lot number is not as important as organizational consistency. The most important aspect is to be able to retrieve the accompanying process control charts, X-rays, and even samples and link them to the body

Table 8.1. Responsibilities of the quality records manager in process control activities.

1. Define records requirements for process control activities.
2. Ensure that process control procedures and work instructions (documents) fall under the jurisdiction of the document control center.
3. Create records for testing and validation activities pertaining to equipment accuracy.
4. Create records that capture information about environmental conditions.
5. Ensure that all reference standards and codes are available in-house, that they are organized, and that they are readily retrievable.
6. Ensure that process control records are being maintained.
7. Ensure that criteria for workmanship are clearly identified, and that they are readily available where they are used.
8. Ensure that records are being maintained of preventive maintenance of equipment that contributes to quality. Ensure that a planned schedule of preventive maintenance exists.
9. Develop records for special processes—qualification records of personnel and prequalification of process capability.
10. Develop a system for handling records in various formats and sizes. This may require special equipment.
11. Develop access schemes to link process monitoring records with inspection and testing results.

Table 8.2. Examination of process control records.
Questions to ask about process control records
1. Are all of your procedures (documents) for process control, special processes and their qualification, equipment, and personnel under the jurisdiction of controlled documents?
2. Do you maintain records of the qualification of personnel, special processes, and equipment?
3. Do you create and maintain records when the customer is informed of any significant changes to the process, the procedures, or quality?
4. Do you have records of the training of personnel for their job requirements?
5. Do you have calibration records of all equipment that can affect quality?
6. Are your process monitoring records organized well, and are they readily retrievable?
7. Where are the process control records housed?
8. Have you defined retention times for all process control records?

of quality records that define the attributes of the product. Table 8.2 is provided to assist those organizations that are currently examining their process control records.

Conclusion

Process control records include not only those that monitor the process but also records about calibration, training, inspection, testing, and document control. In order to comply with the records requirements of this section of the ISO standards, records from the other enumerated activities also must be in place. Furthermore, because process control records can differ physically from other categories of records, they pose special challenges in organizing, storage, and retrieval.

Notes

1. Kaoru Ishikawa, *Introduction to Quality Control* (Tokyo: 3A Corporation, 1989), 236.
2. Ibid., 237.
3. Ibid., 288.
4. R. S. Bingham, Jr. and Clyde H. Walden, "Process Industries," in *Juran's Quality Control Handbook*, 4th ed., ed. J. M. Juran (New York: McGraw-Hill, 1988), 28.5.

CHAPTER 9

Inspection and Testing Records

Q9001—Section 4.10
Q9004-1—Section 12

Introduction

Not unlike most quality operations, the ISO standards require that inspection and testing be performed (1) on incoming product, (2) in-process, and (3) on finished product. The purposes of these activities are to

- Ensure that the raw materials or components to be used in the final product are of the quality that the organization has ordered (see chapter 7—"Purchasing Records").

- Determine if the process is producing material that conforms to specification.

- Ensure that the finished products conform to specification.

Records are critical in all inspection and testing activities, and, if there is any place in the quality loop where accuracy and timeliness are important, it is in the records that pertain to all inspection and testing activities. It is in these activities that records serve their strongest evidentiary role, proving to the organization that

(1) it knows what it is doing and (2) it has control over what it is doing. At the same time, records prove to the customer that the finished product is exactly what was ordered. Data collected during inspection and testing are employed by the organization to make significant decisions about whether to use incoming materials, whether to continue the process, and whether to ship the product. It is not an exaggeration to state that inspection and testing records are the glue that binds together the myriad activities and decisions pertaining to process and product quality. Their importance can be clearly understood if they were to be disallowed. How would the organization know if the process was working at all? How could anyone, supplier or customer, be assured of characteristics of the finished product? It is an understatement to say that the handicap would be intolerable, and the result would be complete ignorance and chaos.

As critical as records are in these activities, they are not clearly delineated in the ISO standards. In fact, many implied records are prevalent in this section of the requirements. The revised standards do provide more information than the original standards about what types of records should be created and maintained. In fact, the paragraph about inspection and testing records, 4.10.5, provides three times as much information about the types of records to maintain.

> The supplier shall establish and maintain records which provide evidence that the product has been inspected and/or tested. These records shall show clearly whether the product has passed or failed the inspections and/or tests according to defined acceptance criteria. Where the product fails to pass any inspection and/or test, the procedures for control of nonconforming product shall apply.
>
> Records shall identify the inspection authority responsible for the release of product.

In addition, an introductory paragraph to this section, 4.10.1, entitled "General," makes an additional requirement that was not part of the earlier version.

> The required inspection and testing, and the records to be established, shall be detailed in the quality plan or documented procedures.

This requirement specifically states that those records to be used to capture information about inspection and testing—the activities conducted, the results, and the requirement against which the results are compared—are to be referenced in the document describing the procedures themselves. This requirement necessitates the creation of inspection and testing records either in conjunction with the preparation of the procedure or preceding the preparation of the procedure, since the records themselves must be documented in the procedure.

To provide a blanket overview: All tests and inspections conducted on incoming materials, during in-process inspection, and on finished product compose the records of this category. All records of tests and inspections must be compared against an acceptable requirement—for example, internal company specification, customer specification, and so forth. These specifications also form part of the records of this category.

Records of Incoming Product

Depending upon the requirements of the organization, inspectors should test or inspect incoming materials against the purchase orders and specifications. Release of incoming product depends to a great degree upon the results of the inspections. Often a raw material sampling and analysis plan addresses the required analysis, if any, and the results are compared to the raw material specification for the material. Once decisions are made, records of results should be sent to the quality records department. They can be filed (indexed, microfilmed, and so forth) so that they are retrievable against the specifications and purchase orders that were placed. For the sake of convenience, a CAR microfilm system or an optical disk system can permit one-time entry of a specification or purchase order to which multiple, continuous, incoming orders apply. Cross referencing or indexing the criteria documents against the results provides convenient, ready access to the resultant data with referent criteria. Simplifying the comparison between specification and results sets the tone of being in control during audits and during the registration process and positively influences examiners' attitudes.

Questions usually posed by auditors concerning test and inspection records of incoming product revolve around being able to demonstrate that inspectors as well as those who release the product have access to specification requirements. Typical queries involve requests for retrieving the in-house inspection results of a given incoming batch or lot by different variables, that is, supplier name, batch/lot identification, and so forth. Records personnel are subsequently expected to retrieve the referent criteria (purchase orders and specification requirements) and demonstrate an identification linkage between the documents. This is done to assure examiners that access to referent criteria is easy and that correct criteria can be accessed readily and applied to the inspection or test results to ensure valid comparison.

According to Q9001, the organization does have a degree of discretionary latitude regarding the activities and resultant records pertaining to incoming product. Paragraph 4.10.2.1 states,

> Verification of the specified requirements shall be in accordance with the quality plan and/or documented procedures.

This is unlike the calibration records, wherein the organization is specifically required to conduct certain activities and to create and maintain records resulting from those activities.

Paragraph 4.10.2.3 permits the organization to release incoming product if it is needed for "urgent production purposes."

> Where incoming product is released for urgent production purposes prior to verification, it shall be positively identified and recorded in order to permit immediate recall and replacement in the event of nonconformity to specified requirements.

In other words, the paragraph requires strict adherence to the identification and recording requirements of the product in the event that it fails to meet specification requirements. Unspoken, but logically assumed, is that no inspection or testing has been conducted prior to emergency release, thus making the issue of adherence to identification procedures all the more important. As is described in chapter 7, the identification of incoming product forms the first step in the chain of subsequent material traceability, and adherence to incoming product identification should be a practice in the organization anyway.

Records of inspection of incoming product should be utilized for purposes in addition to releasing the product into the system.

The inspection results of vendors' products should be analyzed and compared with the inspection results of competitive vendors' products to determine the best incoming quality. Results should also be examined for each vendor's products over a period of time to determine the consistency of supply as well as any possible decline or increase in the quality of the incoming product. As with other types of quality records, valuable information resides on the records of inspection results of incoming products—information that results in more informed decisions.

Inspection Records and Process Control Records

The interrelationship between process control records and in-process inspection and testing records is not always apparent, unless the organization belongs to an industry that is regulated by a government body and has experienced detailed quality system and supplier audits. Whether the process is in control will be revealed not only in process monitoring, but also in the inspection and test results of in-process quality control activities. Working in tandem to ensure that process activities are resulting in the intended outcome, the two activities are interdependent. It stands to reason, therefore, that the records of these activities should support the checking and monitoring that does occur. Process control records reveal that upper and lower control limits are being respected as operational boundaries, while in-process inspection and testing records support this finding by furnishing hard data on materials emanating from the process. In their own way, records of in-process inspection and testing provide ongoing internal audit checks and reveal that the process is in control by demonstrating that sampled materials have the performance or other characteristics that should be inherent in the materials at that point. In-process inspection and testing records, in fact, can serve as an early warning to a deviation in processing that can then be corrected in a timely manner. These two categories of records serve as excellent examples of those quality records that should be utilized in tandem—analyzed and cross-verified to determine whether reported data on both sets of records coincide and are providing information that is consistent and compatible.

All inspection and testing records, in-process and final, reveal the relationship between process variables or parameters and final product results. The overall purpose is to enable planners to establish controls over variables in order to achieve specified product results.[1] Records of final inspection results should bear no surprises. They should be capturing data that was planned for and is anticipated. Records of final inspection and testing should be a mere confirmation of the expected outcome, rather than a revelation about weaknesses that have gone undetected upstream. If this occurs, examination of both process control records and in-process inspection and testing records should be conducted to determine why product characteristics deviate from expected results.

In-Process Inspection and Testing Records Versus Final Product Inspection and Testing Records

Q9001, Paragraph 4.10.5, clearly mandates the creation and maintenance of records pertaining to inspection and testing activities. When compared to the earlier version, it is apparent that this paragraph has been greatly expanded. Requirements indicate that it is not enough simply to record the results of the inspection and testing activities, but information on the records must clearly show whether or not the product has passed or failed the inspections and tests. This means that there must be a space on the records for a "pass–fail" indication. In addition, the defined acceptance criteria should be specified or referred to someplace on the record. In many instances, even though records provide results of the specified activities, it is not clear from the records whether or not the results were according to specifications.

The statements in Paragraph 4.10.5 are all *shall* statements, meaning that these are all mandatory records requirements. The standards, however, do permit a certain degree of discretionary latitude regarding the exact types of records that are created and maintained. Paragraphs 4.10.3 ("In-Process Inspection and Testing") and 4.10.4 ("Final Inspection and Testing") both permit the organization to determine the appropriate inspection and testing activities. It is the organization's responsibility to specify those inspection and testing activities that it deems necessary and to describe those in the quality plan or in procedures. A sampling and analysis plan, a check sheet, or a similar document often communicates the specific requirements. Adherence to its own internal specifications, then, is what the standards require. In these instances, it is the organization's responsibility

- To define the inspection and testing activities that will result in quality product
- To conduct those inspection and testing activities that have been specified in the procedures
- To create and maintain records of the results of the inspection and testing activities that have been conducted

In organizations where products are complex, inspection and testing records can be formidable, especially if the industry is also under the jurisdiction of a government regulatory authority. Where product safety is a strong concern, inspection and testing records can also be voluminous. The number and types of records vary widely from company to company. For example, in the process and manufacture of zirconium, which is used in the cores of nuclear reactors, sampling will occur at each phase of the chemical process during which the metal is extracted from the raw material, formed into a metal sponge, combined with scrap metal, and melted into an ingot. At that point, fabrication into specific customer-ordered products precipitates a series of further inspections and tests. After the metal is heat-treated, beta-quenched, rolled, extruded, and formed into a variety of final products, further testing is conducted—chemical, metallurgical, X-ray, ultrasonic, dye penetrant, and so forth. Each one of the tests produces a record that reveals the characteristics being examined. Inspections also produce records: visual inspection, measurements for thickness, width, surface texture, and so forth. Each activity—each inspection and each test—produces a record on which appear results that must be compared with specified requirements to reveal conformance.

Organizations that need to determine which and how many records to create and maintain to satisfy the requirements of 4.10.5 would be well advised to first define those steps in the process that must yield inspection and test results, that is, those places in the process after which testing or inspection must be conducted to preempt irreparable or costly product discrepancy. Many books have been written on process control and it is not the purpose of this publication to explain the development of process planning or sampling methods. The required records will emanate from the decision points that are determined by the organization. What is important is the documentation or description of exactly where in the process the inspection and test activities will occur, the adherence to the procedures, and the creation and maintenance of records for those inspection and test activities.

The same logic holds true for final inspection and testing. Often dictated by customer specifications, final inspection and testing records can be more readily identified, since they frequently are clearly delineated. Q9001, 4.10.4 has the following requirement for final inspection and testing.

> The supplier shall carry out all final inspection and testing in accordance with the quality plan and/or documented procedures to complete the evidence of conformance of the finished product to the specified requirements.

A record must be created, again, for each type of test that is performed and for each inspection activity that takes place. As mentioned earlier, in a well-controlled quality environment, final inspection and testing should be a mere formality. It is, however, the final point in the quality process where out-of-spec product can be detected and it should be taken seriously. It can happen that material will be found to be out-of-spec for a number of reasons. Some tests and inspections can be conducted only at the end of product manufacture. Prior to final inspection and testing, several critical processing steps might be required that could transform the properties of the product. Tests conducted after such processing can be crucial in revealing product performance characteristics. Records of such tests and their results, when compared to specification requirements, are the strongest evidence that the final product complies, in every way, with customer requirements.

Key Elements of Inspection Records

In order for records to be able to demonstrate product conformance, they must possess key elements. A quality records manager can ensure that these key elements are incorporated into inspection and testing records. Most important, the quality records manager can develop a system that includes all necessary requirements of the standards as enumerated in Table 9.1.

Records must clearly identify the material and final products, and they should enable the organization to trace materials. Personnel also contribute significantly to validity of information. Inspectors must be duly authorized members of the quality function, and often evidence must be provided of their expertise and knowledge in conducting the inspections required of them (see chapter 14, "Training Records"). In addition, evidence must exist on the

---

Table 9.1. Responsibilities of the quality records manager in inspection and testing activities.

1. Define the records requirements for testing and inspection activities.
2. Manage the creation of testing and inspection records to ensure that required elements are incorporated into records.
   a) Are specifications cited on appropriate records?
   b) Do records contain a pass/fail indication?
   c) Is there a category indicating release?
   d) Do records require identification of material?
   e) Do receiving inspection records indicate the parameters checked and the sample and lot sizes?
   f) Do final inspection and test records show that the finished product conforms to specified requirements? Is there evidence of
      —final test procedures?
      —qualified personnel?
      —identification of test equipment and test status?
      —temperature and humidity conditions (if appropriate)?
      —test data?
      —acceptance criteria?
3. Develop a system for retrieving receipt inspection results against specifications and purchase orders.
4. Develop a system for organizing in-process and final inspection and test records that links them to specific material identification/customer orders for material traceability.
5. Provide checks of all inspection and testing records.
6. Control inspection stamps.
7. Conduct training sessions on data collection for and proper completion of inspection and testing records.
8. Ensure that all inspection and testing documents fall under jurisdiction of the document control center.

records themselves that the inspection and test results have been reviewed by a knowledgeable individual and that the results revealed conformance to requirements. As was discussed on page 174, records must show clearly whether the product has passed or failed the inspections or tests, and they should also provide or refer to the defined acceptance criteria. In addition, release authorizations must be evident, whether the release is for in-process material (from one step to another) or for final product.

Product Release

The standards deal indirectly with the concept of *release*. Paragraph 4.10.5 states simply,

> Records shall identify the inspection authority responsible for the release of product.

Included someplace in the quality assurance manual or in inspection and testing documents should be information that (1) details the product release criteria and (2) assigns authority to release product at different stages in the process or for shipment.

Release is a common practice in organizations and extends through the release for shipment of final product. Release involves designating key areas in processing, wherein the product or material cannot continue in the process until it has been tested or inspected and released for movement. Records that release in-process material can be the same as those that report the results of the inspection or test activity. Release under these circumstances can be accomplished with an inspection stamp—a tightly controlled artifact that identifies the inspector who released the material or product.

Release rights are accorded only to those individuals who have the expertise or knowledge to evaluate the results of inspection or testing and can determine that all specification requirements have been satisfied. Release authority extends into Section 4.15 of Q9001, "Handling, Storage, Packaging, and Delivery." Some customers require specific marking of the packaged product and packaging. Requirements can include the materials that are used, the kind of crating material to be used, and even how the items are to be arranged in the package. Release records of product for shipment can—like a checklist—specify elements that are required according to contract. Using this checklist, the authorized individual then signs the document and dates it. The creation of release records per contract requirements is not uncommon. Data elements to include on such release records are

- Customer name
- Contract or specification number
- Material identification (to be shipped)
- Name of person verifying the release
- Name of person or department authorizing release

If the crating material and internal arrangement of the product in the package are part of the specification requirements, it may be necessary for the person who will release the shipment to witness the packing of the product or to view the opened shipping container so as to verify compliance with those aspects of the contract.

Release for shipment is based on all of the cumulative records that have been created and gathered about the product. Collection of all records and their review and comparison of results with specification requirements should be standard before shipment is considered. Centrally gathering all such quality-related records in the quality records department simplifies the process of ensuring that all records have been received, that they have been reviewed, and that all is in-spec. Developing a records collection system for each order at the outset, the quality records department functions as a clearinghouse that can be contacted for information pertaining to the status of the process and to the specification requirements that yet need to be satisfied and recorded. With appropriate training, quality records personnel can compare the inspection and test results against customer specification requirements to further ensure adherence to requirements. Although laboratory and other quality personnel usually provide the initial examination of results and make determinations about product compliance, second-level checks by other individuals are often made.

Product Certification

In industries where product certification is required, the quality records department should prepare the certification. In those instances, it is necessary for all pertinent processing and product records to reach the quality records department before shipment. Depending upon the industry, certifications can include all of the test and inspection results of a particular customer's order. The certification technicians (working as part of the quality records personnel) extract certification reporting requirements from the customer specification and prepare certifications that provide test and inspection results required by specification. The certification itself becomes an important record that can be legally binding. Inaccurate results reported on certifications can carry severe legal penalties, because the product, in essence, is being misrepresented to the client. In some industries, certifications become the acceptance factor for the product. In other words, the information (extracted results from records) reported on the certifications determines whether or not the customer will accept the product. The certification can be required prior to product shipment or, at the very least, with the shipped product. If the certification must be included with the shipped product, its attachment to or inclusion in the shipment must be verified before the product is released for shipment.

As backup to the testing records that report the actual results of the tests, the laboratory maintains internal records about the tests, with the names of the individuals who conducted them, the dates, the types of tests, a clear identification of material (perhaps a sample), the conditions under which the test was conducted, external standards or test methods that were used, and so forth. These records provide the much needed and often requested traceability or audit trail that anchors the reported results. Laboratory notebooks and logs are considered vital records—an extremely important type of record to the organization (see chapter 16). Because records about inspection and testing are so critical, it is important to examine the current system to determine if all required aspects are being satisfied. Table 9.2 provides a series of questions pertaining to inspection and testing records.

Records and Inspection Stamps

Although inspection stamps are not discussed nor are they required in the ISO standards, the use of such stamps is common-

Table 9.2. Examination of inspection and testing records requirements.

Questions to ask about inspection and testing records

1. Do you have in-process and final inspection and testing records for all activities that you have designated?
2. Do your inspection and testing records demonstrate that the product or service has passed all required inspections and tests?
3. Do you maintain a list of approved sources that reflect a vendor's or subcontractor's quality performance rating?
4. Do receiving inspection records indicate evidence of acceptance or reasons for rejection of incoming materials?
5. Do receiving inspection records indicate the parameters checked and the sample and lot sizes?
6. Are records maintained of incoming material that has been released for "urgent use" prior to inspection and testing?
7. Do you have written procedures for all in-process inspection and test points, and are they all controlled documents?
8. Can you readily compare the receipt inspection results with specification or purchase order requirements?
9. Can you readily retrieve a given test or inspection record that reports information for a specific customer order or shipment?
10. Do you have backup for all test and inspection records?
11. Have retention times been defined for all test and inspection records?
12. Do you have records on inspection stamps that have been issued? How tightly controlled are they?
13. Do your inspection and test records identify the personnel responsible for the inspection or test?
14. Do your inspection and test records identify the type of inspection or test performed, associated requirements, and acceptance criteria?

place in many industries. Controlled inspection stamps are thought to be more reliable than initials or signatures that can be forged easily. Authorized quality control inspectors are issued a stamp with a unique number or code assigned to each inspector. The stamp is tightly controlled in the sense that it can be used only by the inspector to whom it is issued. The inspection stamp replaces the inspector's initials or signature on records that represent significant release points in the process. Because of the critical nature of inspection stamps, records play an important role in the control process. Records must be maintained on the issuance

ISSUED INSPECTION STAMPS

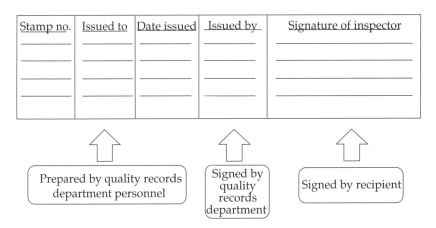

Figure 9.1. Example of a record of issued inspection stamps.

of inspection stamps to individuals and must clearly identify the person to whom the number or code was issued (see Figure 9.1).

If an inspection stamp is misplaced or lost, the quality control inspector is responsible for immediately reporting the loss to the quality records department and to all release points. This prevents unauthorized personnel from using the approval stamp to pass materials or products that have not been adequately and independently inspected. The lost inspection stamp number is taken out of circulation and no records should bear that lost stamp number from the date of loss forward.

Uncontrolled Inspection Stamps

Without thorough, current, and accurate records about the issuance and ownership of inspection stamps, there is little control in this critical area. The following case illustrates this point. An article appeared in February 1989 in the *Austin American-Statesman* concerning the use of a phantom Inspector 11, who existed only as a rubber inspection stamp in an organization that was a leading manufacturer of aerospace fasteners—Voi-Shan Aerospace Products, located in the San Fernando Valley. A federal task force investigating how defective nuts, bolts, screws, and other fasteners worked their way into the supply system for U.S. aerospace manufacturers led to a national probe of parts fraud that involved the FBI, the Defense Criminal Investigative Service, and the Internal Revenue Service, as well as investigators from the Air Force and the Navy. During the investigation, Voi-Shan employees described a system in which required test data for high-tension parts were routinely forged because test equipment was broken or a backlog of parts to be tested had piled up. Employees told investigators that, whenever fasteners failed to meet tests, or the required tests were falsified, the material was shipped out of the factory with the Inspector 11 stamp. Former Voi-Shan employees told investigators that false test results were routinely supplied for parts sold to aviation manufacturers—Boeing, General Dynamics Corporation, Lockheed, and McDonnell Douglas, as well as GE and Pratt & Whitney, jet engine manufacturers. Voi-Shan describes itself as "the largest manufacturer of aerospace fasteners in the world."

The FAA disclosed that it had fined Boeing, the nation's leading producer of commercial aircraft, $125,000 for allowing self-locking nuts that failed to meet the company's own specification to be installed on 22 Boeing 767 jets. The defective bolts were installed on a critical system that controls the rudder and wing flaps. The FAA levied the fine because Boeing "failed to ensure that its suppliers maintained a quality-assurance program capable of verifying" that parts met specifications.

Concern over the use of substandard parts in critical high technology was initiated in 1986 when investigators for the Defense Criminal Investigative Service began probing how substandard and defective bolts had found their way into the Bradley Fighting Vehicle, produced by FMC Corporation, in San Jose, California. Representative Ron Wyden (D-Oregon), member of a House Energy and Commerce oversight subcommittee that had been investigating the problem, stated, "The issue is no longer confined just to the defense sector. Every sector we've investigated, whether it's been nuclear safety, defense, aviation, you name it—in one sector after another, we've found the problem."[2]

Methods of Prevention

Records of inspection and test results that have been falsified for expediency and profiteering result in false customer expectations.

Certification documents based on such data are meaningless. Instead of providing the mental assurance that purchasers of certified products expect, the certifications become opportunistic records that actually can result in the loss of human lives.

This excerpt illustrates a number of records activities that have already been discussed in previous chapters and provides support for the activities that are required in the ISO standards as well as for the records that are required of those activities. It also supports the concept of a quality records department that controls the gathered and disseminated information, serving as an independent third-party check to detect and prevent any activities designed to circumvent the established controls. For example, Boeing was fined $125,000 because it allowed the defective parts to enter its system. Requiring receipt inspection and collecting records pertaining to that activity would have filtered the defective units out of the system. It is not clear whether or not receipt inspection was being conducted or how the comparative analysis of inspection and test data against Boeing's internal specifications was being handled. In any case, sending the receipt inspection results to the quality records department, where records personnel would at least have seen them, could have alerted Boeing management that the results were out-of-spec.

The entire concept of a phantom inspector would have been more difficult to carry out had the quality records department controlled the records of stamp issuance. If it had maintained a list of inspection stamp numbers, together with the names of the inspectors to whom the stamps were issued, the quality records personnel would have been able to notify someone when quality-related records entered their department bearing an inspection stamp that had not been issued.

This situation also raises questions about the internal and external audits that should have been conducted in these organizations. By verifying information through the audit trail that quality records provide, auditors should have been able to detect the problem of the nonexistent inspector.

Conclusion

Inspection and testing records provide evidence that materials and products conform to specified requirements. From incoming materials and components through supplier-finished product, inspection and testing records make possible the comparison of attributes with specifications—both internal company specifications and customer specifications. Without information about the product characteristics, it is impossible to make any determinations about whether or not the product conforms to the desired requirements. The value of inspection and testing records is clearly understood by those who wish to circumvent the controls.

Notes

1. Frank M. Gryna. "Manufacturing Planning," in *Juran's Quality Control Handbook*, 4th ed., ed. J. M. Juran (New York: McGraw-Hill, 1988), 16.9.

2. Knight-Ridder *Tribune* News Service. Michael Zielenziger, "Faulty, Untested Nuts, Bolts, Turn Up in Civilian Aircraft," *Austin American-Statesman*, February 19, 1989, D1, D5. Excerpted with permission.

CHAPTER 10

Inspection, Measuring, and Test Equipment Records

Q9001—Section 4.11
Q9004-1—Section 13.0

Introduction

As with most quality-related activities, control of inspection, measuring, and test equipment is intertwined with activities from other quality-based functions. Equipment that is used to monitor processes and measure products provides strong evidentiary value that validates the entire quality system. If the units of measurement are inaccurate, nothing else matters, because the results are not what they purport to be.

What the Activity Involves

Unlike other portions of the ISO standards, requirements pertaining to inspection, measuring, and test equipment are detailed and clearly delineated. In its broadest charge, the introductory sentences in 4.11.1 specify the following.

> The supplier shall establish and maintain documented procedures to control, calibrate, and maintain inspection, measuring, and test equipment (including test software) used by the supplier to demonstrate the conformance

of product to the specified requirements. Inspection, measuring, and test equipment shall be used in a manner which ensures that the measurement uncertainty is known and is consistent with the required measurement capability.

The remaining portions of 4.11 enumerate the specific types of actions that are required. The word *shall* in the statements denotes a requirement in all instances, for all suppliers, and not merely activities that the supplier may elect to perform. Table 10.1 is reprinted from Q9001 and enumerates all of the required activities pertaining to equipment calibration.

Calibration

In some contexts, the word *calibration* is used to designate the combination of checking the instrument and adjusting it to bring

Table 10.1. Calibration requirements in ANSI/ASQC Q9001-1994, 4.11.2.

The supplier shall:

a) determine the measurements to be made and the accuracy required, and select the appropriate inspection, measuring, and test equipment that is capable of the necessary accuracy and precision;

b) identify all inspection, measuring, and test equipment that can affect product quality, and calibrate and adjust them at prescribed intervals, or prior to use, against certified equipment having a known valid relationship to internationally or nationally recognized standards. Where no such standards exist, the basis used for calibration shall be documented;

c) define the process employed for the calibration of inspection, measuring, and test equipment, including details of equipment type, unique identification, location, frequency of checks, check method, acceptance criteria, and the action to be taken when results are unsatisfactory;

d) identify inspection, measuring, and test equipment with a suitable indicator or approved identification record to show the calibration status;

e) maintain calibration records for inspection, measuring, and test equipment;

f) assess and document the validity of previous inspection and test results when inspection, measuring, and test equipment is found to be out of calibration;

g) ensure that the environmental conditions are suitable for the calibrations, inspections, measurements, and tests being carried out;

h) ensure that the handling, preservation, and storage of inspection, measuring, and test equipment is such that the accuracy and fitness for use are maintained;

i) safeguard inspection, measuring, and test facilities, including both test hardware and test software, from adjustments which would invalidate the calibration setting.

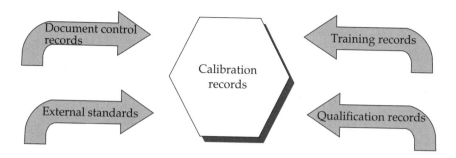

Figure 10.1. Records from other sections of ISO standards that affect calibration.

it within its tolerances for accuracy.[1] Usually, however, testing the instrument to see if it is within calibration limits is referred to as *checking* while the actual adjustment to the instrument is called *calibration*. The ISO standards are unclear about which definition is used in this series, but that is not the issue, nor is it important. The fact remains that both activities—the checking and the adjustment—must be conducted. In order to know if the instrument is in calibration, it is assumed that some checking process is in place. It is also assumed that, if the checking reveals an instrument that is out of calibration, that instrument will be adjusted. The concept of calibration comprises both activities.

The Role of Records

The main role that records play in the inspection, measuring, and test equipment arena is one of evidentiary value. Records provide evidence that all of the specified activities have been performed. Records also identify the actual pieces of equipment about which proof is provided. As Figure 10.1 illustrates, records from other sections of the standards are brought into play in calibration requirements. For example, document control records satisfy the requirement that procedures exist describing the calibration methods. Personnel training and qualification records indicate that the individuals who calibrate instruments and use them as measuring devices are qualified to do so. Equipment records are necessary to the sane functioning of any organization, regardless of the ISO requirements. For internal operating knowledge, it is necessary to know if measurements are accurate and if test results are revealing in-spec or out-of-spec conditions.

Types of Records to Maintain

Calibration records can be numerous and tedious to maintain. They often require capturing myriad data elements about hundreds, and sometimes thousands, of pieces of equipment. For this reason, manual recordkeeping is strongly discouraged for schedule adherence and for recording calibration results. Automation should be used to control the schedule and to trace the performance history of the equipment. Because of the large numbers involved and the methods that can be used to develop calibration schedules, it is easy to understand why some instruments pass their calibration due date. The most important aspect of calibration records is the development of a schedule and strict adherence to that schedule. Just as the process of calibration validates the entire process and the products themselves, adherence to the schedule validates the calibration system.

Development of a calibration system is the composite effort of all functions and units that are involved. Managers of the work areas, inspectors, and testers who use calibrated equipment, together with the quality records manager, can devise a schedule that is workable, meets requirements, and ensures accurate recordkeeping.

Identifying Equipment

As with the development of any major schedule, gathering information and planning for the system are the most laborious and time-consuming portions. Crucial to the schedule development process is the identification of each piece of inspection, measuring, and test equipment that will have to be calibrated. As Table 10.1 indicates, Subparagraph "b" specifies that all inspection, measuring, and test equipment that affects product quality must be identified. The reason is that, before procedures for the calibration system can even be written, the items that must be calibrated must be known. Subparagraph "b" also requires that the equipment be calibrated and adjusted against certified equipment that has a known valid relationship to internationally or nationally recognized standards. The importance of first identifying the equipment, again, is evident. Before the organization can even select the recognized standards, it must first identify the types of equipment that it must use.

Designing an identification scheme for equipment is similar to developing an identification scheme for quality records, or an indexing scheme for information. The input of the quality records manager is desirable and useful, because knowledge of identification guidelines is part of the working repertoire of a records manager and is one of the responsibilities delineated in Table 10.2. Each piece of inspection, measuring, and test equipment that will fall under a calibration program must bear a unique identifier, and this identifier must be used for one and only one item. The unique identifier is the link between all of the records about a single piece of equipment and, through it, the organization has access to the entire performance history of that item. Unique identifiers are commonly etched onto the instruments themselves, so that they cannot be altered or removed.

As is true of other identification schemes, a variety of approaches is possible. Straight numeric, alphanumeric, or serial

---

Table 10.2. Responsibilities of the quality records manager in calibration activities.

1. Define calibration records requirements from the standards.
2. Ensure that calibration procedures fall under the jurisdiction of the document control center.
3. Ensure that all external standards necessary for calibration activities are in-house, that they are organized, and that they are readily retrievable.
4. Assist in developing a calibration schedule.
5. Design any records necessary for calibration activities.
6. Coordinate the development of unique identifiers for all pieces of equipment that must be calibrated.
7. Design any labels that may be used to physically identify items.
8. Develop an oversight overcheck system within the quality records department.
9. If inspection and test results must be validated because of out-of-calibration equipment, ensure that all records are created and maintained, and that they contain all information pertaining to the process or product.
10. Develop a system for organizing, storing, and retrieving all records pertaining to calibration activities.
11. Develop records for calibrated items that must be checked in and checked out, to ensure control over measurement indicators.

codes are some of the most common methods of identifying calibrated items. Once a system is designed and selected, it should be applicable to all current and future items.

Developing a Schedule

A calibration schedule must be developed for each piece of equipment based on the requirements for the particular class to which that equipment belongs. The accuracy of equipment deteriorates over a period of time or with frequent usage. It is necessary to determine how long a particular instrument can provide accurate readings within acceptable ranges, and the instrument must be calibrated before inaccurate readings occur. Whatever schedule is developed for a particular piece of equipment, it is important that the quality records manager be notified and be provided with a list of the items and their calibration schedules. The quality records department can monitor the schedule to ensure compliance and can serve as the custodian of carefully scheduled calibration results.

The calibration schedule should be devised to permit a window of time for adherence. In other words, it is important to notify the managers of the work areas and the calibration laboratory that an item is approaching its calibration deadline. A tickler system works well in notifying responsible parties that given items are nearing their calibration due date. Although it is possible to develop manual tickler files for calibration schedules, a more efficient approach is to develop an automated tickler file, so that a computer can automatically generate notices concerning approaching calibration due dates. It is good practice to generate a notice 30 days prior to the calibration due date. Early notices permit the effective scheduling of calibration equipment and personnel and also allow adequate time before the calibration deadline to accommodate scheduling conflicts.

Developing an automated tickler file requires collecting and entering into the system all information pertaining to the calibration process. The same pieces of information must be recorded about the calibrated items, whether the system is manual or automated. Although developing an automated calibration system may seem like a formidable task, it simplifies the notification and recordkeeping processes and ensures more reliable adherence to the schedule. Regardless of the type of system, the following data elements should be recorded for each item requiring calibration.

- A unique identifier
- A brief name or description
- The location, department, or area
- The document control procedure number
- The frequency of calibration
- The last calibration date
- The next calibration date
- The date of actual calibration
- Results
- Calibration personnel
- Acceptance criteria

Recording these data elements complies with the requirements in subparagraph "c."

A calibration notice should be issued to the party or parties responsible for calibrating the item—either a standards laboratory or inspection and testing personnel, depending upon the procedures established in the organization. Issued as a multipart form, one copy of the calibration notice is sent to the calibrator, another to the manager of the area using the item, and a third to the quality records department. If the item is calibrated within the 30-day period, the copy of the notice that resides with the department performing the calibration is completed and sent to the data entry personnel who enter the calibration results into the calibration file, thus clearing the item. If the system permits, data can be entered at the point of calibration, thus eliminating the need to submit them to data entry. The completed, signed, and dated copy of the calibration record is sent to the quality records department where it is filed, microfilmed, or placed onto an optical disk system and indexed (see Figure 10.2 for a flowchart of activities). It is important to include a delinquency notice as part of the system. If the

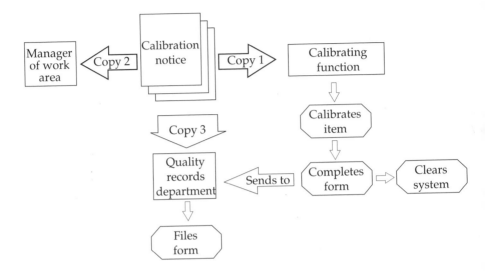

Figure 10.2. Flowchart of a calibration records system.

30-day grace period lapses, the automated tickler system issues a delinquency notice to all three recipients about the lapsed due date.

If the results of calibration are unsatisfactory, it is necessary to take action. The procedure for the type of action to be taken must be described in a document. In some instances, it may be necessary to reinspect or retest material that was checked by the equipment before calibration. In fact, subparagraph "f" requires that, if measuring or test equipment is found to be out of calibration, the validity of previous inspection and test results must be assessed and recorded.

Ensuring Calibrated Equipment

Because of the large number of pieces of calibrated equipment within most quality arenas, it is necessary to establish a systematic, organized procedure for calibration, and it is important to incorporate checks and balances into the system. Modern organizations operate within fixed financial constraints, and a card-based, manual record system for monitoring and recording required calibrations is labor-intensive and costly. If a new calibration records system must be developed, it is both cost-effective and efficient to automate either the entire process or a large portion. Those organizations that currently use manual record systems for calibration data can transfer existing information to an automated one. The quality records manager, working either in conjunction with information systems personnel, or, if qualified, alone, can design the changeover to be completed in phases, with designated categories of equipment entered into the system at prescribed intervals.

The effectiveness of the calibration program will depend, in large part, on adherence to the schedule and on the ability to identify quickly those items that are nearing or have passed their calibration due date. The quality records department, as ultimate recipient of the calibration records, is well positioned to ensure compliance with predetermined schedules. Quality records department personnel can monitor adherence to the schedule and notify the quality records manager of delinquencies. Putting the quality records department in the calibration loop provides a check as well as further assurance that effective controls are operating in the quality system.

Records to Create and Maintain

Because calibrated equipment is central to ensuring quality in processes and products, it is important that calibration records be thorough, accurate, and current. The data elements to be recorded span all information pertaining to the identification, checking, and adjustment of the calibrated items. This includes the following records and information.

- The identification number (code) for each item
- The calibration schedule for that item
- Dates of checks
- Names of personnel
- Results of checks
- The equipment against which the calibrated item was checked, and its relationship to nationally recognized stan-

dards, that is, the basis for calibration, the method of checking that was used

- Any adjustments that were made
- Any deficiency in the equipment
- If required, the time out for repair
- If results were unsatisfactory, the action taken
- If results were unsatisfactory, whether or not previous inspection and test results were invalidated
- The results of the initial calibration of the item, prior to its first use
- The item's current calibration status

The last piece of information, current calibration status, should be displayed on the equipment itself. Subparagraph "d" requires that the equipment bear an indicator or identification record showing its calibration status. A calibration sticker or label, showing the date when the item was calibrated, with the initials of the authorized individual, is commonly affixed to the item. By providing an immediate visual indication to the user that the equipment is in calibration, a physical label precludes any questions concerning its calibration status.

As Figure 10.1 indicates, calibration records are intertwined with records pertaining to document control and personnel/training. Calibration procedures fall under the aegis of the document control center and belong to that category of documents that must adhere to formalized procedures for creation, authorization, distribution, and retirement. The types of procedures that are prepared must cover the aspects specified in the ISO standards, Section 4.11. The amount of detail in the procedures is left to the discretion of individual organizations and industries. Some lines of business must prepare very detailed procedures, because, in addition to complying with ISO 9000, they must satisfy the requirements of regulatory agencies. The ISO standards require that the following information be included in the calibration procedures (Q9001, 4.11.2, c).

... details of equipment type, unique identification, location, frequency of checks, check method, acceptance criteria, and the action to be taken when results are unsatisfactory.

Training records for personnel who are to use calibrated items as well as for the calibrators themselves are important in validating the calibration process. Individuals who lack the expertise to use or to check calibrated equipment raise doubts about the quality system. Once again the interconnection of records pertaining to the quality process is evident. The maintenance and updating of records pertaining to personnel qualifications is easier to manage, and to retrieve during audits and during the registration process, if they are centralized in the quality records department (see chapter 14—"Training Records"). As seen in this explanation, they affect and are related to the calibration process.

The internal housing of externally produced standards also comes into play in the calibration process. As described in chapter 3, it is common to utilize industry standards as the reference point for certain activities generally conducted in the quality department. For example, some ASTM standards may be necessary for the test methods used in calibration, such as temperature or humidity controls. Part of the responsibility of the quality records department is to ensure that the required industry standards are in-house, that they are current, and that they are readily retrievable. It is not possible to demonstrate to an auditor that the item was checked utilizing a particular ASTM standard when that standard is not in the organization, or when it has been superseded by a newer version.

To summarize, therefore, the kinds of records that are required for calibration are those that

- Document the calibration process itself and track the historical performance and results of all calibrated items.
- Cover the procedures pertaining to calibration, that is, document control records.
- Reveal the expertise and training of individuals who use or calibrate the items.
- Provide access to the referenced industry standards and the standards themselves.

The Consequences of Not Being In-Calibration

The consequences of equipment that is *out-of-calibration* are obvious. The recorded results do not indicate the actual conditions.

This is true of in-process activities as well as final product in-spection and testing. An annealing furnace thermometer that is out of calibration can be registering 600 degrees Fahrenheit, when the furnace temperature is actually less than 500 degrees. And certain assumptions are made about the metal that was annealed in the furnace—its molecular structure, strength, and performance characteristics. Granted, the differences will be revealed in further testing on the metal, but the entire annealed lot will remain flawed, and the production process will be delayed, postponing promised shipment dates. At the very best, uncalibrated equip-ment will result in embarrassment and will require renegotiating shipment dates.

The earlier in the process that the uncalibrated item is used, the less chance there is that the result will be defective product. Checking systems throughout the process most likely will reveal the discrepancy before the product is shipped. Uncalibrated in-spection and testing equipment at the end of the line, however, can mean shipment of defective product. A gauge or caliper used to measure the thickness of metal strip product can erroneously read in-spec dimensions, resulting in the shipment of out-of-spec metal pieces.

Records serve to control the process by keeping track of each calibrated item. They also serve as a check to ensure that delin-quent items are brought to the attention of responsible individuals in the quality organization. Records provide the results of calibra-tion, thus reinforcing trust in the quality system. They also reveal the performance history of calibrated equipment, supporting and raising the level of confidence in the quality system. It is impor-tant, therefore, to ensure that calibration records requirements are being satisfied. Table 10.3 provides a series of questions pertaining to calibration records.

Storing and Maintaining Inspection and Test Equipment

Although responsibility for the appropriate storage and mainte-nance of inspection and test equipment is not the jurisdiction of the quality records manager, there are some activities that the

---

Table 10.3. Examination of calibration records requirements.

Questions to ask about calibration records

1. Do you have a unique identification number for each piece of inspection, measuring, and test equipment?
2. When equipment is found to be out of calibration, do you have records revealing that you have assessed the validity of all previous inspection and test results?
3. Do you have a calibration schedule, in writing, indicating the frequency of calibration for all items?
4. Do you have calibration reports, data sheets, and/or certificates that support the accuracy of your reference standards?
5. Do your calibration records contain the
   a) item name, identification number, location of use?
   b) frequency of calibration?
   c) reference to calibration procedure?
   d) date last calibrated, by whom, and date of next calibration?
   e) identity of the standard used to perform calibration, or identity of the certification document?
   f) results of the last calibration and any deviation from standard values?
   g) results or indications of crosschecks or periodic inspections, maintenance, or repairs, if any, conducted between calibrations?
6. Do you have records of new or reworked measuring and test equipment calibrated prior to usage?
7. Do you have labels or markings on your measuring and test equipment to indicate
   a) item identification?
   b) date last calibrated, by whom, and date of next calibration?

---

quality records manager can contribute to and some records that can be maintained that help elevate the credibility of the calibration system. Working in conjunction with appropriate personnel, the quality records manager can help devise a system for identifying stored items by linking them to the storage equipment or facility. A system similar to that used to establish bibliographic control over library materials is well within the purview of most records managers. Designating a fixed location for storing calibrated equipment and developing a system that requires checking the desired item in and out helps ensure that the items are always stored appropriately. Conducting a periodic inventory of equipment that should be in storage provides further assurance that the system is working.

A log can be maintained at storage locations, revealing when equipment has been checked in and checked out. Such records then can be deposited with the quality records department and maintained as part of the calibration records system.

Conclusion

Calibration records provide assurance that inspection, measuring, and test equipment is operating properly. Records consist of calibration schedules, identification of the items themselves, evidence that appropriate checks have been conducted, and the results of the checking. By proving that all equipment affecting quality is in calibration, records support the information captured during the process and recorded during inspection and test activities.

Notes

1. Joseph J. Zeccardi, "Inspection and Test," in *Juran's Quality Control Handbook,* 4th ed., ed. J. M. Juran (New York: McGraw-Hill, 1988), 18.76.

CHAPTER 11

Nonconforming Product Records

Q9001—Section 4.13
Q9004-1—Section 14

Corrective and Preventive Action Records

Q9001—Section 4.14
Q9004-1—Section 15

Handling, Storage, Packaging, Preservation, and Delivery Records

Q9001—Section 4.15
Q9004-1—Sections 10.4, 16.1, and 16.2

Introduction

The topic of nonconforming product is closely tied to the discussion of inspection and testing presented in chapter 10. Because the activities are closely connected, so are the records. Corollary to identifying acceptable material and product, from receipt through

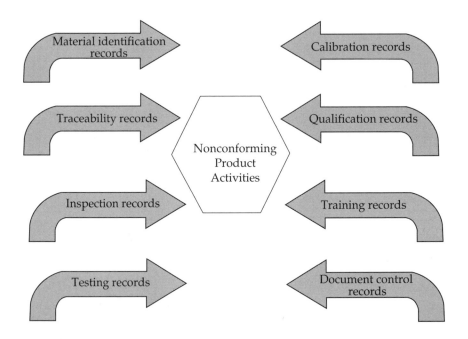

Figure 11.1. Records from other sections of ISO standards that affect nonconforming product activities.

shipment of final product, is identifying materials and products that are unacceptable or nonconforming. There would be no need to identify acceptable or conforming material if there was no such thing as nonconforming material.

The Role of Records in This Activity

Just as it is important to prove that material or product is acceptable, it is important to identify unacceptable material. Records serve multiple roles in controlling nonconforming product. They function as identifiers, as notification, as disposition, and as corrective action. Earlier chapters of this book and prior sections of the Q9001 standard must be brought to bear on the process of controlling nonconforming product. Unless the records described earlier are in place, instituting measures to control nonconforming material will be difficult, if not impossible. Once again, as Figure

11.1 illustrates, the interconnection of quality records and activities is evident in this section of the standards.

Sections 4.13 and 4.14 skirt the issue of those quality records that should be created and maintained to adequately conduct the activities that are specified. Reading these sections can lead to an erroneous assumption that only the following needs to be recorded.

> The description of nonconformity that has been accepted, and of repairs, shall be recorded to denote the actual condition (4.13.2).

Records necessary to control nonconforming material actually begin with the appropriate identification of all material, so that nonconforming product can easily be identified. Uniqueness is an important feature of material and product identification because it eliminates confusion. In addition, the nonconforming product is designated to be nonconforming because of inspection or testing, and, therefore, inspection and testing records enter the picture. The evaluation methods used to make the determination must be recorded, and the validity of those methods depends on appropriately calibrated equipment as well as on the skill and expertise of the inspectors and testers. Paragraph 4.13.1 of Q9001 specifies the following:

> This control shall provide for identification, documentation, evaluation, segregation (when practical), disposition of nonconforming product, and for notification to the functions concerned.

Identification encompasses not only the unique identification of the batch, material, or products, but, in this requirement, means identifying the product *as* nonconforming product. It means the *designation* of the material as nonconforming. The *Guidelines* (14.2) suggest that

> Suspected nonconforming items or lots should be immediately identified and the occurrence(s) recorded.

The safest method is to attach some sort of physical designation, in the form of a label or tape or whatever is deemed appropriate for the type of product. The product should be visibly, clearly identified as nonconforming. A further form of identification is the record created to capture the pertinent information about the nonconforming material or product. The record should include the following items of information.

- The product identification
- The reason(s) for nonconformance (test results, inspection, and so on)
- The present physical location of the product
- The name of the individual who detected nonconformance or who designated it as such
- The date
- The disposition of the nonconforming product
- The reason for disposition (for example, customer acceptance)
- The name of the person who reviewed the disposition decision

Records as Notifying Agent

Because nonconforming product must be pulled from further processing or prevented from being shipped, the procedures established to handle it should provide for an orderly and systematic method of notification to all pertinent functions. Nonconforming product is unplanned; obviously no sane organization purposely builds in processes to develop a product that is nonconforming. Because a nonconformance is unplanned, its identification and designation causes disturbances that can ripple through the organization and beyond, to its customers. On the other hand, although nonconformance is unplanned, it should not be unanticipated. If it remains both unplanned and unanticipated, chaos results. The ISO standards thus insist on documented procedures designed to address all of the necessary actions that should be taken when a nonconforming product is identified.

One of the important facets of procedures in this instance is to develop concrete methods for notifying those functions and individuals whose schedules and activities are affected by the nonconforming status. Records serve as the concrete proof that all notifications have taken place. The first to be notified should be the customer. Notifying the customer about the nonconforming status of the order is necessary because shipment deadlines most likely will be affected. In addition, discussing the nonconformance with the customer helps to determine the disposition of the product. Records must be kept of customer notification, whether the notification is done orally or in writing. The standards require that, if the nonconformity has been accepted, its description must be recorded to denote the actual condition. Usually, because of time constraints, notification may be handled initially by telephone, so that detailed discussions can take place. The discussion, as well as the customer response, should be put in writing and faxed (or mailed) to the customer, with a request for a return confirmation of the decision, again in writing. Faxes in both directions can be used for expediency. Keeping records of customer notification and response is important because these will be the only records that prove that appropriate contact was made, and they reveal the customer's decision about product acceptance or rejection. If faxes are used, it must be remembered that incoming faxes gradually fade over time. The information becomes illegible, and the record will be of no use to the organization. If important faxes are received and the record must be retained for any length of time, they should be photocopied and the photocopies should be retained as the record copies.

The quality department, of course, must be notified. In most instances, this is the department that has detected the nonconforming product. Usually the quality department notifies all pertinent functions. Procedures developed by the supplier should specify the level of authority in the quality department that must be notified. A place can be prepared on the record that identifies nonconforming material to indicate that the appropriate quality personnel have been notified.

The next area in the processing and production chain that was to receive the material or product must also be notified about the nonconforming product, because it, too, is affected. The established production schedule now must be changed, and the identification of nonconforming product may mean a change in personnel requirements as well as working hours.

Records of Review of Nonconforming Product

The standards require that nonconforming product be reviewed. The *Guidelines*, Q9004-1, elaborate on the review activity in 14.4.

> Nonconforming product should be subjected to review by designated persons to determine whether it can be accepted with or without repair by concession, repaired, reworked, regraded, or scrapped. Persons carrying out the review should be competent to evaluate the effects of the decision on interchangeability, further processing, performance, dependability, safety, and aesthetics.

Records of the review process must be created and maintained. These must reveal that the nonconforming product was reviewed to determine its disposition and that it was reviewed by authorized, designated individuals, who have the expertise to evaluate the effects of the disposition.

Records of Repair or Rework

If the decision is to repair or rework the nonconforming material, records must be created and maintained of the repair or rework activity. The information that must be captured is

- The identification of the material or product
- The nature of the repair or rework, cross referenced to the disposition of the product
- Reinspection or retesting of the material or product

Multiple records may be necessary, especially if inspection and testing require numerous actions. Usually one record is generated for each type of inspection and each type of test conducted. The same pieces of data must be recorded about repaired or reworked products as is recorded for conforming products. The difference is that inspection and test records of repaired or reworked material should be clearly designated as such to distinguish them from the original testing and inspection records. These new records should be retained together with the records of prior testing and inspection. It is the responsibility of the quality records manager to design a records system that accommodates such records. Further responsibilities are delineated in Table 11.1.

Because shipment release will be made at the point of the latest inspection and testing, it is important that records be identified

---

Table 11.1. Responsibilities of the quality records manager in nonconforming product activities.

---

1. Define the records requirements for nonconforming product activities.
2. Develop the records that are required.
3. Ensure that the records contain the necessary data elements, such as
   a) details of deficiencies.
   b) dispositions.
   c) corrective actions.
4. Ensure that records are developed to report on investigations of nonconformities and on the analysis of causes.
5. Ensure that records are created and maintained about all communications with the customer concerning the disposition of nonconforming products.
6. If nonconforming material has been reworked, repaired, or modified, ensure that appropriate records of reinspection and retesting have been completed. Develop a system for incorporating the records of reworked material into process and product records.
7. Design identification materials (stamps, tags, and so forth) if they are needed to label segregated, nonconforming product.
8. Ensure that records have been created of the review of nonconforming product.
9. Design a system for organizing, storing, and retrieving all records pertaining to product so that records about other products that were designed or processed following the same procedures as the nonconforming product can be readily retrieved.
10. Assist in designing or design the automated system for nonconforming records.

---

clearly. It is also important for the audit trail and for records traceability that all actions, decisions, and results of nonconforming product be logically organized so as to provide a chronological history of exactly what transpired. Records of nonconforming product that are scattered or dispersed or that cannot be retrieved in a unit undermine confidence in the handling of nonconforming product and can even call into question the ultimate quality of shipped material that was repaired or reworked.

Records of Other Actions

Identifying nonconforming product may precipitate additional actions that should be recorded. Other products that were designed or processed following the same procedures as those used to create the nonconforming product may have to be reviewed. If such

Table 11.2. Examination of nonconforming product records requirements.

Questions to ask about nonconforming product records

1. Do you have rejection forms that indicate the nature and extent of the nonconformance?
2. Do you have records of conducting material review?
3. Do records about nonconforming material specify the disposition?
4. Do you have records of repetitive discrepancies?
5. Do you have records of management review of nonconforming product records and reports?
6. Do you have records of reinspection and retesting on material that was reworked, repaired, or modified?
7. Do your nonconforming product records and material review records contain details about the deficiencies, dispositions, and corrective actions?
8. Is information about nonconforming product analyzed to determine the cause of nonconformity? Do your records reflect this information?
9. Do you have records of all contacts with customers pertaining to the disposition of nonconforming products?

material is reviewed, records should be created and maintained of both the review and the results. Previous lots of the same product may also need to be reviewed, and, again, records should provide information about this review activity. To ensure compliance with records requirements for nonconforming product, organizations are encouraged to ask themselves the questions presented in Table 11.2.

Identifying nonconforming product may precipitate the recall of completed product. If recall is necessary, the value of well-organized quality records becomes evident. It would be virtually impossible to pinpoint exactly which items should be recalled unless records are accurate and unless they identify material and products clearly enough that they can be traced.

Corrective and Preventive Action Records

Identifying and disposing of nonconforming product is only part of the task. The remaining portion is eliminating the root causes of nonconforming products. It is readily understood that corrective action activities are critical in preventing chronic nonconforming products. Although the supplier is required to establish procedures for investigating the causes, analyzing the processes, initiating preventive actions, and applying controls to ensure that corrective actions are effective, there is no provision in the standards that requires all of the activities that have taken place to be recorded. An organization would be hard-pressed to prove that any of these actions have been taken unless it had records containing the information that serves as evidence.

Corrective Action Records

The procedures for corrective action, described in Q9001, 4.14.2 should include records that prove that the activities have taken place. Subparagraph "a" requires

> the effective handling of customer complaints and reports of product non-conformities

Records to support these activities include the customer's complaints as well as evidence that the complaints are being handled effectively. Reports of product nonconformities are also a category of records.

Subparagraph "b" requires

> investigation of the cause of nonconformities relating to product, process and quality system, and recording the results of the investigation

Here, the types of required records are specified clearly: results of the investigation of the cause of nonconformities. Records serve as evidence that the cause has been investigated. Data elements to be recorded would be very similar to identification of nonconforming product. In fact, if feasible, the cause and corrective action could be included on the same record that was used to identify the nonconforming product, because most data elements remain the same. A section of the record, physically separated from the identification of nonconforming product, can include the cause and the corrective action that will be taken. If information capture is automated, the data elements can be entered on that product lot and logically accessed according to appropriate variables.

Subparagraph "c" requires

determination of the corrective action needed to eliminate the cause of nonconformities

Records should provide information about the corrective action that has been determined to eliminate the cause.
  Subparagraph "d" requires

application of controls to ensure that corrective action is taken and that it is effective

Records should reveal that controls have been applied and that the corrective action is effective. In other words, records provide evidence that the corrective action system is working.

Preventive Action Records

At the next step, beyond corrective action, the standards require that procedures for preventive action be developed to eliminate the causes of the nonconformities. Paragraph 4.14.3 is devoted to preventive action requirements and specifies in subparagraph "a"

the use of appropriate sources of information such as processes and work operations which affect product quality, concessions, audit results, quality records, service reports, and customer complaints to detect, analyze, and eliminate potential causes of nonconformities

This statement is all-encompassing and can be labor-intensive for any organization. Logically, records of continuous, ongoing process activities are being consistently monitored under the aegis of process control. Records, thus, are already being created and maintained. Work operations that are being conducted according to documented procedures, by trained operators, with calibrated equipment, should result in acceptable product. Because work operations encompass a variety of rather intricate and elaborate record types, those records, according to this statement, should exist and should be analyzed. In reality, such examinations become the crux of internal audits. Records of concessions, by default, already exist, if nonconforming product has been discussed with customers and disposition has been made. Analysis of nonconforming product records is an important facet in developing corrective actions that will be preventive in nature. A single type of repeated nonconformity can often be traced back to a root cause or several root causes that, then, can be addressed and corrected. The *Guidelines* discuss problem analysis and determination of root cause in paragraph 15.5.

> In the analysis of a quality-related problem, the root cause or causes should be determined before corrective action is planned. Often the root cause is not obvious, thus requiring careful analysis of the product specifications and of all related processes, operations, quality records, servicing reports and customer complaints.

The *Guidelines*, therefore, recommend analysis of the same records that are part of the requirement in 4.14.3.

Analysis of concessions should be documented in a record to prove that preventive actions are a normal part of quality operations. Analysis of customer complaints and service reports, as well, should be recorded. The same logic holds true as does for concessions. The clustering of complaints and service reports around a particular defect or nonconformity can lead to faster resolution of the problem. This is the rationale behind the recommendation in the *Guidelines*, 15.5.

> Consideration should be given to establishing a file listing nonconformities to help identify those problems having a common source, contrasted with those that are unique occurrences.

Because of their very nature, quality records should be viewed and examined consistently. Under normal circumstances, the information on them precipitates further processing and production. Unless quality records are analyzed, the product cannot be shipped or the material cannot continue for further processing. In most organized quality environments, such records already exist, and, in the normal case of business operations, they are being reviewed and analyzed.

Subparagraphs "b" and "c" of 4.14.3 require the

> b) determination of the steps needed to deal with any problems requiring preventive action;
> c) initiation of preventive action and application of controls to ensure that it is effective.

The types of records required to satisfy these subparagraphs must provide information on the exact nature of the preventive actions that have been initiated and the problems that those ac-

---

Table 11.3. Responsibilities of the quality records manager in corrective and preventive action activities.

1. Define records requirements for corrective and preventive action activities.
2. Design any necessary records.
3. Design records system for customer complaints, linking the handling of the complaint to the complaint to show effectiveness.
4. Ensure that records are being created and maintained that report on the results of investigations about the causes of nonconformities.
5. Ensure that records about corrective actions are maintained.
6. Develop a records system that assists in identifying root causes by clustering complaints, concessions, and service reports that have a common source.
7. Ensure that records provide information on the exact nature of preventive actions and the controls that have been established.
8. Develop records for management review of nonconformities and corrective and preventive actions.

---

tions have been designed to address. The orderly preparation of a method designed to keep a current listing of nonconformities goes a long way toward presenting a logical cause-and-effect record system. All nonconformities should be organized by type and traceable to the following variables: customer order, date, nonconforming product record, disposition, investigation of cause, and determination of cause. The preventive actions can be plugged in, adjacent to the type of nonconformity, if the cause has been determined to be identical for that nonconformity. Organizing such information is one of the responsibilities of the quality records manager, as specified in Table 11.3. Presenting information in this manner simplifies the understanding of those preventive actions that have been initiated for given nonconformities and also permits detection of those that are effective and those that are not.

Not only must the records state that controls have been applied, but they must also specify what those controls are. Vagueness and generalities should never be characteristic of quality records. Rather, specificity and exactness are key features of good quality records. Effectiveness can be demonstrated through an elimination of the nonconformity. In other words, the corrective actions have been effective because the nonconformities have ceased or have been reduced significantly.

The last subparagraph of 4.14.3 requires

d) confirmation that relevant information on actions taken is submitted for management review.

This requirement directs the quality function in the organization to develop a system for the retrospective analysis of nonconformities, as well as the corrective and preventive actions that have been taken. In order to prove compliance with this requirement, records must be created and maintained revealing that the information has been presented for management review. Records should also exist proving that management has reviewed the information and reporting on any decisions emanating from that review. Organizations can use the questions posed in Table 11.4 as guidelines to determine the current status of their corrective and preventive action records.

Effect on Document Control Records

The standards require that procedures be changed if actual activities are now being conducted differently as a result of the corrective and preventive actions that have been implemented. In other words, the written procedures should reflect reality and not past practice. The requirement in 4.14.1 to "record any changes to the

---

Table 11.4. Examination of corrective and preventive action records requirements.

Questions to ask about corrective and preventive action records

1. Do you have records of customer complaints? Do your records demonstrate that the complaints are being handled effectively?
2. Do you organize the information from your nonconforming product records to reveal repetitive discrepancies or unsatisfactory trends?
3. Do you have records revealing that you investigate the causes of nonconforming products?
4. Do you have records revealing that you analyze all processes and records to eliminate the causes of nonconforming products?
5. Do you have records of preventive actions that have been taken?
6. Do your records reveal that the preventive actions have been effective?
7. Do you incorporate changes that have been made in the processes in your controlled documents? Or are your documents not reflective of reality?
8. Do your records reveal that you have established time limits for corrective actions? Do you monitor implementation?

documented procedures" is a blanket requirement for all changes in all procedures, and the requirements specified in Section 4.5 on document control should be followed. The *Guidelines* elaborate on this point in 15.8.

> Permanent changes resulting from corrective action should be recorded in work instructions, production-process documentation, product specifications, and/or the quality-system documentation. It may also be necessary to revise the procedures used to detect and eliminate potential problems.

If the organization is effectively implementing the document control function, there is nothing new or additional that is required here. Frequently, what happens, however, is the gradual obsolescence of documents as a result of procedural changes that are never incorporated into them. Documents that are not updated to reflect reality are weak points during audits.

Automating Nonconforming Records

If a database is created of all variables pertaining to nonconforming product, recordkeeping will be easier and more effective. By being able to reconfigure the data and generate topic-specific reports, the quality department can use the information in the records to conduct analyses, to trace causes, to detect causes, and to identify those corrective actions that have been effective. The automated information system can also integrate disparate pieces of information that would be separated on different records if a manual, paper-based system were utilized. Rather than have records that confuse, the quality function would have records that illuminate the situation and can effectively contribute to analysis and better decisions.

Handling, Storage, Packaging, Preservation, and Delivery Records

Records to satisfy this section of the ISO standards are not as numerous or tedious as those required for other activities. Post-production activities are important in safeguarding the quality that has already been built into the product and accepted. Documents are important in these activities to reveal to auditors that measures are taken to protect the quality of the finished product. Compliance with this section depends to a great degree on the procedures and condition of the areas where finished product is stored and packaged, as well as on the handling and packaging techniques employed. Rather than retrieving a large number of records to demonstrate compliance with this section, the quality function actively demonstrates compliance by showing auditors the areas where finished product is stored, how finished product is handled, and how it is packaged.

Some records may be required if the product is stored for a period of time, during which time it can deteriorate. If such is the case, Paragraph 4.15.3 requires that

> In order to detect deterioration, the condition of product in stock shall be assessed at appropriate intervals.

Such assessments and their results must be recorded. When auditors examine postproduction activities, they focus on how accurately the activities reflect the written procedures, and how customers' requirements are addressed in the packaging, preservation, and marking procedures.

Some typical records-related audit questions are

- What sort of packing requirements are in the customer specification for this product (order)? (This necessitates retrieving a copy of the customer spec.)
- How are these requirements made known to the packaging personnel? (This necessitates indicating that a procedure exists that describes the packing requirements.)
- Do the packing personnel have an authorized copy of the procedure? Have they read it? What proof do you have?
- Can I (we) see how the packing personnel pack the product according to the procedure and customer's requirements?

Questions can also involve controlled documents. For example,

- Is this the latest revision of that packing procedure?
- Has the previous one been retrieved?
- What changes were made in this latest revision?
- Who else receives this document?

The most important aspects of Section 4.15 regarding records is having the ability to prove to auditors that measures exist to protect finished product, that personnel are aware of those measures, that the measures are applied, and that they are effective.

Conclusion

Records play important roles in identifying nonconforming product and, subsequently, in corrective action and preventive action activities. For the credibility of the organization, it is imperative that it has the ability to identify product that is nonconforming and that it institutes measures revealing that the problem has been remedied and procedures have been developed to prevent future occurrences. Records enable the organization to exert control over deviations, to determine root causes, and, thus, to maintain credibility.

CHAPTER 12

Quality Records

Q9001—Section 4.16
Q9004-1—Sections 5.3.4 and 17

Introduction

The section on quality records in the standards is one of the smallest, yet the space it occupies is misleading. All records requirements do not appear in 4.16. Section 4.16 simply provides a blanket overview requirement, specifying the records management activities that must be applied to *all* quality records that are required throughout the standards. This includes all supplier records and all subcontractor records.

Records Procedures Required

The revised version of the standards has a significant change in Section 4.16 requirements.

> The supplier shall establish and maintain documented procedures for identification, collection, indexing, access, filing, storage, maintenance, and disposition of quality records.

In other words, procedures must be written describing how the organization conducts these records management activities, and the procedures must fall under the document control umbrella. Procedures that define how each of the records components is handled can be lengthy, depending on the amount of detail included. Where time is short, organizations can prepare sketchy procedures to satisfy the registration process and then elaborate on them later. It is unwise to leave the procedures sketchy permanently, as they can and should be used by the quality records management staff to implement the activities. Procedures for indexing, for example, should be detailed, so that employees who are responsible for that activity can follow the instructions that have been prepared. The approach toward documented procedures for records management components can follow the pyramid model that is used for all quality documentation. The top tier can consist of a records management policy, and this document can be at the most general level. The second tier can be more specific, and the third tier should be the most specific with actual work instructions and steps included.

The documented procedures must apply to all records that pertain to product quality, not just to some record categories or to some record types within a category. To clarify: All quality records must be identified, collected, indexed, filed, stored, maintained, and, finally, disposed of. Section 4.16 also stipulates that

All quality records shall be legible and shall be stored and retained in such a way that they are readily retrievable in facilities that provide a suitable environment to prevent damage or deterioration and to prevent loss.

In addition to the legibility requirements, all quality records should be stored in such a way that they are protected from deterioration or destruction. Applying techniques from vital records protection programs (see chapter 16) ensures compliance with this requirement. Section 4.16 further requires that

Retention times of quality records shall be established and recorded.

Because development of a records retention schedule is a major undertaking, a detailed explanation of how to develop one is presented in chapter 16.

Not all subactivities that comprise the records components just mentioned are delineated in the standards or in the *Guidelines*. It is assumed that the supplier knows what those are. In addition, a complete list of records that the quality function should create, maintain, and manage does not appear anywhere in the standards or the *Guidelines*. The *Guidelines* provide examples of some types of quality records that require control in 17.2.

    inspection reports
    test data
    qualification reports
    validation reports
    survey and audit reports
    material review reports
    calibration data, and
    quality-related cost reports

By no means is the list inclusive, as this book points out. All required records are not explicitly mentioned anywhere in the standards. It is by implication that the standards allude to the records requirements. Because the records requirements are condensed and records themselves are implied, the ISO representative or the quality records manager must interpret and amplify each of the records-related statements that pertains to the quality activity. Satisfying the quality activity requirement frequently necessitates keeping records.

Retrieval and Format

The inability to retrieve records is the single biggest records problem that organizations face. They may be unable to retrieve records in a timely manner, or they may be unable to retrieve some records at all. The requirement that quality records be readily retrievable, therefore, is not a light charge. Retrievability encompasses the aforementioned activities of identification, collection, indexing, filing, storage, and maintenance. To a great extent, all of these activities depend on the format of the record—whether the record is in paper or hard copy, on microforms (microfilm/microfiche), on an optical disk, or stored on computer. Depending on the format, different activities, different skill sets, and different facets of knowledge apply. Also, the format affects the resources required, the kinds of equipment necessary, the implementation time frames that are realistic, and the expertise required.

Filing, as a term, is applied to each of the formats. Yet each format has storage equipment that is specific to it; each requires different storage conditions; each utilizes different methods of access; and each requires different supplies and different environmental conditions. As a requirement, *maintenance* of quality records also is linked closely with format, since some formats do not endure as long or as well as others. Q9001, Section 4.16 contains the following note about format.

> Records may be in the form of any type of media, such as hard copy or electronic media.

Because medium or format affects many decisions that must be made in satisfying the ISO records requirements, some important considerations are presented here that are applicable to specific media.

Paper Format

The word *record* conjures up mental pictures of paper documents, housed in four-drawer vertical file cabinets; and, as a matter of course, information or data captured on paper are what normally come to mind when records are discussed. According to a study commissioned by the Association for Information and Image Management (AIIM), 95 percent of information in American businesses is stored on paper.[1] Most literature devoted to managing information, however, has disregarded this fact. Companies continue to create about one million documents during every minute of business, yet ignorance about managing paper records is as prevalent as the medium itself.[2]

Mismanagement often begins by selecting inappropriate housing—the file cabinets. A file cabinet is the very first piece of equipment that comes to mind when individuals need to house records. Four- and five-drawer vertical metal file cabinets dominate every office environment. Yet, the traditional file cabinet is the most expensive type of equipment to buy and maintain. For the number of records that it can accommodate, a vertical file cabinet is not cost-effective. It occupies more floor space than its actual size; because the drawers must be pulled out in order to access the records, the floor space beneath the opened drawer must be left open—it cannot be used. Additional space must be provided to allow individuals to stand in front of the open drawer to access

Open-Shelf Filing Units

Requires: 14 inches for cabinet
            25 inches for aisle space
Total: 39 inches
            No open drawer space required

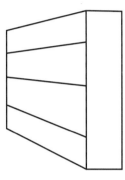

Vertical Three-Drawer File Cabinet

Requires: 28 inches for cabinet
            28 inches for open drawer
            25 inches for aisle space
Total: 81 inches

Figure 12.1. A comparison of space required by open-shelf and vertical file storage units.

the records in the file cabinet. Figure 12.1 illustrates the difference in space needed between the traditional vertical file cabinet and an open-shelf filing unit.

Selecting appropriate housing for active paper records involves a knowledge of the filing equipment that is specific to the types of records that an organization retains, as well as retrieval patterns and costing issues. There is equipment for every size and shape of paper record that exists. Equipment can be selected from a bewildering array of choices: vertical files (two, four, and five drawers, with or without locks), lateral files, open-shelf files, hanging files, mobile shelf units, flat files, box files, rotary files, and special purpose files such as pigeonhole files. Each type of equipment has features and advantages suited to specific kinds of records in particular surroundings, and a record is best housed in equipment that has been designed specifically for that type of record. Flat files, for example, are used to store maps and engineering drawings. Box files come in various configurations and sizes and are used to store inactive records, magazines or catalogs, and even microcomputer floppy disks. Letter-size (8½-inch by 11-inch) records should be placed in letter-size filing equipment. Legal-size (11-inch by 14-inch) records should be housed in legal-size filing equipment, or, better yet, should be eliminated.

Purchasing decisions about filing equipment should be based on cost-effectiveness and suitability, taking into consideration the following factors.

- The initial cost of the equipment, as well as its maintenance cost
- The design of the equipment
- The floor space required
- The frequency of use
- The efficiency of equipment operation
- The degree of protection and security offered

Supplies such as file folders, labels, and file guides also should be selected for use in the specific equipment for which they were designed. Access and retrieval are more difficult if the wrong supplies are used. For example, top-tab file folders instead of side-tab folders in open-shelf files makes the search process harder. Retrieval in open-shelf files is rapid and refiling is highly accurate, but only if side-tab file folders are used.

Organizing schemes must also be designed to take advantage of the physical equipment configuration. Open-shelf filing illustrates this point. Side-tab folders work best when color coding is combined with a meaningful alpha, numeric, or alphanumeric identification on the tab. Side-tab folders in open-shelf files do not function well when plain white labels, or color-striped labels, designed for use on top-tab cut folders, are affixed to them. They are difficult to read, and they serve no meaningful purpose in facilitating rapid and accurate storage and retrieval of records.

Decisions about organizing schemes for paper files are difficult, because there is no one perfect way to intellectually organize paper records. The main problem is that individuals request or seek records by using one of several possible identifiers, while the physical paper record can reside in only one location, under one main identifier. To copy the records and establish files for each possible identifier is ludicrous. Paper files require external indexes or multiple cross references so that the record can be located under a variety of possible terms. However, because indexes and cross references are not used regularly, retrieving paper records is highly problematic. Deciding on an organizing scheme—alphabetic, numeric, subject, or some other—is difficult, and it solves only part of the problem. Regardless of the method that is used, additional retrieval devices, such as indexes, are required to provide ready access to records. Otherwise, the records department is perceived as a black hole, and, because users do not trust the records department, they create their own insurance copies of records that they need to use regularly.

Optical Disk Technology

Because of the inherent problems of paper-based systems, many organizations are using optical disk document management systems. The required activities of access, filing, storage, and maintenance of quality records must be handled quite differently in an optical disk environment. Because records are digitized and read to an optical disk, access depends completely on the indexing scheme. If it is designed effectively, the computer-based index permits multilevel or relational searching, and access to optical disk records is vastly improved over paper records. Because the system is electronic, it allows for random access of records and the assignment of multiple index terms to one record. However, the design of the indexing scheme becomes much more critical in an optical disk environment, because the index is the *only* access to that record. Hunt and search methods, frequently used when paper records cannot be located, do not work in an optical disk environment.

With optical disk, the speed of access to records is vastly improved, with access times varying from one second to several minutes. Also, multiple users in different locations have access to the same record simultaneously. This is not possible with paper records unless they are copied and distributed. Furthermore, unlike paper records, records on optical disk cannot be misplaced, misfiled, altered, or inadvertently destroyed.

However, conversion to this new electronic medium is not a cure-all for the paper records problems that most organizations face daily. For optical disk technology to be successful, a system must be established, procedures must be developed, and, most important, the current paper-based system must first be cleaned up. Before an organization can install an optical disk system, certain activities must be conducted. The first need is to understand what is being replaced—the current paper system. This is the task of records management professionals, whether they be consultants or staff.

Microforms

Mention of the word *microfilm* causes many adverse reactions—groaning, shuddering, grunting, expletives, and so forth. Yet microfilm has moved into the 21st century because of its marriage with computer technology. It is a viable option to paper and optical disk and can be used very effectively to store and retrieve active quality records, not only those records that must be retained as backup or for the archives. Several publications provide thorough descriptions of micrographics products and also present approaches to implementing microforms in the organization for active records management (see the selected bibliography).

Much literature is available today about CAR systems, digitized microfilm systems, and even hybrid systems. Just as with records in other formats, knowledge about access, environmental storage conditions, and equipment that is specific to microforms is necessary in order to achieve the expected results. Because of their long history and gradual evolution, microforms do not present many of the concerns that are still expressed about optical disk systems. A wide variety of products are available, including various types of microforms, cameras, and even films.

The ISO requirements for indexing, accessing, filing, storing, and maintaining as well as ready retrieval must be addressed differently with microforms because of the format. Again, format affects the type of intellectual access that is developed; it affects the selection of equipment (readers, reader/printers, cameras, and storage cabinets); it affects the type of environment in which the records are housed and stored; and it dictates very different maintenance activities.

Indexing

Marc R. D'Alleyrand defines *indexing* as "a generic term used to describe the processes that lead to the identification and location of documents and/or the information they contain."[3] According to D'Alleyrand, *indexes* are "lists arranged in a specific sequence, that link attributes to documents and provide the information necessary for retrieval."[4]

Good indexing is essential to the management of information in any records system, regardless of the format of records. Whether an organization is using CAR systems, optical disk systems, or paper, or even a combination of media, some type of indexing is required if the records are to be retrieved by more than one identifier. The reason is simple: Users request information by using more than a single term in their query. For example, an engineer may request records of tensile test results from Ajax Chemical Company's order by supplying both the name of the customer (Ajax) and the number of the ingot—A-12345. A quality control inspector may request the same tensile test results in a different way, by shop order number. Since is is not feasible or logical to duplicate the test results and establish a physical file for each type of identifier and query, access must be provided by indexing—assigning multiple terms to the record. This permits access to one copy of the physical paper record through multiple parameters.

Developing an indexing scheme (or schemes) for quality records requires (1) an understanding of the subject matter and (2) knowing the retrieval needs of users. The subject matter of quality records is limited. Records in any organizational environment, by their very nature, have a predefined scope. This can be by function, by department, by purpose, or by use. The subject matter is readily understood by those working in the organization. In retrieving a record, a user automatically thinks in terms that are pertinent to that record and automatically requests the record by a highly appropriate term. The subject matter of quality records is predetermined and clearly self-defined.

The second aspect, knowing the retrieval needs of users, is easy to determine. How users request records is part of the information that can be gathered either during a records inventory or afterwards, for the purpose of constructing indexing schemes. Questions such as the following can be asked.

- How do users request the records?
- What are the actual terms (words) that they use to request a given category of records?
- How would they like to be able to retrieve the records?
- What are the parameters by which the records should be identified?

Development of a good indexing scheme results from knowing the users, their needs and their wants, and how they would like to retrieve the records. No matter how large the organization and how diverse its products may be, the user population is still finite, and the quality records are still finite. Determining user needs and wants, therefore, is possible. It can lead to a solid, well-constructed indexing scheme for records, one that instills confidence in the records system. In most cases, records themselves are bearers of the indexing parameters. In other words, the actual possible index terms are on the records, and the designer of the indexing schemes determines which parameters become candidates for index entry terms.

Records Technologies and Indexing

Indexes can be devised for records stored on paper, on microforms, and on optical disk; however, an external index for paper is used differently than indexes for CAR systems and optical disk systems. Regardless of which medium is being used, the index terms themselves are stored and manipulated in index databases. The difference is at the point of record retrieval. An external index to paper records can only identify the record and its location. Indexes to CAR systems and optical disk systems actually function as records retrievers, because they are electronically linked to the record itself. This is an advantage of CAR and optical disk systems, because the user does not have to physically walk over to the record and retrieve it. These systems also permit electronic routing and transmittal. In addition, they maintain the integrity of records, because records cannot be removed or misplaced, either while they are in use or when they are refiled.

When designing indexing schemes for records, it is important to remember that often it is *not* necessary for the requester to view the record. The requester needs information *from* the record. Indexing schemes should be designed to provide those essential pieces of information that are frequently requested from the record. This precludes having to retrieve the record, whether it be from a paper file, a roll of microfilm, or an optical disk system. In other words, index terms for records are items of information in and of themselves. The user can operate with these terms as pieces of information because they provide answers without requiring that the actual record be viewed.

Indexing costs can become a significant portion of quality records operating expenses. The extra cost, however, is minor when compared to the costs of not finding the record and also when compared to the costs of storing and retrieving the records during their life and use. Because of the costs of indexing, however, techniques are being developed to accelerate the indexing process. Automatic methods of indexing currently require that either the index field be in the same place on each document or that the index term be printed on a cover sheet. Two very different approaches are being used: optical character recognition (OCR) and bar code indexing.

OCR and Bar Code Technologies

OCR software converts information in a predefined area of the record into ASCII text for indexing purposes. Two popular OCR techniques being used are matrix matching and feature extraction. Some advanced feature extraction systems use artificial intelligence techniques to provide a degree of judgmental capability, and

they possess the capacity to "learn" the characteristics and idio-
syncrasies of a new font. Some newer systems are reading handwriting.

Bar code indexing is simpler and more reliable than OCR. It
is appropriate for applications in which documents are already
indexed on a computer database and a correspondence must be
established between each existing index entry and each document
page. Bar codes are more standardized and more consistent than
text characters. Bar code labels can be generated in-house and applied to records to identify them. If a laser wand or laser detector
is attached to a microfilm camera, records can be indexed at the
same time that they are being microfilmed. Several large, reliable
organizations provide such equipment, including 3M, Bell &
Howell, and Kodak.

Records Management Subactivities

The numerous subactivities that must be conducted to satisfy the
ISO requirements in Section 4.16 depend, to a great extent, on
what already exists and on the record format that is being used.
If an organization elects to use the ISO standards as an opportunity to revamp its records operations, converting from one medium to another, activities can include everything from collecting
literature about the new format to contacting vendors, educating
oneself and the organization about the proposed change, conducting feasibility studies, selecting a vendor, selecting equipment, designing the system, converting to it, training users, and,
eventually, implementing the system. If an organization wishes
simply to purchase new file equipment, activities can be limited.
It is necessary to develop long-term plans for what the quality
records system should be designed to accomplish. Taking into account the requirements of the standards, organizations should ask
themselves, "How do we best achieve this, so that we are not only
complying with the standards but improving our internal operations as a result?" It is with this goal in mind that a quality records
system should be developed.

The amount of time required depends on the goal of the organization. Centralizing quality records from various areas to a
quality records department may take several months, depending

---

Table 12.1. Examination of quality records requirements.

Questions to ask about quality records

1. Do you have documented procedures for identification, collection, indexing, access, filing, storage, maintenance, and disposition of all quality records?
2. Do you know where all of your quality records are?
3. Do you know what quality records are being created and retained in each of the quality-related functions?
4. Are all of your quality records clearly identified?
5. Are all of your quality records legible?
6. Do you have organizing and access schemes for all quality records so that they are easy to retrieve?
7. Do you have a retention schedule for all of your quality records?
8. Do you dispose of your quality records as dictated by the retention schedule? In other words, is the retention schedule being implemented?
9. Are your quality records stored in appropriate equipment?
10. Are your quality records maintained in an environment that protects them against deterioration and/or destruction?
11. Do you have a backup system for your quality records?
12. Are your quality records filled out accurately and completely? Do you have anyone who checks this?
13. Are all departments and individuals clear about how to route quality records?
14. Are your quality records collected in each department or in a centralized records department? Are they collected at all?
15. Are all appropriate signatures and stamps affixed to quality records?

---

on the size of the organization, the volume of records, and the amount of identifying and reorganizing that needs to be done. A possible alternative is to adopt a *day-one approach:* From a given date forward, the quality records are to be managed according to new procedures. The natural life cycle of existing records eventually causes them to become outdated, at which time they can be destroyed (see chapter 16). Some organizations that are converting their records from one medium to another take this approach. They find that conversion is less costly and can be accomplished in less time by using a day-one approach.

Conclusion

The most important point is that a qualified professional records manager must spearhead the compliance process for records. The examination questions presented in Table 12.1 reveal how the requirement must be applied to all quality records, and they further support the contention that it is best to have a quality records manager who can devote full attention to records activities. Because of the many records-specific approaches that are available and the number of decisions that must be made regarding the development of a workable quality records system, it is important that someone with records expertise be the responsible authority. A great deal of compliance rests on quality records and how well they are managed. How records are handled, how they are identified, accessed, and so forth affects the compliance activities of each section of the standards.

Notes

1. Association for Information and Image Management, *Information and Image Management: The Industry and the Technologies* (Silver Spring, Md: Association for Information and Image Management, 1987), 23.

2. David Black, "The New Breed of Mixed-Media Image Management Systems," *IMC Journal* 25 (January/February 1989), 9.

3. Marc R. D'Alleyrand, *Image Storage and Retrieval Systems* (New York: McGraw-Hill, 1989), 19.

4. Ibid., 21.

CHAPTER 13

Internal Quality Audit Records

Q9001—Section 4.17
Q9004-1—Section 5.4

Introduction

The basic reason for conducting internal quality audits is so that the organization can regulate its quality system and activities. The purposes are

- To prevent potential trouble spots before they are found by cutomers and external auditors
- To assess how the quality department follows the approved procedures
- To comply with the ISO standards and any other federal or regulatory requirements

As with any system or set of activities, what has been planned in writing and in the boardroom may not be effective in actual practice. This is the reason that drills are recommended to test the adequacy, for example, of a disaster plan.

- To determine if it actually works
- To reveal any difficulties in implementation that could not be foreseen
- To determine if the outcome is what the plan intends

Internal quality audits are common in regulated industries, such as the nuclear and pharmaceutical industries. In such industries, where high quality is mandatory, regulatory authorities and customers often conduct external quality audits, often referred to as third-party audits. To police themselves and to prevent any surprises during external quality audits, regulated industries have a long tradition of planned internal quality audits. Ongoing internal quality audits provide valuable information to the organization about problem areas before they get out of control. Very often, internal quality audits result in preventive actions, rather than corrective actions, and, in this sense, they can be viewed as proactive quality activities rather than reactive ones.

Records Requirements

Whereas the 1987 version of the standards did not mention the word *records* even once in the audit requirements, the revised version does clearly specify some instances where records must be maintained. The results of audits must be recorded as well as the implementation and effectiveness of corrective actions that have been taken. This section, however, like other sections of the standard, does not delineate all of the types of records that must be created and maintained to prove compliance. Once again, implied records are involved.

The first requirement pertains to procedures for planning and implementing internal quality audits. Such procedures would fall under the requirements for controlled documents and would necessitate all records that pertain to document control.

The first paragraph in 4.17 actually requires plans for two types of audits—quality system audits and audits of quality activities.

> The supplier shall establish and maintain documented procedures for planning and implementing internal quality audits to verify whether quality activities and related results comply with planned arrangements and to determine the effectiveness of the quality system.

Quality activity audits are those conducted of specific functions or work areas in the organization whose activity affects quality, such as the chemical laboratory or the calibration laboratory.

Audit Schedule and Auditor Qualification Records

The next requirement affecting records is that the quality audits be scheduled and that they be conducted by personnel who are independent of those having direct responsibility for the activity being audited.

> Internal quality audits shall be scheduled on the basis of the status and importance of the activity to be audited and shall be carried out by personnel independent of those having direct responsibility for the activity being audited.

The organization must develop and adhere to an internal quality audit schedule. It is common for the quality function to ensure that each of the quality-related activities is audited at least once each year. Some areas may be audited more frequently, depending on their past audit results and on their relative importance in the quality loop. The audit schedule should be prepared for each activity that is to be audited.

Auditors often ask what the qualifications are of the audit team members. In some organizations, auditor candidates undergo formal training to ensure their competence in the skills required to carry out audits and to manage audits. They can receive training in-house or from an external firm. Training from another organization brings a fresh perspective into the audit program. Auditor candidates can attend seminars and workshops both on the requirements of the ISO 9000 standards and on audit assessment techniques of examining, questioning, evaluating, and reporting. The basis for selecting audit team members must be recorded, whether it be in the form of an audit qualification record or a designation record assigning a member to the team. Regardless of the method that is used, records must exist that identify the basis for selection and the approval of that audit team member by quality management.

Backup records, in the form of a request for approval of designated team members may be necessary. A request for audit team approval can be a form that is completed by an audit coordinator or supervisor and submitted to the quality manager. It is prepared in advance of the audit schedule, so that the actual names of individuals can appear on the audit schedule. The request form lists the names of individuals who have been tentatively selected as audit team members for a given area. It requests an approval signature and date from the quality manager or the substitution of an individual for one that has been proposed. Figures 13.1 and 13.2 illustrate a request for audit team approval and an auditor qualification record, respectively.

Because the standards require that audits be conducted by individuals who are independent of the area being audited, it is helpful to include the department or function of the audit team member on the audit schedule. The audit schedule, therefore, should include the following data elements.

- The area to be audited
- The names of audit team members
- Their departments, areas, or functions
- The date of the scheduled audit

When it is prepared in this manner, the schedule is valuable proof to external auditors that planning has taken place. It is also valuable for preparing a list of internal audits that have already been conducted. Frequently, external auditors ask which audits have been conducted in the past six months or during the past year. The planning schedule, prepared in advance, can easily be transferred to a completed audit schedule, thus providing all pertinent information at a glance.

It is good practice to convene the audit team prior to the performance of an audit, for the purpose of planning the audit. Pre-audit meetings are especially valuable in defining the topics that are to be audited, and a form can be prepared and presented to audit team members at the meeting that itemizes appropriate topics. Pre-audit meetings also present an opportunity to review the purpose(s) of the audit and to present pointers to team members about how to conduct themselves during an audit. Whoever is responsible for conducting the planning meeting (an audit coordinator, the lead auditor, or another quality management representative) should prepare records of the pre-audit meeting.

Records of Audit Results

The most obvious record is the audit report itself which includes a description of all observations and findings. According to the

Request for Audit Team Approval

Area to be audited

Date of scheduled audit

The following individuals have been tentatively selected as audit team members. Please indicate your approval or disapproval. Indicate replacements below for any disapproved individuals.

	Name	Department	Approved	Disapproved
1.				
2.				
3.				
4.				
5.				

Replacement for _____   Replacement for _____

Name _____   Name _____

Department _____   Department _____

_____   _____
Signature of quality manager   Date

Figure 13.1. Example of a request for audit team approval.

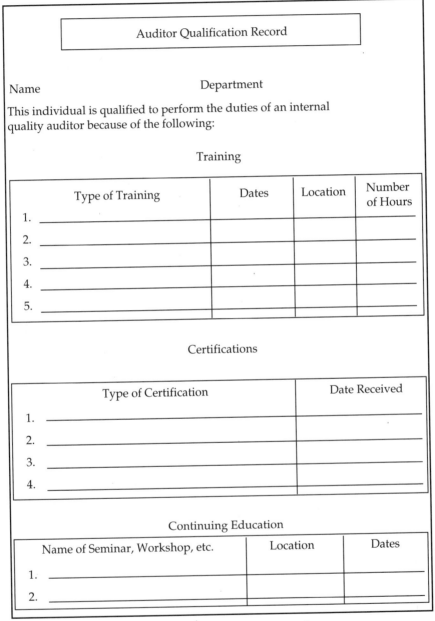

Figure 13.2. Example of an auditor qualification record.

Guidelines, Paragraph 5.4.4, the following items should be covered in the audit report.

a) all examples of nonconformities or deficiencies;
b) appropriate and timely corrective action.

Actually, the audit report itself includes only the items stated in "a'"—the nonconformities and deficiencies. In the report, a request is made to the area manager that appropriate corrective action be taken and that it be done in a timely fashion. It is the responsibility of the area manager to specify those corrective actions that are intended, together with the dates by which they will be completed. This is presented to the audit team or audit coordinator by the area manager in writing.

Attached to the audit report issued by the quality department are usually forms referred to as *requests for corrective action* (see Figure 13.3.) One form is prepared for each separate finding or observation, and a copy is issued to the area manager. The original remains with the original report, in the audit files. Such a form is useful in clarifying each separate item and also in requesting that action be taken on each item. Because the information on the form is presented in chronological order of occurrence, this form is useful in tracing the steps that have been taken pertaining to the deficiency and also in providing a historical picture of the activities that have taken place.

The audit report must be issued to the manager of the area that was audited, and records must indicate the date that the audit report was sent to the area manager. Some record must be retained for timely response from the area manager. A tickler file is often developed to remind the audit coordinator if the response is not received by its due date. In the response, it is expected that the area manager will indicate corrective measures that will be taken to remedy deficiencies found during the audit. This is important for conducting follow-up audits.

The response from the area manager is a record, and an important one, because it lists the intended corrective actions. It is against this record of planned actions that the follow-up audit is later conducted. In some organizations, the response to the audit report must be formally accepted. There may be instances where

| Request for Corrective Action |

To _____ Finding number _____

Area Audited _____ Date of audit _____

Description of finding

Response due date _____ Auditor _____ Date _____
Receipt by auditee _____ Date _____

THIS SECTION TO BE COMPLETED BY AUDITEE

Description of corrective action to be taken

Expected completion date _____
Signature of manager of area audited _____ Date _____
Signature of quality department acceptance _____ Date _____

THIS SECTION TO BE COMPLETED BY AUDITOR OR AUDIT COORDINATOR

Finding is closed ☐ Yes ☐ No

How was corrective action verified

Verified by _____ Date _____

Figure 13.3. Example of a request for corrective action.

the response includes items that are unacceptable to the audit team. Procedures for handling audit responses vary among organizations, from formally disseminating the audit responses to all members of the audit team to acceptance being handled by only one person, the audit coordinator. As in all quality activities, whatever is written in the procedure is what must be done.

The two reports are extremely important records, because they serve as proof that the organization is policing its own quality-related activities, that it is identifying areas needing improvement, that remedial actions are taking place, and that those remedial actions are being verified through follow-up audits. The audit reports and area manager's responses also provide important information for management review activities, as discussed in chapter 4 and required in Section 4.1.3 of Q9001. As has been stated frequently in this book, maintaining thorough and accurate records of quality activities simply makes good business sense. The findings and corrective actions should be reviewed at regular intervals by quality management to determine if repetitive problems remain uncorrected. The audit reports and responses to them reveal if a particular area has recurrent deficiencies, if some deficiencies remain corrected for a period of time and then recur, or if the quality activities continue to experience the upward spiral loop of improvement that should be the ultimate goal of all quality-related operations. The kinds of audit records that exist and how they are organized play important roles in this process. As depicted in Table 13.1, it is the responsibility of the quality records manager to develop a system for organizing audit information so that it reveals meaningful aspects about the quality system.

Audit reports and responses serve as excellent examples of those record types that should be studied over a period of time. They provide information about problems that, otherwise, might go unnoticed. In order to facilitate review of information contained in audit reports and responses, a file of findings and corrective actions should be developed. The basic variables to include are

- The name of the area audited
- The date of the audit
- Findings

Table 13.1. Responsibilities of the quality records manager in auditing activities.

1. Define internal audit records requirements from standards.
2. Design any necessary records.
3. Ensure that auditing procedures fall under the jurisdiction of the document control center.
4. Develop a database for internal auditing information.
5. Function as an audit team member to audit records and documents of audited areas.
6. Develop a system for presenting information on findings and corrective actions
   a) so that it may be easily analyzed in management reviews.
   b) to reveal any repetitive problem areas or departments.
   c) to reveal any repetitive findings.
7. Develop organizing schemes for audit records that are logical, provide ready retrieval, and reveal cogent aspects about the internal audit program.

- Observations
- The corrective actions promised
- The corrective actions taken
- The date of the follow-up audit

It is also possible to include the items of information that pertain to all internal quality audits and thus create a master internal quality audit database. This would include all pieces of data that pertain to scheduling and conducting internal audits. Reports can be generated as desired, based upon the kind of information that is required. A comprehensive internal audit database would also include the items of information that pertain to audit scheduling, such as the scheduled audit date and the names of audit team members.

Follow-Up Audit Records

Follow-up audits verify that the promised corrective actions, specified in the area manager's report, have been implemented and are effective. In order to prove that verification has taken place, records of the follow-up audits must be created and maintained. As was suggested in the previous section, a corrective action file expedites this process. This is prepared by extracting the findings and observations from the audit report and developing a checklist. Rather than working with the documentary form of the reports themselves, a checklist focuses on highlighting those aspects that are to be verified during the follow-up audit. Not only does this expedite the follow-up process, it ensures that a finding is not buried in a body of text and, thus, is missed during the follow-up verification. The findings and observations checklist should include the corrective action that has been promised in the area manager's report. The promised corrective action should be placed adjacent to the finding or observation. Using a table or matrix format is much easier than working with text for the purpose of checking to determine whether or not the item has been completed. The type of record that is created for use in the monitoring process, thus, can contribute to easy assessment in determining the implementation of corrective actions as well as the effectiveness of those corrective actions. On the other hand, the wrong types of records will be an impediment and will contribute only to hostility since, although they must be maintained, they serve only to muddle or confuse the situation.

Working with a checklist and utilizing existing computer technology enables the audit coordinator and quality manager to *close out* deficiencies that are corrected. The concept of closing out a finding is useful in determining that progress has been made as a result of the internal audit plan. Such a system—of findings, corrective actions, and closed out items—establishes proof of continuous improvement, resulting from a well-planned internal quality audit program. Records, thus, serve not only to assist the audit process, but to reveal the progress that is being made and to point out areas where improvement is still necessary. Table 13.2 contains questions about internal audit records that can assist organizations in evaluating their own records.

Organizing the Internal Audit Records

Internal quality audit records are always examined by external auditors and will be examined by registrars. This holds true especially for conformance audits, such as those conducted against the ISO standards. The main reason for this is to examine if the

---

Table 13.2. Examination of internal auditing records requirements.

Questions to ask about internal audit records

1. Do you have a schedule for internal quality audits?
2. Can you prove that you are adhering to the schedule?
3. Do you have records that indicate the qualifications of audit team members?
4. How are audit team members selected?
5. Can you demonstrate that audit team members are independent of the area being audited?
6. Do you maintain checklists as guidelines for conducting audits?
7. Do you have records of any meetings that have been conducted pertaining to audits—pre-audit meetings, opening audit meetings, closing audit meetings?
8. Can your records demonstrate that the audited area has been notified of deficiencies (findings) identified during the audit?
9. Can your records demonstrate that corrective action has been specified for each audit finding?
10. Do your records demonstrate that corrective action has been taken and that it has been effective?
11. Do your records demonstrate that corrective action has been initiated in the time frame specified?

---

organization is complying with the stated requirements. Secondary reasons are to determine how the organization is ensuring that deficiencies are being detected and how it polices the corrective actions that are promised and implemented. Records, therefore, should be logically organized and easily retrievable, designed to reveal the most cogent aspects of the internal quality audit process.

If data are maintained in a computer database, it is important to keep the information current for external audit examination. Those corrective actions that have been implemented and verified through follow-up audits should include the updated actions and decisions. For example, outdated revisions of documents in the fabrication area may have been discovered during the internal audit. If the follow-up audit, conducted two weeks later, verified that the documents were current, this information should have been entered into the database, thus clearing the finding. Currency of information must be given priority. Retrieval of information in ways that are meaningful to the audit process is equally important. Sorting capabilities must be addressed early in designing the system, for logic, for effective use, and for purposes of analysis. Summary reports by area, for example, may be requested, and they should be designed to reveal the number of audits in the area during the previous year and the findings in that area. Ensuring that the system is able to produce such reports is part of the responsibility of the quality records manager.

Other aspects that are closely examined by auditors include repetitive findings and the findings that remain *open*—that have not been corrected. Repetitive findings indicate an ineffective plan of corrective actions, or they can suggest a more serious problem. Those findings that have passed their due date for correction are also problematic. It is important to have quality managers review such instances in order to eliminate the causes or to shorten the time that they remain open. Scenarios such as these are scrutinized by external auditors who press for answers.

Organizing Paper-Based Audit Records. Because internal quality audit records are examined closely, it is important that they be in order and present information in a manner that is consistent with the important reasons for conducting internal audits. If a paper-based manual system is being utilized, more record types must be created in order to configure the audit information in meaningful ways. The schedule for audits to be conducted should appear in a separate file, together with the auditor qualification records or designation of audit team members approved by quality management. Another file category should be the information pertaining to each individual area that has been or will be audited. This should be arranged logically, preferably in some sort of alphabetic order. For each area that is audited, the following files should exist.

- The notification to area management of an upcoming audit
- The notification to audit team members (including any responses from audit team members)
- The pre-audit meeting with audit team members
- Lists of questions prepared by audit team members

- Audit notes taken by audit team members
- The audit report
- Requests for corrective action
- The follow-up audit
- Deficiencies (and a record of whether they are closed or open)

Another major audit file category should be prepared from the findings or observations and corrective actions in each audited area, that is, the list of findings that was discussed earlier. If automated recordkeeping is not being used, it is still important to prepare what are referred to as *secondary records* for internal operating purposes—records that are prepared from other records. Although this is labor-intensive and does not provide the same manipulative capabilities as do automated systems, it does reveal important information at a glance and reduces the level of frustration during external audits.

A variety of statistical analyses may be performed with the internal audit findings. Frequency charts, Pareto diagrams, bar charts, histograms, and scatter diagrams are but a few of the graphic depictions that can be prepared from the data accumulated during internal audits. Visual aids such as these reveal trends that otherwise might remain unnoticed when the information remains in text format. If such analyses are performed, copies should be retained in another category of audit files to reveal to external auditors that analyses are being conducted and to present the results of the analyses.

Check Sheet for Internal Audits. Because many activities must be done to conduct and close an internal quality audit, a checklist can prove to be a valuable asset (see Figure 13.4). The checklist simply lists all of the activities that must be conducted as a reminder to the individual who is responsible for arranging and coordinating the audits.

Checklists are especially useful for internal audit control, because multiple audits and follow-up audits overlap and are at various phases of initiation and completion on any given date.

```
┌─────────────────────────────────────────────────────────────────────┐
│                                                                       │
│        ┌──────────────────────────────────────────────┐              │
│        │        Audit Checklist for Internal Audits    │              │
│        └──────────────────────────────────────────────┘              │
│                                                                       │
│    Area to be Audited  _____  Date _____   │
│                                                                       │
│                                                                       │
│    ☐   1.  Audit team approved by quality manager                     │
│    ☐   2.  Audit team approved by its own departmental managers       │
│    ☐   3.  Audit team members' acceptance received                    │
│    ☐   4.  Pre-audit meeting set                                      │
│    ☐       Performed                                                   │
│    ☐   5.  Audit date and time set                                    │
│    ☐       Performed                                                   │
│    ☐   6.  Closing meeting held with manager of audited area          │
│    ☐   7.  All team member notes received by lead auditor or audit    │
│            coordinator                                                 │
│    ☐   8.  Audit report written                                       │
│    ☐   9.  Corrective action requests completed                       │
│    ☐  10.  Report and corrective action requests formally issued to   │
│            auditee                                                     │
│    ☐  11.  Auditee responses received                                 │
│    ☐  12.  Responses sent to audit team for approval                  │
│    ☐  13.  Follow-up conducted of open items                          │
│    ☐  14.  Date follow-up audit performed                             │
│    ☐  15.  Audit closed                    Date _____        │
│                                                                       │
└─────────────────────────────────────────────────────────────────────┘
```

Figure 13.4. Example of an audit checklist.

Otherwise, it is impossible to remember which steps have been carried out for which audit. As the form depicts, one checklist is prepared for each area on the audit schedule. The activities begin with getting approval for audit team members and end with the date that the audit was closed.

Official Audit Records

The following usually comprise official audit records.

- Auditor qualification records and approval records
- Reports of all meetings
  —The pre-audit meeting of the audit team
  —The opening meeting with the department to be audited
  —The closing meeting with the department that was audited
- Checklists (if used)
- Working papers of the audit team members
- The audit schedule
- Audit reports
- Corrective action requests
- Follow-up audit records
- Any correspondence between the audit team or audit coordinator and the department that was audited

External Audit Records

If audit records are maintained on a database, only one database need be created that encompasses information from both internal and external quality audits. Because the important pieces of data are the same, it makes good sense to simply incorporate the two types of audits into one electronic file. Findings and observations from external audits must be addressed and effective corrective action also must be implemented. Tracking the occurrences of deficiencies from both types of audits by including them in a single database can prove to be extremely meaningful to the quality operation. Weak spots may be brought to the forefront that otherwise might go unnoticed if the information were not integrated, but rather was separated in two different physical paper files.

It is recommended that, even if paper files are the selected record format, summarized findings and corrective action lists be created from information in both the internal and external audit files. The summary serves the function of collocating, or bringing together, data that is physically separated. If paper files are used for external audit records, again, logic and ease of retrieval should be the guidelines for organizing them. Because external audits can be numerous, depending on the type of business that the organization is in, the files should be organized by auditing agency or date of audit. Cross references and indexes will be necessary to provide easy access to information that will be housed across files. Following up on external audit findings and ensuring that corrective action has been effectively implemented are important in remaining qualified as a supplier in many instances. A method must be designed to ensure that open-action items do not get buried in a paper file system.

If the external audit files are arranged by auditing agency, the files should be separated into subtopics.

- Pre-audit communication (correspondence, setting a date, and so on)
- The audit plan (what will be audited)
- The opening meeting with auditors (notes taken)
- The audit report
- Findings (corrective actions taken)
- Observations (remedial actions taken)
- Area managers notified (of findings and observations)
- Open items
- The response to the auditing agency

Whether or not the findings of previous external audits have been closed out is one of the first things that external auditors examine. Using their own previous report and the organization's response as a basis, they verify that corrective actions have been implemented and that they have also been effective.

Conclusion

Internal audit records reveal that the quality system is working as planned. They capture information about troublesome quality areas and provide evidence that remedial actions have been instituted. Results of internal audits prove to the organization and to external agencies that the quality activities and the quality system are in compliance with ISO standards.

CHAPTER 14

Training Records

Q9001—Section 4.18
Q9004-1—Section 18.1

Introduction

There is a Japanese axiom: "Quality control starts with training and ends in training. Training is conducted regularly for top management, middle management, and workers."[1] Unless the entire workforce is trained in the concepts of quality, in how to perform its respective jobs, and in how to constantly seek areas of improvement, nothing else matters. Training is so critical that wise organizations are developing their own internal educational systems, often called *universities*, to provide ongoing training to all levels, across functional lines.

Understanding what to do and how to do it is so fundamental to the achievement of quality that it is difficult to believe that this concept is often ignored and even belittled. Instead of being considered an investment that produces enormous return, training, too often, is considered to be a frill, viewed as an overhead cost—the cost of doing business. Organizations currently invest billions of dollars annually in external seminars and workshops and in internal education. Yet, too frequently, the results are disappointing. Unless the training produces changes in attitudes and results in executives and managers adopting the principles and methods that are presented, improvements in quality are negligible.

Training and documented procedures form the basis of work instructions for technical and production personnel. It is not sufficient to write detailed procedures and expect individuals to be competent in job performance simply by reading the procedures and implementing them. The training requirements of Q9001 are stated simply in 4.18.

> The supplier shall establish and maintain documented procedures for identifying training needs and provide for the training of all personnel performing activities affecting quality. Personnel performing specific assigned tasks shall be qualified on the basis of appropriate education, training and/ or experience, as required. Appropriate records of training shall be maintained.

The *Guidelines*, Q9004-1, present more detail about the kinds of training that should be provided by addressing training for three different personnel categories.

Training for Different Personnel Categories
Executive and Management Training

Just as the attitude toward records management and its importance to the organization originates at the highest levels in the organization and filters down, so does the attitude toward quality. The *Guidelines* in Paragraph 18.1.2, therefore, recommend the following.

> Training should be given which will provide executive management with an understanding of the quality system, together with the tools and techniques needed for full executive management participation in the operation of the system. Executive management should also be aware of the criteria available to evaluate the effectiveness of the system.

Records to Maintain. Records must prove that training has occurred, and they must identify the information that has been presented to the executives and managers. Records also should reveal the qualifications of the individuals who conduct the training and should validate the materials that were used in the training. The kinds of information that should be retained about executive and management training are

- The name of the course

- The names of the individuals who took the course
- The individuals' titles
- The dates of attendance
- The frequency of the training
- The number of hours of training attended
- Signatures of attendees
- Signatures of those conducting the training, to verify the attendance

Qualifications of executives and managers also may be questioned. In order to validate qualified personnel, it is often necessary to present their education and/or work experience. The following type of question may be posed: What qualifies the vice president of engineering to hold that position? Such a question can and should be answered by presenting records of the individual's education and/or work experiences.

Technical Personnel

The *Guidelines*, 18.1.3, present the following recommendations about training for technical personnel.

> Training should be given to the technical personnel to enhance their contribution to the success of the quality system. Training should not be restricted to personnel with primary quality assignments, but should include assignments such as marketing, purchasing, process, and product engineering. Particular attention should be given to training in statistical techniques.

In other words, training for technical personnel should include all activities that pertain to quality. In fact, even though only four categories of technical personnel are specifically mentioned in the *Guidelines*, training should be given to personnel in all functions discussed in each segment of the standards. Taking the sections of the standards from the beginning, this would include personnel in the following functions.

- Management (all of the areas specified here as well as executive management)

- Contract review
- All engineering personnel, including
  - —Design engineering
  - —Process engineering
  - —Product engineering
  - —Quality engineering
- Document control
- Purchasing
- Inspection
- Testing
- Metrology
- Shipping and receiving
- Quality records
- Internal auditing
- Training

Unless personnel in these areas are well versed in their activities, through former education, training, and/or experience, they should be trained. Even though they may be knowledgeable about their function or professional field, they may not be familiar with how their function contributes to quality or what their responsibilities are relevant to the ISO standards. Even if no other training is conducted, personnel should be trained in the requirements of the ISO standards. If they are already qualified to perform their job duties, this should be documented and forms part of the records that are maintained on training.

Training should be formally conducted, with special time periods allotted for the activity. Training also should be conducted by qualified personnel. It is not sufficient to assign a new worker to one who is leaving the position in a couple of weeks, and to consider that to be training. It is true that each organization must contend with employee turnover, but the job-related instructions that are conveyed from the employee who is leaving to the newly hired employee are considered to be specific to that particular slot.

Training, on the other hand, encompasses knowledge of the overall function, how it operates, the role that it plays in contributing to the quality of the product, and knowledge about procedures that must be followed. Training for compliance with ISO 9000 should include information about the standards themselves and a complete explanation of the importance of compliance, as well as the specific activities that are required by that function in order to satisfy its responsibilities.

Training in statistical techniques is specifically mentioned in the *Guidelines* in Paragraph 18.1.3. This paragraph refers the user to a later section—20.2—for examples of the kinds of statistical methods that can be taught. It is important to remember that the list only provides examples and is not mandatory, nor is it all-inclusive. Some of the types of statistical methods are

- Design of experiments and factorial analysis
- Analysis of variance and regression analysis
- Tests of significance
- Quality control charts and cusum techniques
- Statistical sampling

Process Supervisors and Operating Personnel

Paragraph 18.1.4 of the *Guidelines* presents the following recommendations about training for process supervisors and operating personnel.

> All process supervisors and operating personnel should be trained in the procedures and skills required to perform their tasks . . . . As appropriate, personnel should be certified in their skills, such as welding. Training in basic statistical techniques should also be considered.

In addition to training records, the organization may be required to produce copies of certificates for specific skills. For example, in the aviation industry, an Airframe and Powerplant (A&P) license is required to perform certain aircraft maintenance activities. The importance of keeping records of personnel who perform specialized operations cannot be overemphasized. Very often, a certificate, a license, or a record indicating that a person

---

Table 14.1. Examination of training records requirements.

Questions to ask about training records

1. Do you have training and qualification records for all personnel whose work affects quality?
2. Do you have certifications or licenses in the files for special categories of personnel? Are the certifications or licenses current?
3. Do your training records reveal the variable that qualifies the individual to perform the job at hand? Is it education, experience, number of hours of training, or some other factor?
4. Do you maintain attendance records for training sessions?
5. Are the attendance records verified by the instructor or some other authorized individual?
6. Do you have records that indicate the qualifications of your training instructors?
7. If you use examinations at the end of your training sessions, have you recorded the results?
8. Are all personnel trained in appropriate records procedures for quality records (for example, legibility, accuracy, routing, and so on)?

---

has been qualified to perform a certain activity must exist if that activity is to be considered valid. Table 14.1, which presents an examination of training records requirements, includes a question about certificates and licenses.

Certification of a particular skill, field, or profession can be accomplished through a number of channels. Professional organizations often administer exams that, if passed successfully, will result in the individual being *certified*. Such is the case with ASQC. Certified Quality Engineer and Certified Quality Auditor are but two examples of certifications that attest to the professional knowledge and experience of an individual. Being certified or qualified to perform a specific job function can involve steps similar to those required for becoming certified in a profession. The process follows a standardized series of steps.

A formal training program on how to do the job
A formal examination, including a demonstration of successful performance of the job
A formal certificate attesting to the success in the examination
A license to do the job for some designated period of time
A program of audit to review performance and to serve as a basis for renewing the license[2]

The procedures and skills enumerated as examples in 18.1.4 of the *Guidelines* are as follows.

—the proper operation of instruments, tools, and machinery they have to use,

—reading and understanding the documentation provided,

—the relationship of their duties to quality, and

—safety in the workplace.

Training should be conducted on the use of equipment to ensure that each individual who uses an instrument, tool, or piece of machinery for a quality-related activity knows how to use it and is using it properly. Training also should be conducted about the documented procedures and work instructions that process supervisors and operating personnel receive. The intent is to ensure that each person reads and understands the content of the documented procedures.

In some organizations, a special document control record is prepared for each distributed document; this is referred to as a *read and understood form.* This record is part of the document control records, and it requires the signatures and dates of all individuals who have formally received an official copy of the document. It includes a statement to the effect that the individual attests to reading and understanding the document. If the individual cannot understand the instructions or procedures in the document, it is his or her responsibility to seek clarification from the supervisor or manager of the area. The read and understood form remains with the distributed copy of the document until the document is superseded or retired. It then becomes part of the superseded or obsolete file and is retained with the original copy of the document according to procedures established by the document control center (see chapter 6).

Documented procedures and training work in tandem to ensure that things are done accurately. A balance exists between the amount of information included in documents and the amount of information presented in training sessions. In many instances, it is not feasible to include each detail of job performance in a document, but training sessions can be more detailed and can elaborate on many aspects of job tasks. An example of a paper training record is illustrated in Figure 14.1.

Training course	Dates	Location	Trainer	Number of hours	Results

Training Record Summary

Trainee's name _____   Employee number _____

Figure 14.1. Example of a training record summary.

Types of Training Records to Maintain

Training records are similar for all levels of individuals, although some of the data elements may differ. The purpose of training records is to prove that all individuals are qualified to perform their jobs. A higher purpose would be to instill a sense of the importance of quality in each individual, by offering courses on quality to all employees in the organization. What is required in the ISO standards is records that prove capability and attest to qualified personnel. The data elements to be retained are as follows.

- The name of the individual
- The individual's title

- The area in which the individual is qualified
- The reason (training, education, experience) the individual is qualified
- If training,
    - —Name of the course
    - —Location
    - —Administered by
    - —Dates
    - —Number of hours
- If education,
    - —School attended
    - —Dates
    - —Degree or certificate awarded
- If experience,
    - —Number of years of experience
    - —Function or profession
- Requalification required by (date)
- Recertification required by (date)

If requalification or recertification is required, a tickler system must be developed that will notify the training department in advance to allow appropriate time for the process. If training has been conducted in the organization, backup records may need to be retained, such as sign-in sheets for course attendees, proving that the individuals actually did attend the courses.

Organizing Paper Training Records

Training records are often retained in the human resources department. If this is the case, the quality records manager should provide advice and assistance on the most efficient way of organizing the records. Organizations frequently make the mistake of inserting the training records into the employee's personnel file.

In order to retrieve training records that have been organized in this fashion, it is necessary to procure each file.

A better approach is to create a training file category specifically for quality verification that contains all information pertaining to training activities that affect quality. A copy of the training record can, of course, be included in the employee's personnel file. To expedite retrieval, however, and to effectively maintain current training records, a separate training file should be developed for quality purposes.

It can be organized in a number of different ways: by broad categories, by name, by function, or by department. Broad categories would include, for example, all courses pertaining to quality. Subcategories would be the actual names of individual courses such as Introduction to Total Quality Management, Quality Course for Executives, Quality Course for Middle Managers, Introduction to Quality Control, and so forth. Each course should have its own separate folder for each time that it is presented. In each folder would be the names of attendees, together with the sign-in sheets and a record of the total number of hours attended for each individual. Backup records should also include course materials such as videotapes, overhead transparencies, lecture notes, slides, and so forth. Also, interactive compact disks are now being utilized to train individuals in performing their job duties.

Using Technology for Training Records

The simplest approach to organizing information pertaining to training is to utilize a database. Entering the data elements specified earlier enables sorting according to any variable. Printouts of training records can be stored in appropriate computer binders and hung on equipment designed for that purpose. Training information can also be retained on COM or on computer output to laser disk (COLD) if the volume is great. Whichever approach is used, it is easier to create a file specifically to house training information than it is to incorporate this information into an individual's personnel file. Updates can be accomplished more easily on a computer file.

Table 14.2. Responsibilities of the quality records manager in training activities.

1. Define training records requirements from standards.
2. Design any necessary records.
3. Ensure that training procedures for quality-related activities and personnel fall under the jurisdiction of the document control center.
4. Develop a database for training information.
5. Ensure that training records are kept current.
6. Develop organizing schemes for training records.
7. Conduct training sessions about records management and document control requirements.

Training in Records Management and Document Control

However training is administered in the organization, a component of that training should be education in records management and in document control procedures. The quality records manager is the person most qualified to conduct training about these two areas, and training should be one of the responsibilities assumed by the quality records manager, as presented in Table 14.2. This is especially true if these activities are new to the quality arena or new to the organization. Education about records management and document control is the best method of achieving cooperation, and cooperation is essential for successful ISO compliance. Explaining the whys and hows to employees results not only in better, more accurate records, but also in their understanding the reasons behind the specific requirements that, otherwise, might appear arbitrary or frivolous. Training in proper records completion and in records routing is an important topic as well. Unless employees have worked in regulated environments, they might not be aware of the appropriate methods for making changes on records, for example. One-line cross-throughs, accompanied by the initials of the employee making the change, are standard practice for making a change on quality records. Another standard practice is signing and dating all blanks on a traveler or work order. If a particular step is not required, the adjacent signature space should be completed with *N/A*. If there are specific instructions to complete the quality forms only in black ballpoint pen, for example, the reasons should be made clear to employees, who might otherwise find it capricious.

Whatever is decided in the organization about records routing—whether a centralized or dispersed quality records system is developed—this information should be part of any training in records management. Routing instructions should be clear to employees, and, if timeliness of routing is important, this should be emphasized. Regardless of how the records are organized, and regardless of their format—paper, electronic, or microform—their importance to the quality function and to ISO compliance should be stressed.

Another aspect of training should cover document control and the steps and activities that are necessary to ensure a tight, workable system. Again, unless the organization must answer to a regulatory agency, employees may not be familiar with the entire notion of document control, much less with the many details that it encompasses. It is important to explain to employees why documents must be controlled, how this relates to the quality process, why they must sign for a document, why they cannot reproduce controlled documents, why they must relinquish a previous revision before being given a new one, why they cannot change documents whenever they desire, and why they must read the documents that are issued to them. Explaining the reasons results in more cooperative employees, whether they be executives, engineers, or production workers.

Training about document control and records is an ongoing process. Even though formal training may be offered and employees attend it, daily education and repetition of the reasons and the procedures is a fact of life for quality records managers. The beginning chapters in this book can be used to educate employees about the importance of records in the quality arena and, specifically, for ISO 9000 compliance.

Conclusion

Training records provide information revealing the qualifications of individuals that enable them to perform their jobs. Records should be maintained for all personnel involved in activities that affect quality, indicating that they are qualified because of education, experience, and/or training. An important component of in-house training should be education in records management and document control procedures, to be conducted by the quality records manager.

Notes

1. Imai Masaaki, *Kaizen: The Key to Japan's Competitive Success* (New York: McGraw-Hill, 1986), 47.

2. Joseph J. Zeccardi, "Inspection and Test," in *Juran's Quality Control Handbook*, 4th ed., ed. J. M. Juran (New York: McGraw-Hill, 1988), 18.86.

CHAPTER 15

Developing a Quality Records Management Program

Introduction

Organizations that currently have a records manager who is responsible for some or all of the main components of a records management program are infinitely closer to satisfying the records requirements of the ISO standards. The problem, however, is that many individuals have the title of records manager, but do not possess the knowledge or qualifications to adequately perform the function. In many environments, the designation of a records manager is taken lightly, because organizations are unaware of the field of records management. A common misperception is to equate records management with simple filing. If this occurs, the organization believes that a clerical-level person can perform the function of records manager. Not realizing the full importance of a records management program, the organization believes that little specialized training or expertise is required for the position. Therefore, the organization never does reap the benefits of professional records management. Expectations for the records management function are formed by the first person to manage it. If the first person is not an educated or experienced professional, the organization believes the position to be clerical in nature and expects little other than filing activities to be performed.

Often the custodian of a records center is designated as the records manager when no other components of records management exist in the organization. In this instance, as well, the records manager is perceived as a clerk, with a passive role, and is not consulted in information management problems. As discussed in chapter 1, records management, as a discipline, includes the following components: records inventories; records creation management; forms management; reports, directives, and correspondence management; vital records security; records retention scheduling and management; micrographics management; establishment of records centers and their management; files management; integration of information technologies and their applicability in providing cost-effective solutions; and, in some cases, archives management.

It can happen that organizations seeking to become registered under the ISO standards currently employ someone as a records manager, but they still do not have the in-house expertise or education either to function as a quality records manager or to design and direct a quality records management program. If the in-house records manager is not a Certified Records Manager, does not have a university degree, or does not have several years experience in the field, it is unlikely that he or she possesses the knowledge and expertise to effectively design and manage a quality records management program. If this is the case, a number of alternatives are possible.

Alternatives

Depending on the size of the organization, a highly qualified records manager can be hired to serve as the enterprise-wide records manager. The individual who is currently serving in the records management role can work as a supervisor or manager of one of the component areas, for example, as a supervisor of the records center. This is especially convenient in those cases where the individual has been performing precisely that function. The enterprise-wide records manager can enlarge the scope of records management, developing it into a full program that encompasses all of the components.

Another possibility is that an individual can be hired to function as a quality records manager, specifically for the purpose of designing and implementing the records management components that are required in the ISO standards. After the program is working smoothly, this individual can be designated as the enterprise-wide records manager, to develop and implement a full-fledged records management program for the entire organization. Again, depending on the size of the organization, another individual can be selected to manage the quality records department, reporting to the enterprise-wide records manager.

Currently, the trend in organizations is toward a holistic view of information resources, leading to a consolidation of isolated pockets of records management components, by establishing organization-wide programs. The organization's records manager eventually assumes management of the entire records management function, which includes many, if not all, of the components that comprise the field. In large organizations, the records manager assumes management of component managers, such as the forms manager and the micrographics manager, who are directly responsible for their individual units. It is important to remember that the individual who is selected as the enterprise-wide records manager should be qualified to function as a member of the organization's management team and should not be viewed simply as a person who is responsible for custodial activities pertaining to records and information.

Possible Reporting Structures

Reporting structures for records management positions can be as varied as the organizations that employ them. The following are suggestions for organizations that need guidance when establishing a records management function. A records manager can be placed at the same level as the manager of information services/systems, with both functions reporting to a vice president of information resources (see Figure 15.1). Organizations that are not large enough to have a vice president of information resources often do have a vice president or director of administrative services. It is not uncommon for a records manager to report to the head of administrative services.

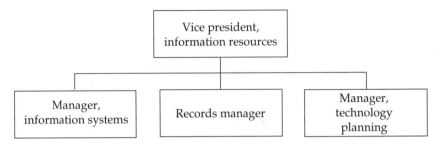

Figure 15.1. Organization chart showing the records manager reporting to the vice president of information resources.

Within the records management function itself, a variety of reporting responsibilities exist. Figures 15.2 and 15.3 present but two alternatives. Depending on the size of the records management function in the organization, the reporting structure can be simple or elaborate. If one of the approaches depicted in Figures 15.2 and 15.3 is taken, the quality records manager reports to the organization's records manager with a dotted line to the quality manager. Under the quality records manager would be the document control center and its personnel, with expertise and personnel brought in from the enterprise-wide records management program to assist with any activities that are similar or that overlap. For example, in developing a vital records program, the personnel from the enterprise-wide vital records section would be consulted and utilized to develop procedures and assist in imple-

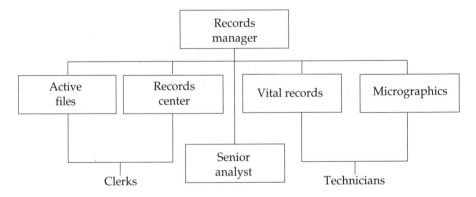

Figure 15.2. Organization chart for records management function: approach 1.

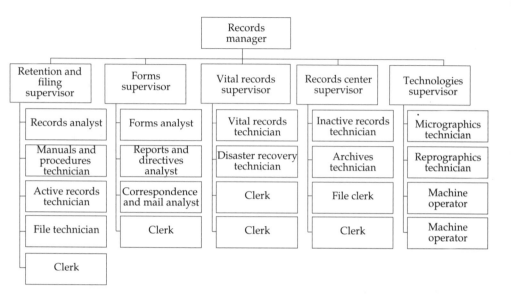

Figure 15.3. Organization chart for records management function: approach 2.

mentation. In any case, a quality records manager should still be a valid position, because, otherwise, attention is not focused specifically on those record activities and record types that ensure compliance with the ISO standards.

Alternatives to an Organization-Wide Records Management Program

Organizations that do not have a comprehensive records management program and are not in a position to develop one at this time yet need to comply with the ISO standards can take another approach. A records manager can be hired to serve as the quality records manager and can report directly to the quality manager.

A staff must be hired to assist the quality records manager. If this is to be done, the limits of quality-related records must be defined clearly, so as not to diffuse the resources of quality records personnel, whose activities will take them across functional lines. For example, if training records are to be brought under the management of the quality records department, it must be made clear that the quality records personnel will not address issues pertaining to other personnel records. Perhaps a records management program for other personnel records can be developed at a later time, *after* the ISO registration process has been completed. When organizations implement a departmental records management program, such as a quality records department, other departments quickly see the advantages, especially in improved access and retrieval of records. Other departments then may request assistance with their records problems from the quality records manager, and this individual becomes an internal consultant to other departments. In the beginning, however, it is necessary to focus solely on satisfying the records requirements in the standards for expedient registration.

Using Consultants

As do all other fields, records management has consultants that are reputable and disreputable, qualified and questionable, strong and weak, ethical and unethical. The best way to select a consultant is to know what to ask for when interviewing prospective candidates. This book provides a thorough explanation of the types of activities that should be conducted in satisfying the records requirements of the ISO standards. Being familiar with those activities and with the records requirements themselves places the quality department in a good position to determine which consultant will provide the best services.

The consultant should be intimately knowledgeable about the records requirements of the ISO standards. If a choice must be made between a consultant who knows the quality aspects of the standards but not records management, and one who knows records management but not the quality aspects, it is better to select the records management expert. It is easier for a records manager to understand the records requirements and the activities that must be conducted in order to achieve compliance. Knowledge of the field is of prime importance in consultant selection.

Another aspect that an organization must determine is what the exact services are that will be required from the consultant. Do you want the consultant to design a filing system? Do you want the system to be implemented? Will the consultant design a system and then oversee implementation by internal staff? Is the consultant expected to contact vendors to gather competitive information about equipment and prices? Should the consultant conduct feasibility studies, comparing different proposed approaches? Will the consultant train in-house personnel to continue the implementation after the consultant leaves? In other words, be specific about the "products" that you expect from the consultant. Do you expect a written report only, describing how a system is to be developed? If so, who will develop and implement the system? Consultants also can be hired just to write the procedures that are specified in 4.16. Be careful about what is written in the procedures—you will have to implement them.

Pricing Structures. Consultants price their services differently. Their rates can be hourly, daily, or by the project. A fee of $100 per hour is not unusual for professional records management consulting. Because the prices can be quoted according to different bases, and the types of services that are provided can vary considerably, it is important to compare apples with apples.

Consulting fees for long-term projects can be hefty. However, this is often a viable solution for those organizations that either do not have the in-house expertise to successfully implement a quality records management program or for those that want the added credibility that consultants often provide. Sad but true is the fact that, although in-house talent is available in some organizations, the outside expert carries greater weight and respect and, because of this, often can accomplish more in shorter periods of time.

The greater the consultant's education and experience, the higher will be the fees. One possibility is to hire the consultant to provide in-house training to records personnel who have some knowledge of records management or who are records managers, but not in the full sense of the term as described earlier. The expertise of the consultant can be leveraged by providing sessions to individuals who are already somewhat familiar with the field. A training session can be conducted initially for two or three days, during which time an overview is presented of required activities. The quality records personnel then can proceed to begin the program. The consultant can continue to provide half-day or day-long sessions, ranging from once a week to once a month. During these sessions, the details of conducting specific activities can be presented. The training time can also be used to answer questions posed by quality records personnel as they are implementing the program.

Determining if a Good Job Is Being Done. One way to determine if the consultant is doing a good job is to prepare a checklist of activities in advance and give a copy to the consultant, asking that it be completed weekly or monthly. Usually, the activities that the consultant is performing are quite noticeable. Are the records being inventoried? Are forms being analyzed for inclusion of appropriate identification and revision numbers? Are records users being interviewed about their records needs and problems? Are the files being gathered and reorganized? The checklist should reflect those duties and activities that have been chosen as the consultant's responsibility.

Recommended Qualifications for Records Managers

Following is a good description of the qualifications that a records manager should possess.

> For a records manager to fulfill his or her duties effectively, certain qualifications are needed. Qualifications for effectively directing a records program are acquired through academic preparation as well as through experience in the business world. Experience in areas of records management as well as in all phases of office work is certainly beneficial to the records manager . . . . Academic preparation for a career as a records manager should include courses in office administration as well as other business courses such as economics, accounting, management, communication, and information processing . . . . In addition, a top priority in preparing for a career in records management is the art of communication . . . . Understanding the principles of effective written communication enables the records manager to write and update records manuals, to write instructions and guidelines that are clear and concise, and to communicate with top management through well-written reports and proposals.[1]

Today, there is no reason to hire an underqualified records manager. Courses in records management are offered in many universities and junior colleges in the United States and Canada.

Some universities offer full-fledged programs in records management with majors available in the field. Graduate-level courses and programs are also available in a limited number of schools. Every year, ARMA International publishes a directory of educational institutions that offer training in records management. Formal education in records retention scheduling, forms management, micrographics, optical disk technology, records appraisal, and other records-related activities is becoming increasingly necessary for managing records in today's information-intensive industries.

ARMA International also publishes job descriptions for various records management positions, from the clerical level to the senior manager level. The position description presented in Table 15.1 describes the job duties for a records and information manager. The description has been modified to include responsibilities for emerging technologies.

In addition, the U.S. Department of Labor publishes the *Dictionary of Occupational Titles*, which describes the following duties for a records management director.

> Plans, develops and administers records management policies designed to facilitate effective and efficient handling of business records and other information. Plans development and implementation of records management policies intended to standardize filing, protecting, and retrieving records, reports, and other information contained on paper, microfilm, computer program, or other media. Coordinates and directs, through subordinate managers, activities of departments involved with records management analysis, reports analysis, and supporting technical, clerical, micrographics, and printing services. Evaluates staff reports, utilizing knowledge of principles of records and information management, administrative processes and systems, cost control, governmental recordkeeping requirements, and organizational objectives. Confers with other administrators to ensure compliance with policies, procedures, and practices of records management program.[2]

Qualifications for consultants vary. In addition to evaluating the number of years of experience in the field and the education of the consultant, it is a good idea to request references of previous assignments. Furthermore, involvement in pertinent professional organizations, attending conferences, making presentations, and writing all provide evidence of the consultant's knowledge and

Table 15.1. Job description for records and information manager.

Title: Records and Information Manager

Function: Develop and manage records management program for entire organization. Develop and manage long-range plans for the organization-wide records management program. Prepare annual reports to top management on the records management program. Plan long-range needs for employee development and education in records management. Prepare fiscal budget and have fiscal planning responsibilities for organization-wide records management program. Provide technical expertise and supervisory staff necessary for maintaining a records management program for the organization. Manage the optical disk system. Possess and demonstrate strong supervisory and leadership skills in managing the records management program. Responsible for organization assets through systematic review and control of records and information. Maintain knowledge of laws affecting the records management program. Evaluate concepts and techniques for manual and automated records systems.

Duties and Responsibilities:
1. Develop records management plan.
2. Develop long-range forecasts for the records management program.
3. Develop methods and techniques for conducting elements of the records management program.
4. Develop procedures for analyzing records systems.
5. Evaluate and approve purchase of equipment, within limits of authority; participate in negotiation of vendor contracts and agreements.
6. Develop and oversee records management budget and cost controls.
7. Develop policies and procedures for implementing the records management program.
8. Manage implementation and operation of optical disk systems.
9. Develop records retention schedule.
10. Design a vital records protection and disaster recovery program.
11. Develop a forms management program.
12. Develop organizing schemes for storage and retrieval of records in all formats.
13. Evaluate, implement, and review manual and/or automated records systems.
14. Ensure adherence to legal requirements that affect the information of the organization.
15. Assist users in controlling costs associated with information storage and retrieval.
16. Plan and coordinate personnel resources necessary for the operation of the program.
17. Provide expertise and guidance on records management issues and on the use of the optical disk systems throughout the organization.
18. Make presentations to the administrators and upper management to justify and support the records management program.

Table 15.1. Continued

19. Determine future needs for skills and experience and conduct relevant recruitment, training, and education programs as these pertain to the records management program.
20. Maintain current knowledge of automated technologies, i.e., optical disk systems, and computer-assisted retrieval (CAR) microfilm systems, computers, and local networking, as well as working knowledge of related technologies.

Principal Contacts:
Interacts with all levels of management, administrators, and staff, both internal and external to the organization, and with the records management staff.

Position Requirements:
1. Must be thoroughly versed in the conduct of professional records management programs.
2. Must possess strong ability to perceive and analyze problems, plan and develop alternatives, and effect innovative solutions based on sound judgment.
3. Must possess demonstrated excellent oral and written communication skills, suitable to a managerial level position.
4. Must have effective management skills.
5. Must have strong organizational and planning skills.
6. Must be able to lead and motivate people.
7. Must be a self-starter.
8. Must be able to work effectively with all levels of personnel with tact and diplomacy.
9. Must maintain professional status through membership in professional organizations.

Education and Experience:
Master's degree in Library and Information Science with an emphasis in Records Management preferred. Certified Records Manager designation acceptable. Minimum of Bachelor's degree plus four years of equivalent or direct experience will be accepted in lieu of a Master's degree. Demonstrated course work in several areas of records management. Excellent understanding of the automated systems and technologies, tools, and equipment pertinent to the management of records.

Source: Modified from Association of Records Managers and Administrators, *Job Descriptions* (Prairie Village, Kans.: Association of Records Managers and Administrators, 1985), 26–28. Reprinted with permission.

his or her expertise. Invitations to speak at conferences provide strong evidence that the consultant not only has kept pace with the changes in the profession, but also is viewed as an authority in the field.

Conclusion

The records requirements of ISO 9000 require the expertise of professional records managers for smooth implementation and continued operation. Formal university education, Certified Records Manager status, and experience form the basic qualifications of those who are equipped to design quality records management programs that will contribute to higher success rates.

Notes

1. Patricia E. Wallace, JoAnn Lee, and Dexter R. Schubert, *Records Management: Integrated Information Systems*, 3rd ed. (Englewood Cliffs, N.J.: Prentice Hall, 1992), 38–39. (Reprinted by permission of Prentice Hall.)

2. *Dictionary of Occupational Titles*, 4th ed. (Washington, D.C.: U.S. Department of Labor, 1977), 93–94.

CHAPTER 16

Developing a Records Retention Schedule and a Records Protection Program

Introduction

Developing a records retention schedule and a vital records protection program are resource-consuming activities. Entire books have been written on each of these records management components. This chapter can present only a brief, condensed overview of the process. The reader is referred to the selected bibliography at the end of this book for detailed instructions in each of these areas.

The Records Retention Schedule

A records retention schedule is a listing of records within the organization, together with the time that they must be retained for legal or operating purposes. It is the underpinning of a records management program and its preparation defines how information activities are conducted within the organization. Operating without a records retention schedule is foolhardy, because its existence and implementation literally protects the organization in a variety of ways. In some industries, organizations are required by regulatory authorities, such as the FAA and the Nuclear Regulatory Commission (NRC), to develop and implement retention schedules. In such regulated environments, it is necessary to record and to maintain the information pertaining, for example, to aircraft manufacture, maintenance, and modifications for the life of the aircraft. If and when problems with the aircraft do occur, the records are immediately examined to determine if any weakness existed in the structure of the aircraft itself and if all maintenance operations were performed correctly and according to schedule. The same holds true for the manufacture of components that comprise the core of a nuclear reactor. The processing of zirconium and hafnium and the subsequent fabrication of these metals into products must be thoroughly and correctly recorded. All testing, inspection, processing steps, and even packaging are recorded to document the quality of the materials. Maintained for the life of the products, the records serve as evidence that the metal products conform to specifications regarding such characteristics as hardness, tensile strength, chemical composition, and so forth. If a zirconium tube were to crack in a nuclear reactor, the information on the records would be critically important in determining the quality of the fabricated tubes. Thus, quality records can protect the supplying organization by proving that the product did pass all quality requirements and did conform to specifications. Organizations that retain their records according to well-researched retention schedules are thus protected if their products were to malfunction.

The ISO standards are very clear about requiring the development of retention schedules for quality records. Section 4.16 of Q9001 states,

> Retention times of quality records shall be established and recorded.

Developing and implementing a records retention schedule for all quality-related records, however, makes good business sense, regardless of any external authorities or requirements. All states recognize the concept of product liability. An organization is responsible for injury resulting from any products that it manufactures or distributes.[1] It is important, therefore,

> ... for manufacturers and others in the chain of distribution to develop record-retention techniques to create and maintain documents that can be

used to defend them if accidents and lawsuits do occur. . . . In order to plan for the defense of a potential lawsuit, a manufacturer must identify the records that could be used to rebut a plaintiff's allegations and affirmatively show how a product's design was developed and finally approved. These documents detail initial design specifications, engineering evaluations, design reviews, prototype testing, design assurance testing, final design selection, quality control and inspection procedures, sales and marketing efforts, and product service and performance history.[2]

The retention schedule ensures that all records bearing on the quality of the product have been identified and that they are retained for as long as necessary—to satisfy either legal or regulatory requirements or internal operating needs. As important as the retention schedule is, it remains the least understood component of records management by those outside the field, and its importance is downplayed, especially by senior level management. It is not uncommon for upper management to mistakenly assume that a retention schedule can be developed overnight by clerical staff and to view it as a cost to the organization. Operating without a records management program and, especially, without a retention schedule, is a cost to the organization, and examples abound supporting this. Developing a records retention schedule will result in a minimum return on investment of 20 percent per year for those organizations that have been operating without one.

Because the development of a retention schedule can be time-consuming, those organizations preparing for ISO registration should devote attention to its preparation early in the process. Depending on the size, age, and complexity of the organization, the preparation of a retention schedule can take from six months to several years.

Developing a Quality Records Retention Schedule

The following steps, listed in order, must be performed in order to develop a sound records retention schedule.

1. Conduct a records inventory.
2. Interview key personnel.
3. Research records retention periods.
4. Appraise the records.

5. Prepare a draft schedule.

6. Discuss the schedule with affected departmental managers and legal counsel.

7. Obtain the necessary signatures.

8. Duplicate and distribute the records retention schedule.

Step 1—Conduct a Records Inventory

A records inventory serves as the basis for the entire records management program. A well-designed inventory collects information necessary not only to develop the retention schedule but also to establish other aspects of records management required in the ISO standards: vital records programs, indexing schemes, retrievability, filing systems, and access schemes. It is logical to conduct a records inventory as the basis for a retention schedule, because it is impossible to define retention times for quality records if the organization does not know what records it maintains.

Because of the comprehensive nature of the records inventory, it has sometimes been referred to as an *information survey*.[3] The more thoroughly the survey is conducted, the less time will be spent diagnosing records problems and instituting other components of records management. Some elements of information that are needed for retention schedule development are also needed for other aspects of records management required in the standards. For example, developing a vital records protection program requires identifying the records, their volume, location, medium or format, and current equipment use. The same elements of information must be gathered about the records in order to develop a records retention schedule.

If the volume of records is very great and resources are limited, it might be easier to collect information in stages. During the initial information survey, data can be collected that pertain only to records retention schedules. Although it would mean returning to the same locations and recording some of the same data elements, compartmentalizing the activities may prove to be more manageable. If at all possible, it is recommended that one major survey or inventory be conducted that will collect all data elements necessary to apply to each of the records management phases to be instituted.

Because most organizations today operate with some degree of automation, the most efficient approach is to develop a master database into which all data elements from the inventory can be entered. Once the information is entered, it can be sorted various ways—each one providing the information necessary to develop a separate facet of a records management program. Inventories themselves can be conducted with the assistance of a laptop computer, thus eliminating the need for handwritten paper forms.[4]

The Inventory Form. In order to develop a retention schedule, it is necessary to identify the quality records that exist. Certain data elements should be recorded about each quality records series. A records series is a category or group or records that are used and filed together as a unit. Document control records, for example, include all supporting records that pertain to the documents, as well as the documents themselves. The distribution list for each document, the record of revisions, and the annual review record are part of the records series called *document control records.* All records of the same series have the same retention period. In an inventory, records are not identified at the individual record level or by the name on the file folder. A master list should be developed that includes the names of the individual records that compose the series. This is done by the records management staff as part of its internal controls and can be included in a procedural manual.

The inventory form is a working document—a worksheet. If the records manager realizes that it must be revised during the inventory, this should be done. The inventory, after all, is a means to an end, and the inventory worksheet is a tool toward that end. The following data elements should be recorded during the inventory when it is being conducted only for retention schedule development.

- The name of the department or unit
- The titles of records series (the contents should be recorded once, in a master list of all records series contents)
- Format or medium (paper, microfilm, optical disk, floppy disk, and so forth)

- Volume or quantity (inches, cubic feet, linear feet, number of floppy disks, number of microfilm reels, and so on)
- The location (where the records are stored)
- Equipment (the type of housing—open-shelf files, four-drawer vertical file cabinets, microfilm cabinets, and so on—and the number of pieces of equipment)
- The periods of time covered by records (use dates, for example, 1985–1991, 1993–, January 1987–June 1987)
- Retrieval frequency (how frequently the records are used)
- The administrative or operating retention need for the series

In addition to collecting these data elements, it is good practice to provide space for the name of a contact in the department, together with a telephone number in the event that questions arise when the information is being analyzed. The worksheet should also include the name of the individual who conducted the inventory and the date or dates on which the inventory was conducted.

A physical inventory of the quality records provides accurate information on which to base retention schedule decisions. Distributing a questionnaire to departments in order to collect inventory information is discouraged. The basic purpose of the inventory—to identify which quality records exist, where they are located, and how many there are—is best served when the records management staff physically examines the records. It is not uncommon to find records in places that (1) are not obvious and (2) were not designed for records storage. Records are housed in coat closets; in basement rooms infested with insects and vermin; on the floor in empty offices; on top of file cabinets, chairs, and computer terminals; in grocery cartons stacked in warehouses; along the walls of hallways and offices; in mini metal storage units; and elsewhere. Without a records management program, most records that are so stored are unidentified, mixed with various records series, and often not protected from deterioration. They are also not readily retrievable. Both of these latter aspects are required by the ISO standards—protection from deterioration and ready retrievability.

Part of developing a workable records management program for ISO registration is paying attention to the appearance of records. If the storage scenarios mentioned in the previous paragraph are typical, there is an immediate impression that the quality system is in disarray. It is difficult to convince auditors or registrars that control is being exercised over product quality if records are spilling out of every nook and cranny and if they lack a professional appearance.

Quality Records That Must Be Inventoried. In order to satisfy the ISO 9000 requirements, attention should be focused on the records that have been identified in this book. A records inventory should be performed for the following quality records.

- Design control and review records (includes the designs themselves)
- Contract review records (includes the contracts themselves)
- Document control records (includes the documents themselves)
- Purchasing records
- Processing records (can include samples of product)
- Inspection records (includes receipt, in-process, and final inspection records)
- Testing records (includes receipt, in-process, and final testing records)
- Calibration records
- Nonconforming product records
- Audit records (both internal and external audits)
- Training records
- Corrective and preventive action records
- Management review records

Dispersed or Decentralized Quality Records. If quality records are dispersed, it is extremely important to identify all locations where they are maintained. When retention times are satisfied, all copies of the record must be destroyed, including convenience copies.

Retention schedules and adherence to them may become the subject of litigation. The validity of the retention schedule will be undermined if all copies of records are not destroyed when retention times have been satisfied (see Appendix E—Carlucci et al. vs. Piper Aircraft Corporation).

Step 2—Interview Key Personnel

Because it is not possible to gather all pertinent information by physically examining the records, it is common to interview users and keepers of the records. In each organization there are usually *key informants*—those users and custodians of records who can provide the most information about them. It is not necessary to interview all of the individuals in each department. Key informants can be those employees who have worked for the organization for a long time and/or those who designed the current records systems. Interviews are conducted for the following reasons.

- Procedural issues—to define the process and determine how specific records and series of records are used; to understand the interrelationships across records

- Analytical issues—to understand actual or perceived problems with the records and actual or perceived barriers to productivity

- Retrieval issues—to determine the characteristics of retrieval such as frequency, access points, active time frames, and so forth

- Historical issues—to understand when and why specific records procedures were developed

- Retention issues—to determine the administrative need for the information

When interviews are conducted regarding the operating or administrative use of quality records to determine retention times, it is preferable to determine the age of the information that users have had need for in past operations, rather than to ask them outright, "How long do you need to retain these records?" Because most individuals are unaware of the life-cycle concept of records, they tend to believe that it is best to retain all records and information indefinitely. The following types of questions serve as examples to determine accurately the need to retain quality records.

- How old are the records that you need or use to operate?
- What is the oldest record that you have ever had to retrieve?
- Does this happen often, or was it unusual to need a record that was that old?

Step 3—Research Records Retention Periods

A basic rule is that there is no single source that provides an organization with all of the information about retention times for records. In fact, many records are not specified at all in any type of requirement. It is assumed, mistakenly, that (1) all requirements for records retention are clearly stated somewhere and (2) these (non-existent) requirements form the basis for most retention schedules. Both assumptions are false. There are multiple sources that provide information about records retention, and they must be unearthed. The records manager must be aware of all of these sources.

Federal rules and regulations exist; regulatory authorities publish their own requirements; state statutes can include retention requirements; municipal laws can affect records retention; and foreign governments' requirements can even enter the picture if the organization has operations in other countries.[5] Donald S. Skupsky provides a clear explanation of the legal requirements for recordkeeping. He covers records in all media—paper, electronic, microform, and optical disk.[6] The bibliography at the end of this book provides helpful resources for researching retention requirements.

The basic federal rules and regulations are published in the *Federal Register* and in the *Code of Federal Regulations* (CFR). In addition, some agencies and regulatory authorities may have jurisdiction over the type of business that the organization provides, and they have separate guidelines that must be consulted. As an example, the FAA regulates the airlines industries and publishes its own requirements concerning records creation and retention.[7] State statutes and municipal laws must also be reviewed. Finally, the type of business an organization does or provides may be supervised by a self-regulatory organization, and their guidelines and rules can have the authority of law to member organizations.[8]

Purging. One of the immediate results of conducting a records inventory and researching records retention requirements is the destruction of records that have outlived their usefulness and retention times. Such items can be destroyed immediately, thus providing additional space and equipment as well as simplifying the retrieval and organization of the remaining records. It is not uncommon to destroy 30 percent to 40 percent of records after conducting the intitial inventory. In addition, usually 30 percent of the records are identified as inactive and can be removed from prime office space to an offsite storage facility. (Active records are those that are used or retrieved regularly and must be kept inhouse for convenience. Inactive records are not used as frequently, perhaps once a month or less, but still must be retained to satisfy legal or operating criteria specified on the retention schedule. They should be moved to an offsite location where they can be retrieved as needed.) This leaves 30 percent of the original volume of records to organize and house in the operating facility. Immediately, improvement in access and organizing will be noticeable, because only one-third of the records remain. Table 16.1 presents some guidelines for determining the retention times for records

Step 4—Appraise the Records

After the inventory and interviews have been conducted, and the research into requirements has been completed, the records are appraised for their value—that is, whether they are being retained for legal reasons, to satisfy administrative or operating needs, or for historical reasons. A records appraisal is an examination of the data gathered through the records inventory, interviews, and research to determine the value of each records series.

Table 16.1. Principles for making valid retention decisions.

Principle Number 1: Avoid the *every conceivable contingency syndrome*. A records retention program cannot and should not be designed to accommodate every conceivable need for information at any future time, however remote the probability of the need might be.

Principle Number 2: Information should be retained if there is a reasonable probability that it will be needed at some future time to support some legitimate legal or business objective, and if the consequences of its absence would be substantial.

Principle Number 3: Records retention policies should generally be conservative in the sense that they do not expose the organization to an inordinate degree of risk. If the only benefit of a short retention period is savings in space, a substantial degree of risk is usually not justified to attain this reward.

Principle Number 4: Retention decision-makers must be mindful of the fact that the presence or absence of information can be either helpful or harmful to an organization, depending on specific legal or business contingencies that may arise at any time in the life of the business. It is difficult to predict the occurrence of these contingencies with any certainty. Therefore, the best way to minimize the risks associated with document retention is to provide for their systematic disposal immediately after the expiration of their value for legal and business purposes.

Principle Number 5: A retention period is most likely to be valid if it is based on a professional consensus of persons most knowledgeable about the value of the information and the costs, risks, and benefits of its disposal after varying time periods.

Source: David O. Stephens, CRM, "Making Records Retention Decisions: Practical and Theoretical Considerations," *ARMA Quarterly* 22, No. 1, (January 1988), 7. Reprinted with permission.

Step 5—Prepare a Draft Schedule

A draft copy of the schedule is then prepared and presented to the legal counsel and department heads for review. If the retention times have been based on cited requirements, a copy of the appropriate pages from the requirements with highlighted regulations should be attached to the recommended retention schedule to facilitate legal review. After the draft copy is reviewed, any necessary changes should be incorporated into the retention schedule.

Step 6—Discuss the Schedule with Affected Departmental Managers and Legal Counsel

Step 7—Obtain the Necessary Signatures

When consensus is reached on retention times, signatures of the records manager, the department head, and the legal counsel should be affixed to the retention schedule or to a retention authorization form. At this point, the retention schedule is ready to be published and distributed.

Step 8—Duplicate and Distribute the Records Retention Schedule

There are two distribution methods, depending on the size of the retention schedule and the decision of the records manager: (1) The entire retention schedule can be distributed to each affected unit and to the legal counsel, or (2) Only those portions that contain a department's records can be distributed to each department.

At a minimum, the retention schedule should contain the following information.[9]

- The department name
- The schedule number
- The revision number
- The effective date
- The page number
- The records series title and description
- The office that holds the original copy
- The media on which it is kept
- The records retention period
- The period in active use
- The period in inactive use
- The total retention period

It is also a good idea to include a column that provides the source or citation of the retention time.

The records retention schedule is not a fixed item. Because there are constant changes in the law and in the organization's operations, it is continuously open for revision. It is a dynamic document that must be updated regularly to incorporate any changes in record type, status, and retention periods.

Implementing the Retention Schedule

Just as important as its development is the active and attentive implementation of the retention schedule. Depending on the type of records management function in the company, implementation can be accomplished by liaisons in each of the affected departments or by the records management staff. If the schedule is to be implemented by the departmental liaisons, they must be appropriately trained in the importance of diligent adherence and in the methods that have been selected to purge the records and to move the inactive records to a storage facility. Because the records manager bears the ultimate responsibility, it is important that adherence to the authorized retention schedule be monitored.

Disposing of Records

Part of the implementation process of a retention schedule is the periodic, scheduled destruction of records that have satisfied their retention periods. To maintain legal acceptability and demonstrate compliance, records must be destroyed according to schedule. If records are not destroyed according to schedule, but instead are destroyed whenever the organization gets around to it or runs out of storage room, the motives for records destruction will be suspect. It can appear as though the organization has attempted to destroy unfavorable evidence, perhaps anticipating litigation or government investigation. This point is to be emphasized especially concerning quality-related records that provide evidence of product performance and product safety. (More detailed information pertaining to records retention programs, records destruction, and legal requirements for recordkeeping, and legal issues regarding records management programs and destruction of records is available.[10])

Various methods can be used to destroy records that have satisfied their retention requirements. They can be shredded, pulverized, or incinerated. Several issues must be considered when deciding on a destruction method. If the records are classified or carry sensitive government information, there may be a requirement that they must be incinerated. The issue of confidentiality and security also needs to be addressed. How damaging could the information on the record be to an individual or an organization if the record were to be made public or were found by an unscrupulous person? For this reason, simply tossing records in a trash bin is discouraged. Medium or format is another consideration. Microform records (microfilm or microfiche) cannot be sent through a shredder because the images would remain intact and readable. Such media should be pulverized.

Scheduling records for destruction requires developing a timetable and preparing records that document the individuals involved and reveal that appropriate review processes have taken place. Under no circumstances should records be destroyed that have been requested for litigation or government investigation, regardless of the time indicated on the retention schedule.

Transferring Inactive Records

Implementing the records retention schedule involves developing procedures and records to transfer inactive records to another location. Keeping the records organized during the transfer process is necessary so that they can be retrieved if needed during transfer. As with the destruction process, transfer records must be created that list the records being transferred. If storage is provided by a commercial facility, acknowledgment in the form of a receipt is required (see appendix H for examples of transfer records).

Transfer procedures should be developed so that the process is orderly and systematic and so that the organization is protected. The following steps provide guidance.[11]

1. Decide when records are to be transferred.

2. Identify the records to be transferred.

3. Use only transfer cartons provided by the records center.

4. Pack the cartons properly so that files can be easily retrieved and refiled.

5. Mark the cartons only in the required location with specific, predetermined data.

6. Complete a records transfer document, and send it to the storage facility with the records.

7. Contact the records center for specific shipping instructions. Records storage center personnel normally pick up the records and transfer them to their facility.

Records Protection

The standards and the *Guidelines* both address the issue of records protection. Q9001, 4.16 states,

> All quality records . . . shall be stored and retained . . . in facilities that provide a suitable environment to prevent damage or deterioration and to prevent loss.

Q9004-1, 17.2 states,

> While in storage, quality records should be protected in suitable facilities from damage, loss and deterioration (e.g., due to environmental conditions).

The *Guidelines* concern only damage due to environmental conditions. Granted, this can be substantial, and the examples in Table 16.2 provide considerable evidence of this possibility. The statement in Q9001 can and should be interpreted in a different way, with the word *environment* used in its more generic sense to convey the meaning of *the overall conditions*—not just those caused by nature.

Protection of important or vital records usually is not given prime attention by an organization until *after* critical records are lost, damaged, or destroyed. There are numerous commercial disaster prevention and recovery services that handle electronic information or computer records. Little attention, however, has been paid to information that resides on paper and microforms. Considering that 95 percent of America's business information still resides on paper, the consequences of lack of protection can be

Table 16.2. Possible disasters that can destroy or damage records.

- Power fluctuations causing corruption or loss of data on computers
- Rats eating through wiring causing shorts and fires
- Air conditioners breaking down causing computer failures
- Explosions in neighboring buildings causing fires and damage
- Leaking pipes dripping water on to files
- Flash floods taking away whole file rooms
- Transport vehicles crashing or being stolen causing loss of files, letters and tapes
- Military or airport radar equipment causing computer data corruption
- Employee negligence or malice causing security leaks
- Vermin nesting in and devouring files
- A cup of hot coffee tipping over and into a personal computer causing a breakdown
- The incomprehensible minds of vandals causing any damage that is fairly easy to inflict

Source: Ira A. Penn, Anne Morddel, Gail Pennix, and Kelvin Smith, *Records Management Handbook* (Brookfield, Vt.: Gower Publishing Co., 1989), 136. Reprinted with permission.

disastrous. When records protection programs are developed, they are almost exclusively designed after a disaster has occurred, and, then usually, they address only the vital records of an organization. Vital records are those records essential to the continued functioning of an organization during and after an emergency and those records that protect the rights and interests of the organization, employees, stockholders, customers, and the public.

Although some quality-related records that should be protected according to the ISO standards are vital records (engineering drawings, contracts), many of them are not. They are, however, very important records. If the quality records are damaged or destroyed, many organizations simply could not reconstruct the information that they contained. Being aware of the disasters that can affect an organization's quality records helps determine the methods that can be instituted to provide protection for important information pertaining to quality.

Recent headlines prove that it is not necessary to wonder whether or not a disaster could destroy an organization's memory. The bombing at the World Trade Center in 1992, Hurricane Andrew in 1993, the 1993 floods in the Midwest, the 1989 San Francisco earthquake are all recent events that underscore the importance of planned protection for records. Statistics continue to indicate that, of those organizations whose vital records are destroyed or cannot be reconstructed quickly after a disaster, *40 percent* fail within the first year following the disaster. (See appendix F for a description of how the records management vital records program enabled Dean Witter Reynolds to resume business after the World Trade Center bombing.)

Developing a Records Protection Program

Developing a records protection program involves considering and knowing about the following.

- The potential hazards to the organization and to its quality records
- The various protection methods available
- The protection of records stored on alternative media
- The storage facilities available
- Security
- Equipment needed
- Salvage procedures

Potential Hazards

A clear evaluation of the types of hazards reveals the kinds of measures that must be taken to protect quality records. In general, disasters may be either natural or caused by human beings either accidentally or intentionally. Table 16.3 categorizes the potential hazards that should be considered. The geographic location of an organization must be considered when establishing a records protection program. Records in places with high humidity must be protected against mold and mildew. Insects and vermin are more

---

Table 16.3. Evaluating potential hazards.

Environment: What problems are common in a given area? Tornadoes, floods, brush fires, earthquakes, electrical storms, heavy snowfalls, insect invasions, power failures, regular warfare, invasions, high winds, tidal waves, etc. By far the most common hazards to records safety in most places are fire and the water or chemicals used to extinguish it.

Enticing vulnerability: What, by the very nature of the organization, would make it particularly vulnerable to attack or sabotage? A bank in an area where people are starving, a military installation, an innovative research facility whose secrets would be valuable if stolen, a political organization, a key national utility or communications installation, a high publicity or glamour business appealing to lunatics, etc.

Unpopularity: (This is closely related to the above.) What organizations might be particularly unpopular to some people? The police, the tax collection agency, the courts, companies that have just made many people (or only one vengeful or desperate character) redundant.

Technical vulnerability: What part of the organization's equipment and technology is both vital and so highly sensitive that a minute occurrence could cause a major disaster? (For example, one human hair in a computer disk causing a total crash.)

Source: Ira A. Penn, Anne Morddel, Gail Pennix, and Kelvin Smith, *Records Management Handbook* (Brookfield, Vt.: Gower Publishing Co., 1989), 138. Reprinted with permission.

prone to attack records in some environments than in others. Vandalism and theft may be more of a threat in some areas than in others. Protecting quality records from the effects of the environment relates to all of these disasters and not only to those resulting from "acts of God."

Methods of Protection

The most common methods for protecting records are dispersal, duplication, and storage. Dispersal is the practice of duplicating records and storing them in another location. This method is based on the premise that it is unlikely that the same records stored in two different locations would be destroyed in the same disaster.

Duplication is the scheduled reproduction of records specifically for the purpose of records protection. Because it is the information on the records that is actually being protected, duplication does not have to be on the same medium as the original. It can be done in any medium: floppy disk, microforms, optical disk, paper, or photocopy. Table 16.4 presents six forms of records protection.

Protection for records can also be provided by well-constructed onsite storage facilities and offsite storage. For those organizations considering onsite storage protection, ARMA's publication, *Vital Records*, provides valuable information and

---

Table 16.4. Forms of records protection.

1. *Existing dispersal*: Dispersal is the practice of duplicating copies and storing them in another location. Built-in or existing dispersal occurs as a result of normal business operations. That is, vital record copies are stored in another location as a matter of procedure. Copies of a document that originate in a branch office, for example, are often stored in the home office.

2. *Improvised dispersal*: This type of dispersal occurs by making an extra copy of a document for vital records protection. Thus, the duplication of an extra copy for storage in a second location is improvised dispersal. An example of this is the photocopying of formulas to be stored in an offsite location such as the vital records center.

3. *Evacuation transfer*: The original source document of a vital record is transferred to the vital records center for storage and protection in evacuation transfer. Thus, this protection method is for vital records that are referred to infrequently but still considered vital. The original copy is evacuated to the vital records depository, and, if limited reference is needed, no duplication is required.

4. *Duplication*: This protection method for vital records simply insures that a second copy of a vital record is made. Such duplication may be made by electronic tape, floppy disk, microform, optical disk, or photocopy. The backup is stored in the vital records center.

5. *COM*: Another popular method of protection is computer-output microfilm (COM), which permits information to go directly from computer tape to microfiche and requires limited storage space.

6. *Vaulting*: This method uses a heavy-duty combination lock vault to store vital records on site. Placing documents in a fire-resistant vault protects them from possible hazards.

Source: Patricia E. Wallace, JoAnn Lee, and Dexter R. Schubert, *Records Management: Integrated Information Systems,* 3rd ed. (Englewood Cliffs, N.J.: Prentice Hall, 1992), 277–78. Reprinted with permission.

sources.[12] Adequate onsite protection is only possible in a fireproof record vault. Otherwise, onsite storage is acceptable only if it is temporary. Tables 16.5, 16.6, and 16.7 present valuable information when decisions are being made about whether to choose onsite or offsite storage. Offsite storage in a commercial or company-owned facility provides the best measure of protection.

Equipment and Media

If records are protected in a medium other than paper, equipment to read the information must be available. Microforms will require readers and/or reader/printers. Electronic information—tapes, floppy disks, and optical disks—will require pertinent hardware, software, and operating systems. The purpose of providing additional protection for quality records is so that they are available quickly, should the records within the organization be damaged or destroyed. Planning for all necessary equipment facilitates ready access to the records and allows the organization to resume its business quickly after a disaster.

Table 16.5. Evaluating an onsite records storage facility.

The following questions should be asked when contemplating onsite storage.

- Will the storage area have proper heat ventilation and humidity levels?
- Is there a sprinkler system in the area which could allow water to damage records?
- Are there electromagnetic fields nearby which may affect magnetic tapes or discs?
- What security measures are in effect to stop unauthorized entry into the storage area?
- Is the facility safe from fire, floods, earthquakes, and other natural disasters?
- Are the filing cabinets, safes, and vaults able to give adequate protection from fires, floods, earthquakes, and employee sabotage?
- If you are storing microforms, is there air circulation and a filter system to provide a clean environment?
- If this is the only copy of the vital record, would you feel safer storing it onsite as opposed to storing it offsite at a record storage facility?

Source: Association of Records Managers and Administrators, *Vital Records: A Guideline,* 2nd ed. (Prairie Village, Kans.: Association of Records Managers and Administrators, 1984), 14–15. Reprinted with permission.

Table 16.6. Advantages of an offsite records storage facility.

- In an emergency, records can be retrieved quickly because they are in one location.

- Offsite storage facilities are usually designed to store vital records and have environmental controls for temperature, humidity and air filtration and circulation and various other detection and monitoring devices as necessary.

- The staff of these facilities are trained in records management and, thus, are acquainted with professional storage techniques.

- The security in an offsite facility usually has state-of-the-art detection devices. Access to the records is restricted to those whom the organization designates.

- A facility can be selected far enough away so that it would not be affected by a disaster in your immediate area.

Source: Association of Records Managers and Administrators, *Vital Records: A Guideline,* 2nd ed. (Prairie Village, Kans.: Association of Records Managers and Administrators, 1984), 16–17. Reprinted with permission.

Microforms

Microforms (microfilm and microfiche) provide excellent protection of quality records, because they can be stored offsite at low cost and also serve as the backup copies that organizations should have, regardless of any required compliance. Microforms can be converted easily to hard copy (paper) if necessary, they are relatively easy and inexpensive to duplicate, and they can be transported easily. For those organizations that do not have or wish to invest in microfilm cameras and processing equipment, many commercial services are available that will microfilm records at a reasonable cost.

One alternative to storing computer tapes that contain quality records is to convert the information to COM. The cost of producing COM is less than the cost of printing the computer data onto paper as the information is transferred directly from the computer tape to microfiche.

Conclusion

It is foolhardy for organizations, large or small, to operate without records retention schedules and records protection programs, regardless of any external standards requiring them. Developing such programs can be very time-consuming and can demand large

Table 16.7. Evaluation of an offsite records storage facility.

- If your organization had a disaster or needed the records, how quickly could you receive them?
- What controls are there for limiting access to your records?
- How does the facility control temperature, humidity, air filtration, and electromagnetic fields? Does it meet the American National Standards Institute (ANSI) standards for storage?
- What type of insurance is available for the records and facility?
- Is the facility constructed and maintained to minimize the risk of damage from floods, fires, earthquakes, winds, and other natural disasters?
- How does the facility protect against unauthorized entry?
- Does the facility have a program to control insects, rodents, and mold?
- What type of fire prevention system does the facility have?
- What type of filing and index system does it have?
- How is receipt of records acknowledged?
- Is the facility equipped with auxiliary power to operate humidity and temperature controls and security equipment in the event of the loss of the main power source?
- Does it have a disaster plan to restore records?
- Does the facility have equipment to reproduce your records should the need arise?

Source: Association of Records Managers and Administrators, *Vital Records: A Guideline*, 2nd ed. (Prairie Village, Kans.: Association of Records Managers and Administrators, 1984), 17–18. Reprinted with permission.

amounts of resources. For those organizations who are seeking registration under ISO 9000, it is wise to begin addressing both records retention schedules and records protection programs early in the process.

Notes

1. Donald S. Skupsky, JD, CRM, *Recordkeeping Requirements*, (Denver, Col.: Information Requirements Clearinghouse, 1988), 93.

2. Jamie S. Gorelick, Stephen Marzen, and Lawrence Solum, *Destruction of Evidence* (New York: John Wiley & Sons, 1989), 343.

3. Ira A. Penn, Anne Morddel, Gail Pennix, and Kelvin Smith, *Records Management Handbook,* (Brookfield, Vt.: Gower Publishing Co., 1989), 42 ff.

4. Donald Read, Caryl Masur, and Kurt Shinn, "Automating the Inventory Process," *The Records and Retrieval Report* 7 (April 1991), 9.

5. Johanna Jacobs Kruse, "Retention," *The Records and Retrieval Report* 5 (September 1989), 12.

6. Donald S. Skupsky, *Legal Requirements for Business Records: Federal Requirements* (Denver Col.: Information Requirements Clearinghouse).

7. Federal Aviation Administration, Department of Transportation, *Code of Federal Regulations—14 CFR,* Chapter 1, (Washington, D.C.: GPO, 1985).

8. Kruse, "Retention," 12.

9. Association of Records Managers and Administrators, *Developing and Operating a Records Retention Program: A Guideline* (Prairie Village, Kans.: Association of Records Managers and Administrators, 1986), 13.

10. Gorelick, Marzen, and Solum, *Destruction of Evidence;* and Skupsky, *Legal Requirements for Business Records.*

11. Patricia E. Wallace, JoAnn Lee, and Dexter R. Schubert, *Records Management: Integrated Information Systems,* 3rd ed. (Englewood Cliffs, N.J.: Prentice Hall, 1992), 109.

12. Association of Records Managers and Administrators, *Vital Records: A Guideline,* 2nd ed. (Prairie Village, Kans.: Association of Records Managers and Administrators, 1993).

A Self-Evaluation Questionnaire for Organizations Wishing to Determine Their Records Readiness

1. Do you have procedures for each of the following activities pertaining to quality records?
   a. Identification
   b. Collection
   c. Indexing
   d. Access
   e. Filing
   f. Storage
   g. Maintenance
   h. Disposition

2. Do these procedures describe what is actually being done? Do they work?

3. Are the procedures part of the document control system?

4. Do you have a retention and disposition schedule?

   a. Do you know the legal, administrative, fiscal, and historical or archival requirements for the various records categories that you have?

   b. Are you following the retention schedule?

5. Has a records inventory ever been conducted?

   a. Do you know where *all* of the quality records are located?

   b. Do you know which records are active and which are inactive?

   c. Do you know all of the storage media that house records—microform, electronic, and paper?

6. Do you have a standardized method of identifying records in your organization?

   a. Do the records and forms have clear, meaningful titles?

   b. Do the records and forms have unique numbers, revision numbers, and dates?

   c. Are users notified of obsolete record types or forms?

7. Does the collection of quality records work?

   a. Is there a routing system?

   b. Do senders of quality records follow the system?

   c. Do recipients of collected quality records know if there is something missing?

   d. How thorough and complete are the quality records?

8. Is it easy to retrieve the records?

   a. How long, on the average, does it take to retrieve records?

   b. How much time is spent searching for records?

   c. How much is this costing your organization?

   d. How does this look during audits and registration?

   e. Have you ever lost a record—temporarily or permanently?

9. Are you currently storing *all* quality records in prime office areas?

   a. How much space are the records consuming?

   b. How much are you spending on new filing equipment each year?

c. How protected are the records from fire, water, theft, and so on?

10. Are you storing records in an offsite storage facility?

    a. Are all of the records needed?

    b. Are they easily retrievable?

    c. Were the obsolete records and the nonrecords removed *before* the records were sent offsite?

    d. How much are you paying to store records that may not have to be retained?

    e. Do you keep records on what is stored offsite so that you can retrieve the quality records when you must?

    f. How do you implement your records retention schedule when records are stored offsite?

11. Do you have a records protection program?

    a. What sort of special provisions have been made to protect the quality records?

    b. Do you *believe* that they are protected if they are in fire-retardant equipment or in a safe that is located in-house?

12. What kinds of organizing schemes exist for quality records?

    a. Are there indexing schemes?

    b. Are there filing systems? Do they make sense?

    c. Are there directories for electronic information?

13. Do you have any policies or procedures for circulating the quality records?

    a. Do the procedures address removal of records from the organization?

    b. How do you ensure that records are returned to their rightful storage place after they have been circulated?

14. Do you have a forms management program?

    a. How is the design of forms handled?

    b. How is the request for a new form handled?

    c. How is the ordering of forms handled?

    d. Is forms processing, printing, stocking, and distribution centralized and systematic, or is it dispersed and chaotic?

15. Do you use microforms of any type in your quality operations?

    a. Do they work for you?

    b. How satisfied is everyone with them?

    c. Are they an asset or a hindrance?

16. What sorts of technologies do you use for quality records?

    a. Do you use databases for storing and retrieving pertinent information?

    b. Do you use optical disk technology?

    c. Are you networked?

17. How are the security of records and the confidentiality of information being handled?

    a. Does everyone have access to critical quality records?

    b. Has employee sabotage been addressed?

18. What do the quality records offices and work areas look like?

    a. Are records piled inappropriately?

    b. Are physical materials neat?

    c. Are labels clear and legible?

    d. Is the records equipment old or new? Is it functional? Is it broken?

    e. Are there heaps of paper on desks, on file cabinets, on the floor?

    f. Are the records personnel rushed or relaxed?

    g. Does the records department or room look cheap, messy, and frantic, or does it look clean, professional, and calm?

19. Are the quality records personnel trained in their jobs?

    a. Do they have effective or ineffective work methods?

    b. Are they viewed as an assistance or as a hindrance to the quality function?

20. Are quality records duplicated and maintained in various departments?

    a. How prevalent is this? Why is this done?

    b. How much duplication is necessary?

    c. How much is it costing the organization?

Records-Related Questions Commonly Posed by Quality Auditors

Q9001-1994

4.5—Document and Data Control

NOTE: Questions about document control records permeate each of the sections of the ISO standards.

1. Do you have a document control procedure? Show it to me.

2. How do you ensure that documents are reviewed and approved before they are issued?

3. How do you handle controlled documents?

4. Where is the master list of documents? How do you know that this is current? How is it kept current?

5. Can you tell me all of the documents that John Smith has?

6. How do you ensure that all of the recipients have the latest revision?

7. How do you know that operators have read the documents?

8. What prevents people from making copies of controlled documents?

9. How do you determine who the recipients of documents should be?

10. How do you know that previous revision documents are not retained or being circulated?

11. How do recipients know which portions of a document have been revised when they receive a new revision?

12. How do you handle changes to controlled documents?

13. How long are documents allowed to remain valid before they are reviewed for currency? Do they remain valid indefinitely?

14. If I ask Donna Brown for the documents in her possession, will they correspond with your master list?

15. If a document must be customer-approved, how is this handled? How are customers notified of any changes made to documents that must be approved by them?

16. How do you ensure that only valid documents are being utilized?

17. How do you prevent unauthorized changes to documents?

18. Who received documents on–(for example, beta quenching)?

19. How long does it take to distribute documents after they have been approved?

4.6—Purchasing

1. How do you select qualified suppliers?

2. Do you have records of

   a. on-site assessment?

   b. evaluation of a supplier's quality system?

   c. evaluation of product samples?

   d. past history with similar supplies?

e. test results of similar supplies?

3. Show me the purchasing records that describe the products ordered from Ajax Chemical Company.

4. How do you know that the material or product you received was what you ordered?

5. What type of paperwork (records) does the subcontractor send to you about the product that was ordered?

6. Where are the industry standards that are referred to in the purchase order? Do you have the latest revisions? How do you know?

7. How do you verify that the material is of the grade that you ordered?

8. When was the shipment from Ajax Chemical Company released for internal use? Who released it? Why was it released?

9. How do you identify incoming material that is unfit for use?

10. What is the record of acceptable materials from Ajax Chemical Company?

11. How do you monitor the quality of incoming materials from different subcontractors?

4.8—Product Identification and Traceability

1. How do you provide material traceability?

2. Here is tube M23, a finished product. Trace back to raw material what happened to result in this product.

3. How is unique product identification maintained?

4. Here is the record of release of lot AJ-4567—incoming raw material. Show me what happened to it, through final product.

4.9—Process Control

1. Can I see the furnace charts for General Electric's (GE's) order?

2. Have the furnace operators received the latest issue documents?

3. Were the operators appropriately trained to perform their jobs?

4. How do you ensure that the _____ process is in control?

5. How do you qualify your special processes?

6. How are the personnel who work on the special processes qualified?

7. Which equipment is qualified? How is it requalified?

8. Show me the process control charts for _____ .

4.10—Inspection and Testing

1. Can I see the inspection results of material from Ajax Chemical Company's latest shipment?

2. What types of tests were performed on the incoming materials from Ajax Chemical Company?

3. What internal specification were you working to, and how did the results compare to the specification?

4. Who performed the chemical testing?

5. What procedure was used?

6. Where are the industry standards and specifications referred to in this procedure?

7. Against which internal specifications did you conduct your in-process testing? Who checked the results? Who released the material to the next step or process?

8. How do you know that the final product has met specified requirements?

9. Why are the inspectors qualified to release the material?

10. Show me the release records for GE's latest order.

11. What are the criteria for release? How is it determined that the criteria have been met?

12. Who is authorized to release the product for shipment? How is release handled?

4.11—Inspection, Measuring, and Test Equipment

1. Show me your calibration schedule.

2. How was the schedule determined?

3. Do all of the items that must be calibrated appear on this schedule?

4. How is the schedule monitored?

5. Who gets notified when an item is coming up for calibration?

6. Do you have any checks in the system that address passing the calibration due date?

7. Who performs the calibration of _____?

   a. What are their qualifications?

   b. How do they record the results of calibration?

8. Do you have physical evidence on the calibrated items indicating their current calibration status?

9. Do the items that must be calibrated have unique identifiers?

10. What procedures do you have in place for calibration?

11. Are the individuals who use calibrated items trained and qualified to do so?

12. Do you have recognized national or international standards against which the items are calibrated?

13. What do you do if the item is found to be out of calibration?

    a. Show me the documented procedures that explain the actions.

    b. Do you retest or reinspect material that was examined with those items?

14. Show me the calibration results for caliper C1234.

15. Show me the ASTM standard for the test method used for the calibrated item.

16. Must any items that require calibration be stored under special environmental conditions? Show me.

17. How do you control access to these items?

4.13—Nonconforming Product

1. Do you have documented procedures describing how you handle nonconforming product?

2. Do you clearly identify the nonconforming material or product? How do you do that? Show me an example of current nonconforming product or material that is identified like that.

3. What sort of records do you prepare about nonconforming product?

4. How is disposition of nonconforming product handled?

5. How do you notify the appropriate parties when material is nonconforming?

   a. Do you do this verbally? In writing? Show me an example of such notification.

6. Who is authorized to designate material or product as nonconforming?

7. If you decide to repair or rework nonconforming product, do you have records on any reinspection and/or retesting that has been done?

8. Do you review other products that have been designed or processed under the same procedures as the nonconforming product? Where are those records?

9. Have you ever had to recall product? Were you able to do so?

4.14—Corrective and Preventive Action

1. How do you handle customer complaints? Show me the records that prove that investigation of nonconformities has occurred.

2. Do you have a list of the corrective actions that have been taken to prove that they are effective? Or are the nonconformities repetitive and continuing?

3. Do you perform root cause analysis? What methods do you use? What have you determined?

4. Since you indicate in this record that a change was made in the process, show me that the documented procedure has been changed to incorporate it.

5. How soon after the change in the process was the document rewritten and reissued?

4.15—Handling, Storage, Packaging, Preservation, and Delivery

1. This customer specification requires that the material be packed in a certain way. How do you ensure that this is done?

2. Who checks the identification of the packaging before the product is released for shipment?

4.16—Quality Records

1. Do you have a retention schedule for quality records? How were the times determined?

2. Retrieve for me the test results of the latest incoming shipment of powder from Big Bear Company. How do you verify that the results meet the purchase order requirements and the internal specifications for that powder?

3. What methods do you follow to ensure protection of all quality-related records?

4. Where are your quality records stored? If they are in an offsite commercial facility, have you ever visited the facility to ensure that it is providing appropriate protection?

5. How can you be certain that you have gathered all of the processing records on this order?

6. How do you handle changes to final inspection records?

7. How do you back up your quality records?

4.17—Internal Quality Audits

1. Do you have an audit schedule?

2. How frequently is each quality-related area audited?

3. How is the audit team selected?

4. How can you demonstrate that the individuals on audit teams are independent of the area audited?

5. Which audits have been conducted during the past six months?

6. How do you handle the findings?

7. How are corrective actions determined? How are they verified?

8. Are the corrective actions that have been implemented effective?

9. Has management reviewed audit reports and findings? Do you have records of such management reviews?

4.18—Training

1. What sort of training do quality inspectors receive?

2. Has this been documented? Show me the records.

3. How do you determine the kind and amount of training that an individual must receive?

4. Is training offered on quality topics? To whom? How often?

5. Since the operator must be qualified to work on this special process, show me his or her qualification records.

6. A license is required to perform this job function. Do you have a copy of Adam Brown's license in a file?

7. What are the qualifications of Hilda Adams, the instructor for the training course on how to use these calibrated instruments?

APPENDIX C

Companies Providing Products and Services for Electronic Engineering Document Management Systems

Access Corporation
1011 Glendale-Milford Road
Cincinnati, Ohio 45215
Phone: 513-782-8633
Fax: 513-782-8363
Access is a software products and services firm, specializing in technical document management systems. Its products include the following: (1) EDICS (Engineering Document Image Control System), a database application for managing documents and engineering-related information. EDICS handles both text and A-through E-size drawings, whether scanned or electronically imported, (2) EDICS/RM, the Release Management extension of EDICS, which supports the business process of releasing a new document revision, and (3) EDICS-ECC, the Electronic Change Control extension of EDICS, which automates drawing and document change control.

ArborText, Inc.
1000 Victors Way
Suite 400
Ann Arbor, Michigan 48108-2700
Phone: 313-996-3566
Fax: 313-996-3573
ArborText provides SGML-based (Standardized General Markup Language) electronic software and consulting services. Its products include *ADEPT* series, SGML Publisher, SGML Editor, and DOCUMENT ARCHITECT. In 1993 ArborText won the Seybold Award for Excellence for its DOCUMENT ARCHITECT product. Its consultants work with systems integrators to help organizations implement SGML-based information solutions.

Auto-trol Technology
12500 North Washington Street
Denver, Colorado 80241-2400
Phone: 303-452-4919
Fax: 303-252-2249
Auto-trol Technology is a systems integrator. It has recently introduced CENTRA 2000, a database system for configuration management, change management, document management, and workflow. It focuses on technical documentation with features for managing the textual, artwork, and data components of technical manuals.

Cimage Corporation
3885 Research Park Drive
Ann Arbor, Michigan 48108
Phone: 313-761-6550
Fax: 313-761-6551
Cimage develops and markets products that manage the entire document control process, from data capture and storage to document revision, control, and distribution. Its Document Manager provides comprehensive features including security and access control, storage management, revision handling, markup management, check-in and check-out, and document linking, so that related documents or data can be linked to graphical objects on a

document. Cimage's customers include Pacific Bell, Mobil Oil, Ford Motor Company, The Gillette Company, and others.

CIMLINC
1222 Hamilton Parkway
Itasca, Illinois 60143-1138
Phone: 708-250-0090
Fax: 708-250-8513
CIMLINC develops and markets a software called LINKAGE which facilitates the reengineering and integration of manufacturing process information flow. LINKAGE is based on a true compound document structure, in that it can display text, vector, raster, and video images on the same page. It can also display full-motion video and audio. It addresses the interfaces between engineering and production, with a focus on work instructions and shop packets in metalworking, electronics assembly, and other discrete manufacturing processes. (See chapter 6 for a fuller description of LINKAGE capabilities.)

CMstat Corporation
5755 Oberlin Drive
Suite 110
San Diego, California 92121
Phone: 619-552-6600
Fax: 619-546-1473
CMstat is a Configuration Management and Product Data Management System that produces, identifies, documents, records, controls, and reports the functional characteristics and physical configuration baselines of both hardware and software throughout the design-to-ship product life cycle. The CMstat System places a heavy emphasis on configuration management concepts and rules.

CSC Consulting
One University Office Park
Fourth Floor
Waltham, Massachusetts 02154
Phone: 617-899-0232
Fax: 617-891-8970

CSC offers services ranging from consulting and the strategic use of information through systems design and development, system integration, and system outsourcing. In the EDMS area, CSC was awarded the $750 million joint CALS contract by the Department of Defense to reengineer and implement technology to completely automate 30,000 users at more than 300 sites.

Database Applications, Inc.
14 Admiralty Place
Redwood City, California 94065
Phone: 415-593-3477
Fax: 415-598-0255
Database Applications' product, CADEXnet, is a management system for engineering and other documents. It manages current and past revisions, controls security and access to the network, keeps an audit trail as each document evolves, handles workflow, provides for electronic approval routing, and manages components within documents.

Electronic Book Technologies
One Richmond Square
Providence, Rhode Island 02906
Phone: 401-421-9550
Fax: 401-421-9551
Electronic Book Technologies' software product, *Dyna*Text, is an electronic book publishing system that accepts ISO 8879 SGML text directly, allowing in-house publication groups to turn existing reference documentation into electronic books. It has two major components: an Indexer, which accepts source material in a variety of standard formats, and a Browser, which allows users to read, query, and annotate the resulting electronic books over a network or on a standalone personal computer.

FORMTEK, Inc.
661 Andersen Drive
Pittsburgh, Pennsylvania 15220
Phone: 412-937-4900
Fax: 412-937-4946

FORMTEK, a Lockheed company, is a developer and integrator of enterprise-wide information management systems. Its various products allow organizations to manage, capture, store, manipulate, and distribute their engineering documents, and to integrate raster, vector, text, and database information into a single document. The company's products are used for a variety of applications, including integrated product development, shop-floor information access, electronic distribution of information, and process automation.

Hewlett-Packard Company
3404 East Harmony Road
Fort Collins, Colorado 80525
Phone: 1-800-526-1036
Hewlett-Packard's WorkManager coordinates the entire product design and manufacture life cycle, from the initial bill of materials and drawings to the review and approval process, prototype management, and integration of applications. It allows users to manage the content and flow of product development data.

IBM Corporation
ProductManager Development
Department A4W
P.O. Box 2150
Atlanta, Georgia 30301-2150
(No phone number provided)
Fax: 404-835-8032
IBM's ProductManager system helps organizations plan, document, distribute, and track the release of new products and engineering changes while controlling the flow of product and process information. It allows the design department to interact with manufacturing, production, marketing, purchasing, inventory, and all other departments, using the same data. It permits the handling of numerous engineering development, release, and change-related activities in an online, multiple, distribution process.

Image Memory Systems, Inc.
6000 Webster Street
Dayton, Ohio 45414-3434

Phone: 513-890-5022
Fax: 513-890-5080
Image Memory Systems provides document conversion services for engineering drawings by placing them on aperture cards and scanning them to optical disk.

Interleaf, Inc.
Prospect Place
9 Hillside Avenue
Waltham, Massachusetts 02154
Phone: 617-290-0710
Fax: 617-290-4943
Interleaf offers software products, consulting, and training services for document management, intelligent electronic document distribution, and standardized document creation.

International Imaging, Inc.
Corporate Office
701 West Foothill Boulevard
Azusa, California 91702
Phone: 818-969-3078
Fax: 818-334-4809
International Imaging provides conversion services for paper and film conversion of any size and type of media. ScanMobiles bring conversion staff and equipment to the customer's facilities when source documents cannot leave the customer's site. International Imaging offers microfilm conversion, microfiche conversion, aperture card conversion, file folder and technical manual conversion, large format drawing and map conversion, OCR and text conversion, document preparation, indexing, and image enhancement.

Keyfile Corporation
22 Cotton Road
Nashua, New Hampshire 03063
Phone: 603-883-3800
Fax: 603-889-9259
Keyfile's Integrated Document Management software is designed to create, handle, and maintain technical documents (CAD,

scanned-in drawings, and text). It integrates the document handling features found in imaging, workflow, markup, text retrieval, and other document management software. Its Windows-based software offers viewing of CAD drawings in native formats, content-based keyword searches, and automatic tracking and routing of documents and tasks.

Metaphase Technology, Inc.
4201 Lexington Avenue North
Arden Hills, Minnesota 55126-6198
Phone: 612-482-4309
(No fax number available)
Metaphase 1.0 is a suite of products and technologies designed to address the product data management problem. It encompasses applications frameworks, data management, process management, image services, and product structure/configuration management. Metaphase 1.0 is used primarily in the product design and manufacturing markets to track and manage application data.

NMT Corporation
2004 Kramer Street
P.O. Box 2287
La Crosse, Wisconsin 54602-2287
Phone: 608-781-0850
Fax: 608-781-3883
NMT specializes in graphics distribution for engineering communities. It offers a variety of services: (1) software—for distributing, viewing, and printing computer-aided design (CAD) and raster data on workstations and personal computers, (2) scanning services—for converting paper documents and aperture card images to an electronic format, (3) microfilming services—for transferring CAD data to film for a first-generation image or transferring source document to aperture card or microfiche formats, and (4) distribution services—diazo duplicate cards and paper prints for utilities and multisite manufacturers.

NOVASOFT Systems, Inc.
8 New England Executive Park
Burlington, Massachusetts 01803

Phone: 617-221-0300
Fax: 617-221-0465
NOVASOFT offers a suite of document management software that provides workflow management, markup applications, document creation, and editing of scanned raster images to provide capability in concurrent engineering and configuration management.

Optigraphics Corporation
2626 Cole Avenue
Suite 400
Dallas, Texas 75204
Phone: 214-528-5473
Fax: 214-528-5552
Optigraphics designs and manufactures technical document management systems, subsystems, and products. Among the many functions provided by its products are view, markup, edit, revise, print, scan, convert, object storage, and folder management.

Sherpa Corporation
Corporate Headquarters
611 River Oaks Parkway
San Jose, California 95134
Phone: 408-433-0455
FAx: 408-943-9507
The Sherpa Product Information Management System manages, controls, and automates the processes employed to create, review, release, and change product information. The product information can include CAD files, parts and bills of material information, engineering documents, vendor data, work instructions, or any other data or files that describe products. It permits the automatic electronic notification and sign-off of engineering and manufacturing documents, engineering changes, and other controlled information.

Southern Electric International—SEI
100 Ashford Center North
Atlanta, Georgia 30338
Phone: 404-261-4700
Fax: 404-393-9871

The SEI NORMS product is a document control and records management system designed to handle large volumes of both revision-oriented and one-time-reference documents. It controls documents regardless of their media source and supports imaging (raster and vector), paper, film, fiche, and electronic text formats.

Station Software
P.O. Box 816
Kennett Square, Pennsylvania 19348
Phone: 215-444-4061
Fax: 215-444-1777
Station Software offers Sightseer, an information retrieval system for engineering, manufacturing, and management personnel. Users can access, view, measure, print, and redline current engineering drawings directly from the company's CAD system, as well as review associated database records and related documentation from personal computers and workstations.

Universal Systems, Inc.—USI
4510 Daly Drive
Suite 400
Chantilly, Virginia 22021
Phone: 703-803-7550
Fax: 703-803-8130
USI's DOCUMETRIX 3000 platform is an engineering document management system that supports compound document formats including vector (CAD), word processing files, spreadsheets, raster images, and electronic forms. Its functionality supports document scanning and importing (A- through E-size in various source media and formats), indexing (manual or automated), OCR/ICR, quality assurance, archiving, electronic distribution, printing, faxing, searching through database indexing or full text retrieval, workflow processing, document routing and approval, and electronic signature.

The van der Roest Group, Inc.
1535 E. 17th Street
Suite N
Santa Ana, California 92701

Phone: 714-542-2201
Fax: 714-543-4931
The DMS Pro product is a document management system for engineering and manufacturing environments that integrates and tracks multiple document types through their entire life cycle. It prevents changes to the wrong drawings, provides accurate version control, and automatically logs and updates all document activities. It includes workflow, security, capabilities for markup, and electronic routing.

Articles About Electronic Engineering Document Management Systems

Article 1: Document Management Benefits Small Firms, Too
Article 2: Integrating Information for Manufacturing Quality
Article 3: Document Management in Manufacturing
Article 4: Gillette Goes from "Nightmare" to On-Line Control

Article 1

The following article has been reprinted with permission from *IMC Journal* 29 (January/February 1993).

Document Management Benefits Small Firms, Too
by Jim Dick, President
Cimage North America

With companies around the world pushing technology forward at a dizzying pace, the specter of new challenge and opportunity in managing this technology has emerged. Quite simply, as new technical frontiers are forged, there are big problems just keeping track of project status and the latest production revisions.

Traditionally, large companies pioneered techniques for managing vast quantities of data, because their competitiveness, and, indeed, their continuing existence, has depended on it. If you look inside any larger, technology-driven company today, you'll find a sophisticated document management system. Industries like oil and gas, utilities, transportation, and manufacturing have been able to advance rapidly only because of their ability to manage and efficiently distribute their proprietary technical information internally. The application of this technical information singularly differentiates the most successful firms in the marketplace.

Modern computer-based document management has brought forth a framework of desirable capabilities for managing technical information.

1. Ability to input media of all types—drawings of any format and medium, CAD data, textual documents, even video and voice "documents"

2. Ability to store data in multiple locations according to convenience

3. Ability to instantly retrieve desired data from anywhere in the organization without knowing its location or hierarchy

4. Ability to structure an efficient revision control process that can reduce change-cycle time to hours or even minutes

5. Ability to organize data in workflow units, by project, or by team so all related data is always current and immediately available, and communications are instantaneous

The science of data and document management has advanced to the point where companies like Cimage are focused exclusively on providing state-of-the-art solutions for these issues. While we are now used to seeing automated document management systems in large companies, smaller companies are beginning to recognize that the same resource can revolutionize their businesses as well.

I view the fax machine as an example of how a technology has completely changed the way we all do business. Ten years ago, a fax machine was a business luxury. And there weren't many companies you could send a fax to. Today you'll find a fax machine in virtually every business, anywhere in the world. How did we ever get along without this marvelous invention? I believe that document management is on the threshold of driving a similar revolution in the way companies operate.

Principally because of the perceived cost, small- to mid-sized companies have sometimes felt that document management systems are unsuited to their enterprises. Certainly, if you make an investment in technology, you must be able to justify the expense directly, and you also want to improve the efficiency, and, hence, the productivity of your organization.

What size does a company need to be to justify a document management system? Larger companies have reported that it costs more than $1,000 to process a typical document change. This means a technical organization making 1000 changes a year could afford to spend $1 million on a document management system, and would recover the cost in only one year!

Yet this simple payback analysis ignores most of the immense intangible benefits a document management system provides. These benefits are of great value to a company of any size but are difficult to quantify. How much value is there in ensuring that people never again work with out-of-date prints? What are the savings from people being able to get the prints they need in minutes instead of having to wait hours or days? What are the savings when an engineer can instantly pull a document up on his or her PC to check a detail, rather than having to request a hard copy print? What are the increased revenues and profits resulting from a streamlined change control process that lets you get new products to market much more quickly, and error-free? All these benefits and more can be obtained by most firms for far less than the $1 million mentioned earlier.

Most technical firms already have a substantial investment in computers and networks. Thus they already have in place hardware that is fully ready to support document management in addition to the other applications currently served. With the addition of software, they can leverage their investment to reap the benefits of document and workflow management. In this case, the software investment required to service 1000 changes a year may be only $100,000 to $200,000 maximum, as payback times plummet to just one to three months.

What about the organization that has fewer than 1000 changes a year, and fewer than 50 users on the engineering network? Here a small investment in a single-server, multiple-client document management system will produce all the benefits detailed earlier. One of the beauties of even a small system like this is that it can grow virtually infinitely without having to start over.

Technical data and documents are indeed the lifeblood of all our businesses in the 1990s. Companies, large or small, that want to grow and increase their competitiveness are going to have to have a capable system to efficiently manage these documents.

Article 2

The following article has been excerpted with permission from *Quality,* **December 1992, a publication of Chilton Publishing, Capital Cities/ABC, Inc.**

Integrating Information for
Manufacturing Quality
Off-the-shelf technology used to integrate corporate-wide work instructions and SPC
by Michael S. Rudy
Manager, Information Services
ELDEC Corporation, Lynwood, Washington

Many manufacturing companies use SPC. But it is only one of the overall information requirements needed to achieve a competitive advantage. SPC data collection and analysis often have associated work instructions that include reference material such as engineering drawings, bills of material, and downloaded files for test and calibration equipment. These work instructions are different for different sampling points along the manufacturing process. All the associated work instructions in manufacturing must be managed and integrated to meet the challenge of world-class manufacturing.

Sponsoring an ongoing series of improvement projects, EL-DEC Corporation, Lynwood, Washington, a manufacturer of aerospace products and systems, assigned its corporate information services (IS) group to implement a corporate-wide integration of work instructions and SPC, using off-the-shelf technology. Rather than improving and integrating older systems, the IS team chose to standardize on new systems that provide greater capability and easier integration. It was decided that UNIX and X-Windows would be used to deliver the systems throughout ELDEC, including the factory floor. A product data management (PDM) system from Sherpa Corporation, San Jose, California, controls the product and process definition. As different design tools are integrated with PDM, the controlled design information is made available to other disciplines and departments, including manufacturing.

The product structure or bill of material is created within PDM and released, and all documents are assigned to the part that they reference. It is this relationship between parts and documents that organizes the information in the PDM database. At the same time, a data structure is built to organize the work instruction subsystem. The instructions themselves are managed as documents, but they are organized by work center and job step.

The installation of PDM at ELDEC meant that there is one place to manage and release all product-related information. The requirements from manufacturing were to deliver product information to the factory floor in the form of work instructions, and to collect real-time process feedback data. To meet these requirements, ELDEC turned to LINKAGE Multimedia Work Instructions software from CIMLINC, Inc., Itasca, Illinois, and Realtime Quality Management (RQM) from Automated Technology Associates (ATA), Indianapolis, Indiana, for SPC data collection and analysis. LINKAGE serves as the manufacturing interface for information managed in PDM. LINKAGE pulls the bill of material, job steps, engineering and manufacturing drawings, digitized photographs, and raster images from PDM. It displays this information in the LINKAGE forms, which are also controlled by PDM, and delivers it to workers via X-Windows terminals, so they can accurately carry out their assigned tasks. Then, at the designated work steps, LINKAGE initiates RQM and allows workers to call up SPC data entry windows, enter data, and view real-time control charts—all without closing the main work instruction window.

The interaction of this system provides a powerful set of tools for process control, especially in an automated machine shop, notes Mike Oleson, manufacturing manager. "Now we can view our process on-line. Our previous monitoring system was very time-consuming and did not provide real-time feedback to operators," he says. When reviewing a specific machine, Oleson can review individual processes by accessing RQM charts, histograms, and notes of past causes of problems and their fixes. All process notes and measurements are automatically recorded in the corporate database and are immediately available throughout the company. "The data are automatically analyzed and indicate process consistency for key product characteristics. This gives us a way to focus on the process steps that need the most work. We find that we can now budget our time much more effectively," says Oleson.

The benefits have already started accruing with the first implementations. Those areas using RQM have a process visibility never achieved before. The machine shop has carefully documented an achieved payback of less than two years with LINK-AGE. And an immediate benefit of the first PDM usage has been the print-on-demand of engineering drawings. The manufacturing teams control their own work instructions and SPC key characteristics. This effort is proving that it will improve manufacturing yield and reduce manufacturing cycle time.

Article 3

The following article has been excerpted with permission from *Document Management & Windows Imaging*, **2 (September/ October 1992), 36–37.**

Document Management in Manufacturing

In spite of the benefits that document image management has to offer for communication of information for concurrent engineering and manufacturing, the manufacturing industry has been slow in implementing this technology. We believe the members of the National Association of Manufacturers (NAM) may be missing the point about using image management to handle the paperwork in conjunction with all their other computerized systems. This article explores how some manufacturing companies are employing a program called LINKAGE Multimedia Work Instructions software from CIMLINC Incorporated.

Cummins Engine Co.

Cummins is standardizing its manufacturing practices through on-line work instructions routed in a Corporate Computer-Aided

Process Planning (CAPP) system. At Cummins, the factory floor and manufacturing engineers' work instructions are driven by the CAPP system.

General Dynamics Corporation

General Dynamics Corporation, Space Systems Division's problem is to take design information and make it available to launch site users who can't afford to spend many hours a day learning to use a software package. "There are always engineering issues that come up . . . . Whether or not we are going to launch depends on how quickly those issues get resolved. The answers have to be timely and accurate," comments Winston Armstrong, manager of CAED.

The project, called Integrated Smart Schematics (ISS), covers both the hydraulic and pneumatic valves, their electromechanical actuators, all the electronic controls, and the wiring harnesses. General Dynamic's objectives for ISS include

- On-line, real-time design and analysis

- Efficient review and communication for other groups that review system data

- Fast, accurate fault isolation in launch operations (five-second paging)

- Electronic document control (error-checking, configuration, and release) for avionics and fluid-systems parts data

- User-definable GUIs

The key to ISS's fast response is the View & Markup Tool (VMT), which allows rapid access to all CAD drawings associated with either the mechanical or the electrical systems, using either of those engineering schematics as its starting point. Developed with LINKAGE, the hypermedia relationships between schematics and all their underlying information, plus the links between hydraulic and electrical schematics, is the heart of ISS. "Most importantly, hypermedia works with our mechanical CAD and electrical CAD drawings in their (native) vector formats," reports Timothy Brown, a Space Systems senior engineer.

United Technologies Corp.

At the Hamilton Standard Division of United Technologies Corp. in Colorado Springs, Colorado, LINKAGE is being used as the information gathering system for an all-new electronics assembly factory. LINKAGE is the platform on which the manufacturing engineering applications, which include computer-aided process planning and factory-floor data collection, have been built. All applications have a common graphical user interface. Information is generated both electronically (on-line) and on paper, as each work team chooses. The plant is considered "paper sparse" rather than "paperless."

Key documents sent to the factory floor include a Process Parts List, a Summary of Operations, and Operations sheets. These documents are created from the engineering definition of the part which is sent to Colorado Springs from Hamilton Standard's product-engineering which is based on a mainframe in Windsor Locks, Connecticut.

Article 4

The following article has been excerpted with permission from *Managing Automation* **8 (August 1993), a publication of Thomas Publishing, 57.**

Gillette Goes From "Nightmare" to On-Line Control
by George Schultz

Effective management of some 250,000 diverse engineering and technical documents is a tall order for any company. But when The Gillette Company (Boston, Massachusetts) tried to control that many records, from multiple divisions at locations throughout the world, the maker of shaving products, small appliances, and writing instruments knew that it needed help. Simply managing that volume—much less ensuring prompt access to users—was becoming an impossible challenge without automated handling. But now the 250,000 documents are going on-line (103,000 are already there). Already, numerous benefits are being realized.

For example, authorized Gillette personnel can instantly retrieve the latest document revision of every part in a product or subassembly. And whether they are in Boston or Berlin, these employees can view the revisions right on their PCs or CAD work-stations. A high-speed laser printer provides hard copies to the user in various formats, where and when they are needed. Document control and distribution is electronic now—virtually paperless and filmless.

Jay Jellison, manager of the document center in Gillette's North Atlantic Group, explained that the company mated the Document Manager software from Cimage Group (Ann Arbor, Michigan) to Gillette's existing DEC VAX-based bill of materials system. Cimage's sophisticated, network-based system manages and communicates the huge volumes of manually or electronically created drawings, film-based information, and CAD data across multiple sites and different computing systems. Users can retrieve related drawings and documents even without knowing their hierarchy or their location. No longer will active technical documents in paper form have to be passed desk to desk among engineers, designers, and shop managers.

"We're moving rapidly toward having all of our document management, from creation and input through worldwide distribution, under the control of the Cimage system," reports Gillette's document center manager. The procedure is being expanded at the Boston headquarters. About 20 people are on-line there, most of them engineers, and the system is being expanded to the mechanical shops at approximately 20 locations.

Implementation started overseas in Berlin, Germany, and Reading, England, then proceeded to other Gillette facilities worldwide. Connection with Boston is via dedicated telecommunications lines. "And in operation, the system is effectively transparent [to users]," declares Jellison.

Records Retention:
Selective Destruction of Records

From Donald S. Skupsky, JD, CRM, *Recordkeeping Requirements* (Denver, Col.: Information Requirements Clearinghouse, 1994), 4–5. Excerpted with permission.

Clara Carlucci and others (plaintiffs) initiated a lawsuit in 1978 to recover damages resulting from the deaths of three men who perished in the crash of a Piper Cheyenne II at Shannon, Ireland, in 1976. The plaintiffs alleged various design defects which caused the pilot to lose control and crash.

The plaintiff, to prepare the case, subpoenaed various documents from Piper Aircraft Corporation (defendant) relative to the design and testing of the aircraft. Despite repeated requests by both the plaintiff and the judge, Piper failed to provide the plaintiffs with the information. The judge appointed a Special Master in 1983 to review the discovery process and determine why the appropriate records had not been provided to the plaintiff.

Two employees in the Flight Test Department told the Special Master that they, at the request of their supervisor, had selectively "purged" hundreds of records that might be "detrimental" to Piper in future lawsuits. Piper claimed that these records were destroyed under document retention procedures but offered no evidence demonstrating that these procedures were followed by its employees.

William J. Campbell, Senior District Judge, after reviewing the evidence, entered a default judgment against Piper Aircraft Corporation in the amount of $10 million because of the selective destruction of records, without even considering the merits of the case.

> I conclude that the defendant engaged in a practice of destroying engineering documents with the intention of preventing them from being produced in law suits. Furthermore, I find that this practice continued after the commencement of this law suit and that documents relevant to this law suit were intentionally destroyed . . . .
>
> I am not holding that the good faith disposal of documents pursuant to a bona fide, consistent and reasonable document retention policy cannot be a valid justification for failure to produce documents in discovery. That issue never crystallized in this case because Piper has utterly failed to provide credible evidence that such a policy or practice existed . . . .
>
> The policy of resolving law suits under merit must yield when a party has intentionally prevented the fair adjudication of the case. By deliberately destroying documents, the defendant has eliminated plaintiff's right to have their case decided on the merits. Accordingly, the entry of a default is the only means of effectively sanctioning the defendant and remedying the wrong.

The Carlucci case serves as a milestone decision about the destruction of records. The courts will not tolerate the selective destruction of records in anticipation of litigation, especially after litigation starts. While we can be guided by judicial attitudes, it is sad that the ax fell on Piper for the same practice of selective destruction or purging of records followed by most organizations in the United States. Most of us selectively destroy records as part of a "search and destroy mission" without the guidance of a proper record retention program.

Upon closer review of this case, the facts do not support a conclusion that Piper did anything wrong; they only support the conclusion that what Piper did "looked wrong." Piper did have a records retention program, although it did not establish this point in court, and did maintain the official company set of flight test records in the Engineering Department. The records destroyed in the Flight Test Department consisted of valueless, duplicate copies held only in the event test results became lost when sent back to the Engineering Department (the department requesting the tests).

Piper's major indiscretion was its inability to document to the court that records were destroyed in the regular course of business under an approved records retention schedule and that records maintained in the Flight Test Department were valueless duplicate copies that could have been appropriately destroyed at any time. Instead, their so-called "program" appeared to the court as a "sham" and the judge never looked beyond it to the merits of the case.

APPENDIX F

The Importance of Records Protection

From Patricia M. Fernberg, "Staying in Business Despite the Worst," *Managing Office Technology* 39 (February 1994), 10–12. Excerpted with permission.

Whether it's a massive snowstorm crippling the East, the World Trade Center bombings, flooding in the Midwest, the L.A. riots, flu epidemics, or work stoppages, people are affected individually in both their business and private lives. The key to who survives and thrives despite adversity and who fails isn't luck—it's planning.

Disaster planning isn't so much about planning to deal with interruptions; it's planning to keep your business running without interruptions. As Robert Hogan, vice president of the Security Services Division of Banker's Trust Corporation (New York) told his audience at a Cleveland, Ohio, seminar on disaster recovery (sponsored by the Red Cross), "An emergency is an event that threatens to interfere seriously with the organization's ability to maintain critical operations. The objective of your emergency plan is to maintain critical operations as close to normal as possible."

Dean Witter Reynolds' disaster recovery plan had to deal with the most random of crises: a terrorist bombing in its World Trade Center offices on February 26, 1992. The car bomb that detonated in the Center's underground garage at 12:18 P.M. that Friday could have devastated not only Dean Witter Reynolds' ability to serve its clients but also the extensive records it is required by law to maintain. But it didn't. The firm's records management disaster recovery plan responded perfectly.

W. Gerard McKernan, records manager at Dean Witter Reynolds, explains, "When the program was instituted, the charge to the newly formed Records Management Department was to develop and maintain control over the firm's inactive records, ensuring compliance to the limits outlined by the various regulatory agencies and Dean Witter's operational requirements. This necessitated developing procedures and controls that would be applied in both normal operating conditions and those which were much less than ideal. With transactions that could range anywhere from a couple of hundred dollars to a couple of hundred thousand dollars, it was imperative that all necessary precautions be taken to ensure the integrity of our records."

The firm elected to employ a mix of offsite commercial records storage and computer and manual systems with backup for 100 percent accuracy in storing and retrieving inactive records. Inactive hard copy and microform records are secured in a commercial warehouse 120 miles away from the Manhattan offices and were unscathed by the bomb. Back in Dean Witter's offices, McKernan recalls, "Access to our department's PCs and computerized records management system was limited, though we did have access via telephone to the warehouse and its computerized inventory system. That enabled us to provide uninterrupted service to the more than 230 file areas we maintain."

Clients contacted the records management staff at their homes in the first days after the bombing. They, in turn, contacted the offsite warehouse to request services, and warehouse staff delivered the records to the clients before 9 A.M. on the next business day. By layering the levels of records management, the limited computer access was augmented with access to vendors' programs to ensure Dean Witter records management people complete control of records in transit.

McKernan points out that the Records Management Department's contingency plans allowed it to serve its clients uninterrupted between the time of the bombing and the department's return to its Tower offices. "The records program survived this disaster because of the original concepts upon which Dean Witter's records management program was founded, as well as the basic tenets of good management: simplicity, uniformity, education, and discipline," he says.

"The program actually is simple. There is just so much you can do with a box; the same rules apply to everyone, from senior management to mailroom personnel; changes in personnel necessitate retraining of records coordinators (as needed). Discipline is achieved through centralizing the records function in the Records Management Unit. All requests for warehouse records management services *must* come from the unit."

The Records Management Department's disaster recovery plan has been fine-tuned since the bombing, but the changes are minor. Forms samples, retention schedules, operating manuals, user lists, and box counts by file area—the tools needed to run the program—are stored at the warehouse but can be retrieved quickly, when needed. Worst-case scenarios for the department have been developed and are reviewed with department personnel quarterly. Despite the fact that the World Trade Center disaster is unusual, McKernan is convinced that his departmental operations were sustained by its disaster recovery plan. "It worked like clockwork," he says proudly.

Examples of Quality Records from Organizations That Have Successfully Passed ISO Registration

Section 1: Records from Esco Corporation, Portland, Oregon
Section 2: Records from EG&G Instruments Chandler, Tulsa, Oklahoma
Section 3: Records from The Dee Howard Company, San Antonio, Texas
Section 4: Records from FSSL, Inc., Sugar Land, Texas

Section 1
The following quality records have been provided with the courtesy of Esco Corporation, Portland, Oregon. They are reprinted with permission.

MANUFACTURING REQUEST: ☐ PATTERN QUOTE ☐ FOUNDRY ESTIMATE

MFG. QUOTE No. 7933

| PRODUCT ADMIN. (EXT) | CUSTOMER | DIV. QUOTE NO. | DATE SUBMITTED | DATE WANTED | ECN | PATT. QUOTE DATE |
| ( ) | | | | | | |

LAB REPORT REQ'D ☐ YES ☐ NO MPO REQ'D ☐ YES ☐ NO DIMENSIONAL CHECK SHEETS REQ'D ☐ YES ☐ NO CUSTOMER MACHINING ☐ ROUGH ☐ FINISH

PATTERN OWNER ☐ ESCO ☐ CUSTOMER ☐ GOV'T STORED: ☐ ESCO ☐ CUSTOMER REQ'D HARDNESS _____

| ESCO PATTERN NO. | PART NO. | PROD. CODE | ACCT. NO | COST CTR | ITEM DESCRIPTION | DRAWING NO./REV. |

| ALLOY | EST ANNUAL USAGE | | TARGET COST | CASTING COST DIRECT | CASTING COST TRANSFER | NO. ENG. EST NO |

GENERAL INSTRUCTIONS

PATT. DELIVERY REQUIRED FROM FPT RELEASE DATE _____ WKS

PATTERN DESCRIPTION

DESCRIPTION — MAT'L, SIZE, TYPE, KIND, GRADE				CORES		
				GANG #/CAST'G	SAND TYPE	SAND WT.
FLASK SIZE _____ X _____						
COPE/DRAG HT. _____ / _____						
MOLD STA.						
POUR LOC.						
CASTINGS/MOLD						
EST. CL. WT./CAST'G.						
EST. PR. WT./MOLD						
CHILLS						
MOLD'G SAND						
RIGGING						

BY _____ % of EXT. _____ RELEASED BY MFG

FOR CONST. _____ TRIAL CODE _____
☐ DATA BASE CHANGE REQ'D

FINISHING PROCESSES

RISERS	GRINDING	PRESS
☐ BRK OFF	☐ STAND	FIXTURES
☐ BURN	☐ BENCH	HEAT TREATMENTS:
☐ AIR ARC	☐ FLOOR	BRR
☐ SAW	☐ FITTERS	ARR
CLEANING	WELD	POST W.
☐ ROTO BLT	☐ STICK	MACHINING ESCO VENDOR
☐ SAND BLT	☐ WIRE	☐ 1st STAGE ☐ ☐
☐ WHEELABT	☐ SPEC. MAT'L	☐ 2nd STAGE ☐ ☐
☐ RATTLE		

CASTING QUALITY

DIMENSIONAL | Surface

☐ ESCO STANDARD QUALITY

ACCEPTANCE STD'S
☐ SFSA GRADE _____
☐ DWG. TOLERANCES
☐ DIVISION
☐ SUFF. STOCK TO MACH.
☐ CUSTOMER APPROVAL
☐ PER PATTERN

☐ BRINELL _____
☐ MSS-SP55
☐ SIS _____

EXTENT
☐ NONE REQ'D
☐ MII
☐ 100% DWG
☐ PER MARKED DWG
TEST'G FREQ'Y

SURFACE ☐ MII
☐ MT ☐ PT ☐ PER BELOW
☐ NONE ☐ 100% ☐ PER MARKED DWG
PROC.
ACCEPT.
TEST'G FREQ'Y

INTERNAL
RT ☐ NONE ☐ 100% ☐ PER MARKED DWG
PROC.
ACCEPT.
UT ☐ NONE ☐ 100% ☐ PER MARKED DWG
PROC.
ACCEPT.
TEST'G FREQ'Y

COMMENTS:

| PATTERN SHOP | PATT. PRICE | DELIVERY | PATT. PRICE | P/MS/PO NO. | SALES ORDER NO. | REQUISITION SIGNATURE/DATE | AUTHORIZING SIGNATURE |

ENGINEERING CHANGE NOTICE
PORTLAND, OREGON

ITEM
ISSUE HISTORY

ECN NUMBER

SERIAL NO. REQUIRED

MFG SOURCE	ITEM I.D.	REF. I.D. NO.	DRAWING	REV.	ITEM OR LIST NAME	DESCRIPTION OF CHANGE	OBS CODE

1 2 3 4 5 6 7 8 9 10 11 12 13 14 15 16 17 18 19 20 21 22 23 24 25 26 27 28 29 30

REASON

WHERE APPLICABLE
PATTERN FALSIFICATION ☐ PATTERN REVISION ☐

TYPE OF CHANGE

☐ PERMANENT TO BASIC PATTERN

☐ NEW VARIATION NOT PERM. TO BASIC PATTERN

REF. PAR.

REF. RFEA

REQUESTED BY	DESIGN ENGINEER	PRODUCTION ADMIN.	APPROVED BY	E.D.C.	RELEASE	DWGS.	PAGE
	INITIALS	DATE	INITIALS	DATE	INITIALS	DATE	INITIALS	DATE	INITIALS	DATE	ECN NUMBER	

32-3046-B-91

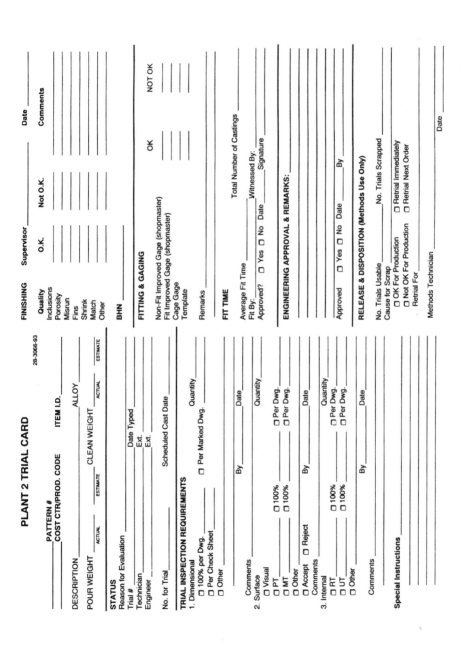

PLANT 2 TRIAL CARD

28-3066-93

PATTERN #
COST CTR/PROD. CODE   ITEM I.D.

DESCRIPTION   ALLOY
POUR WEIGHT   CLEAN WEIGHT
          ACTUAL   ESTIMATE   ACTUAL   ESTIMATE

STATUS
Reason for Evaluation
Trial #   Date Typed
Technician   Ext.
Engineer   Ext.

No. for Trial   Scheduled Cast Date

TRIAL INSPECTION REQUIREMENTS
1. Dimensional   □ Per Marked Dwg.   Quantity
   □ 100% per Dwg.
   □ Per Check Sheet
   □ Other
                    By   Date
Comments
2. Surface   Quantity
   □ Visual
   □ PT   □ 100%   □ Per Dwg.
   □ MT   □ 100%   □ Per Dwg.
   □ Other
   □ Accept □ Reject   By   Date
Comments
3. Internal   Quantity
   □ RT   □ 100%   □ Per Dwg.
   □ UT   □ 100%   □ Per Dwg.
   □ Other
                    By   Date
Comments

Special Instructions

FINISHING   Supervisor   Date

Quality   O.K.   Not O.K.   Comments
Inclusions
Porosity
Misrun
Fins
Shrink
Match
Other

BHN

FITTING & GAGING
                                    OK   NOT OK
Non-Fit Improved Gage (shopmaster)
Fit Improved Gage (shopmaster)
Cage Gage
Template
Remarks

FIT TIME
Average Fit Time   Total Number of Castings
Fit By: Witnessed By:
Approved? □ Yes □ No Date   Signature

ENGINEERING APPROVAL & REMARKS:

Approved □ Yes □ No Date   By

RELEASE & DISPOSITION (Methods Use Only)
No. Trials Usable   No. Trials Scrapped
Cause for Scrap
   □ OK For Production   □ Retrial Immediately
   □ Not OK For Production   □ Retrial Next Order
   Retrial For

Methods Technician   Date

PATTERN # _____ ALLOY _____

CORE EQUIPMENT

Dwg. # _____ Inspected By _____

Equip. Made By □ Altered By □ Shop. □

Equip. Wood □ Metal □ Plastic □ Shell □ Urethane □ Loose □ Other □

COREMAKING

Box No.	Loc./Mach.	Description	Cav/Box	Cores/Casting	Paste	Sand Type	Est. Wt.	Act. Wt.	Type Coats	Drying Inst.	Hooks	Rods	Lightener

(Wash: Type Coats / Drying Inst.)

Supervisor: _____
Date: _____
Comments: _____

Special Instructions/Comments _____

PATTERN EQUIPMENT

Shop _____ Inspected By _____

Due Date _____

Dwg. # _____

□ Cope Drag Boards   □ Other
□ Anti-Shift Feature
□ Loose w/Ramup   □ Loose w/o Ramup   □ Insert

RISERING

Type	#	Dia Ø	Ht. From P/L	Slv Ht.	Cope/Drag Pad	Burn	Removal Arc	B/O

GATING

Instructions/Comments _____

MOLDING   Station # _____

Flask Size _____ x _____ Cope Ht. _____ Drag Ht. _____
Castings/Mold _____ Backing Sand _____
Facing Sand _____
Facing Thickness: Cope _____ Drag _____
Mold Wash: _____ No. Coats _____
Drying Instructions _____
Mold Hardness _____
Chills: □ Stock   □ Special   □ Not Required
Special Instructions/Comments _____

Molding Witness Required: □ Yes   □ No
Call: _____ ext. _____

	OK	not OK	Comments
Molding	□	□	
Core Fit	□	□	
Close Up	□	□	

By _____ Date _____

POURING & SHAKEOUT

Aim Pour Temp. _____ Actual Temp. _____ Heat No. _____ Pour Time _____
□ Single Pour   □ Double Pour   □ Btm.   □ Lip
Instructions/Comments: _____

ESCO CORPORATION

ISO 9002 WORK INSTRUCTIONS

DISTRIBUTION/REVISION CONTROL LIST

DATE: _____

W.I.NO.	TITLE	REVISION	ASSIGNED TO

PAGE 1 OF 1

DEPT.:
REV. DATE:

WORK INSTRUCTIONS

TITLE: _____

REVIEWED AND AUTHORIZED BY: _____

CONTROL RESPONSIBILITY: _____

1.

RECORDS KEPT (IF ANY):_____

OPERATOR TRAINING REQUIREMENTS:_____

PROCEDURE NO.	PAGE #1 OF
REV. A	DATE OF ISSUE:

TITLE:

SCOPE:

PURPOSE:

REFERENCES:

PERSON(S) RESPONSIBLE:

PROCEDURE

WRITTEN BY: _____ **AUTHORIZED BY:** _____
(NAME) **QUALITY ASSURANCE**

PROCEDURE NO.	REVISION DATE AND DEFINITION LOG

REVISION DATE   REASON FOR REVISION

                     ORIGINAL ISSUE

ESCO INSTRUMENT & GAGE CALIBRATION RECORD

Form 89-03081-76

DATE	RESULTS	INSP.	DATE	RESULTS	INSP.

MFG: _____   RANGE _____   ITEM _____   FREQUENCY _____   LOC. _____

TOL: _____   PROCEDURE: CA

ESCO

MII CHANGE REQUEST

A. **MII NO.** _____

B. **SECTION:**

C. **CHANGE REQUESTED:**

D. **REASON FOR CHANGE:**

E. **COST IMPACT COMMENTS:**

_____
_____
_____

F. **CHANGE REQUESTED BY:** _____ **DATE:** _____

G. **REVIEWED BY:** _____ **DATE:** _____

H. **COMMENTS:** _____
_____
_____

I. **DISAPPROVED:** ☐

J. **APPROVED:** ☐ _____ **DATE:** _____

EFFECTIVE:

EXPIRES:

ESCO CORPORATION

MII PROCEDURAL DEVIATION

MII NO.:   ITEM:

DESCRIPTION:

DEVIATION REQUEST

REASON FOR DEVIATION

DEVIATION REQUESTED BY:

DATE:

APPROVED BY

_____ DATE: _____

ElCO CORPORATION
QUALITY ASSURANCE DEPT.

DISPOSITION NOTICE
NO. 8279

TO: _____

PAGE _____ OF _____ DATE: _____

_____

DISCREPANCY REPORT NO. _____

_____

_____   _____

MANUFACTURING ORDER	CUST. P.O. NO.	ITEM/PATTERN NO.	HT. NO.

DISPOSITION

INSPECTION NECESSARY:

COPIES OF THIS REPORT TO:

☐ QA MANAGER   ☐ FINISHING FOREMAN
☐ QAD   ☐ GENERAL FOREMAN
☐ CUSTOM CASTINGS   ☐ OTHER _____
☐ PURCHASING DEPT.   ☐ OTHER _____
☐ MFG. ENGINEER   ☐ OTHER _____

SIGNED X

34-3077-87

DISPOSITION NOTICE

EACO

INSPECTION DEPARTMENT

DISCREPANCY REPORT

No. 2386

To:_____ Item:_____ Ht. No._____

Date:_____ No. Ordered:_____ Lot Size:_____ No. Discrepant:_____

Customer:_____ M.O._____

Vendor:_____ P.O._____

Alloy:_____ Patt./Part No_____ Dwg._____ Rev_____

Discrepancy:_____

Cause:_____

Corrective Action Required   Yes ☐   No ☐ (Respond Within 10 Working Days)._____

Disposition:_____

Copies of This Report To:

___ QA Dept._____

___ Product Supervisor_____

___ Mfg. Engr._____

___ Purchasing_____

___ Corp. QA Mngr._____

___ Inspect. Mngr._____

___ Vendor_____

___ Prod. Control_____

___ Shop Supervisor_____

___ Dispatcher_____

Vendor Insp. P.O. File_____

Other_____

_____
INSPECTOR

_____
Inspection Supervisor

APPROVAL OF DISCREPANCIES AND/OR DISPOSITION MUST BE ACKNOWLEDGED BY RETURN OF COPY SIGNED BY:

_____
Signature

CORRECTIVE ACTION REQUEST   CA# _____

ADDRESSED TO: _____   DATE OF ISSUE: _____

TYPE: QUALITY SYSTEM ☐ PRODUCT QUALITY ☐ CUSTOMER COMPLAINT ☐

STOP PRODUCTION: YES ☐ NO ☐ ALLOY: _____

1. NONCONFORMANCE: PLANT:_____ ISSUED BY: _____

ITEM: _____ PATTERN NO.: _____ HEAT NO._____

_____

_____

_____

_____

2. ROOT CAUSE OF NONCONFORMANCE:

_____

_____

_____

3. CORRECTIVE ACTION TAKEN TO PREVENT REOCCURRENCE:

_____

_____

_____

ANSWERED BY: _____ TITLE: _____ DATE: _____

CAUSE AND CORRECTIVE ACTION RESPONSE TO QA IS REQUIRED
WITHIN 10 WORKING DAYS OF RECEIPT.

4. VERIFICATION OF CORRECTIVE ACTION:

_____

_____

_____

BY: _____ TITLE: _____ DATE: _____

5. APPROVAL: _____ TITLE: _____ DATE: _____

C.A.R. FORM DATE 01/11/93

NO. 3417

REQUEST FOR
ENGINEERING ACTION

ELCO

Form 39-4423-91

AUTHORITY

- ☐ PART CHANGE
- ☐ RECORD CHANGE
- ☐ TEMPORARY DEVIATION

- ☐ URGENT
- ☐ ROUTINE

LOCAL ACTION TAKEN
YES ☐   NO ☐

FROM DEPT./PLANT	DATE	PRODUCT	ITEM IDENTIFICATION

ORIGINATOR

PROBLEM ☐ URGENT ☐ ROUTINE

DEFINE PROBLEM COMPLETELY IN CLEAR AND SIMPLE TERMS. WRITE LEGIBLY. IF APPLICABLE, INCLUDE COSTS. PRINTS, LAYOUTS, LISTS, LETTERS, ETC.

PART DESCRIPTION

RECOMMENDED ACTION: ENTER KNOWN SOLUTIONS OR POSSIBLE ALTERNATIVES.

SUBMITTED BY: _____
PRINT AND INITIAL

AUTHORITY

ACTION TAKEN: ENTER REQUEST TYPE, PRIORITY AND ACTION TAKEN ABOVE. IF APPLICABLE, STATE URGENCY REASON, ACTION AUTHORIZED, DEVIATION EXTENT, EMERGENCY APPROVAL NAME AND DATE, SERIAL NO.

DATE: _____   APPROVED BY: _____
PRINT AND INITIAL

PPES

☐ FORWARDED TO PRODUCT ENGINEERING   ☐ NOT REQUIRED — SEE BELOW   ☐ DISAPPROVED — SEE BELOW

☐ FORWARDED TO MFG. ENGINEERING   DATE _____   BY: _____
PRINT AND INITIAL

ENGINEERING

☐ APPROVED AS REQUESTED   ☐ APPROVED AS STATED BELOW   ☐ DISAPPROVED—SEE BELOW   ☐ UNDER EVALUATION

ECN

DATE: _____   BY: _____
PRINT AND INITIAL

DIMENSIONAL INSPECTION DEPARTMENT

RECEIVING INSPECTION SCHEDULE

DATE: _____

NOTE: List each category of priorities separately with individual headings for each.

P.O. #	VENDOR	ITEM	I.D. P.C.S.	RECEIVING		INSP. NO.	DISPOSITION				COMPL. DATE	DUE DATE	COMMENT
				QTY.	DATE RECEIVED		ACCEPT	REJECT	R.T.V.	HOLD			

EACO INTERNAL AUDIT CHECKLIST

REV. DATE: _____ 5/14/93

SUBJECT: PURCHASER OR GOVERNMENT SUPPLIED MATERIAL (PARA. 4.6)

AREA AUDITED: _____ DATE PERFORMED: _____

AUDIT CONTACT: _____ TITLE: _____

AUDITOR: _____ TITLE: _____

REQUIREMENT	S	U	NA	☐ NONCONFORMANCE ☐ COMMENT
PURCHASER OR GOVERNMENT SUPPLIED MATERIAL (PARA. 4.6) 1. ARE PROCEDURES ESTABLISHED FOR VERIFICATION, STORAGE, AND MAINTENANCE OF CUSTOMER OR GOVERNMENT SUPPLIED MATERIAL? 2. IS ANY LOSS, DAMAGE, OR DETERIORATION OF CUSTOMER OR GOVERNMENT SUPPLIED MATERIAL DOCUMENTED AND REPORTED TO THE OWNER?				

S = SATISFACTORY   U = UNSATISFACTORY   NA = NOT APPLICABLE

PAGE 1 OF 2

EACO

INTERNAL AUDIT CHECKLIST

REV. DATE: _____ 5/14/93

SUBJECT: PURCHASER OR GOVERNMENT SUPPLIED MATERIAL (PARA. 4.6)

AREA AUDITED: _____ DATE PERFORMED: _____

AUDIT CONTACT: _____ TITLE: _____

AUDITOR: _____ TITLE:_____

(EXTRA PAGE FOR ADDITIONAL QUESTIONS)

REQUIREMENT	S	U	NA	☐ NONCONFORMANCE ☐ COMMENT

S = SATISFACTORY   U = UNSATISFACTORY   NA = NOT APPLICABLE

PAGE 2 OF 2

No. _____
(To be assigned by QA)

TRAINING SESSIONS

PERSONNEL: _____
(Area or Dept)

DATE: _____   TIME PERIOD: _____

INSTRUCTOR: _____

SUBJECT: _____

_____

ATTENDANCE:

Name (Print or Type)   Signature

_____   _____

_____   _____

_____   _____

_____   _____

_____   _____

_____   _____

_____   _____

_____   _____

_____   _____

_____   _____

_____   _____

_____   _____

_____   _____

_____   _____

_____   _____

_____   _____

_____   _____

SIGNATURE: _____

SPECIAL TRAINING

DEPARTMENT OR AREA: _____

NAME AND SIGNATURE
OF PERSON BEING TRAINED _____ _____
                            (NAME)   (SIGNATURE)

                        _____DATES_____   _____HOURS_____

                        _____   _____

                        _____   _____

                        _____   _____

                        _____   _____

                        _____   _____

                        _____   _____

                        _____   _____

                        _____   _____

                        _____   _____

INSTRUCTOR(S) _____

TYPE OF TRAINING: _____

                  _____

SUPERVISOR'S
SIGNATURE: _____

RECEIVER TAG: PAGE:1

PART #:   DESC:

PO #:   VENDOR:
VEN LOT NBR: LOT STATUS CD: LOT EXP DT:

INIT: RCVD DT: B/L:
PLNR: BYR: TRANS CARR:
PRNT DT: PACK SLIP #:   FOB:
OF PKGS: P/S QTY:
DOCK LOC: DLVRY PNT: QTY RCVD:
REMARKS:

PO LINE: PART #:   PO DRWG REV:
PUR UOM: DESC:

REQ #:   REQ RCVD QTY:
ACCT #:   DLVR TO: PROJ #:
STOCK DT: COST CNTR: MNTR GROUP:
                         BIN #:

INSPECTION INFORMATION

INSP TYPE: INSP BY: INSP DATE:

QTY INSP: QTY REJ: RDR NBR:
DFCT CODE: DFCT QTY: DFCT DESC:

DISPOSITION INFORMATION

STOCK-QTY   UAI-QTY   RFR-QTY   RFC-QTY

                   SCRAP-QTY   OTHER-QTY   REWORK-QTY

SIGNATURE: COMMENTS:

STOCK ROOM INFORMATION

TOTAL QTY TO STOCK: DATE TO STOCK: RECVD BY:

LOCATIONS:

LOC-QTYS:

COMMENTS:

#_____002016

QUALITY TREND ALERT/STOP PRODUCTION REQUEST

Part/Pattern/Core No._____Description_____

Heat #/Alloy _____ Location: ☐ MF ☐ DH ☐ P3 ☐ NT ☐ DV ☐ CENT ☐ FP _____

No. Items Affected_____ of _____ Location of Parts Now_____ Photo Attached: ☐ Yes ☐ No

Description of Problem: _____

_____

_____

_____

_____

_____

_____

_____

By:_____ Location:_____ Date_____

P R O D U C T I O N	STOP STOP PRODUCTION REQUIRED? ☐ Yes ☐ No If Yes, complete the following:

PRODUCTION CONTROL

1. No. on order_____   4. No. cast last 3 months _____

2. No. to cast _____   5. No. work in process _____

3. Will be cast out by _____   By_____ Date_____

DISPOSITION (WIP/FINISHED GOODS)   By_____   Date _____

_____

_____

_____

_____

CORRECTIVE ACTION   By_____   Date _____

_____

_____

_____

_____

FOLLOW-UP   By_____   Date _____

_____

_____

_____

_____

Trial Required: ☐ Yes ☐ No   Pattern/Corebox Available Date_____Trial Release Date _____

#68-04237-81

FOUNDRY PROCESS & TOOLING

QUALITY CONTROL

DISCREPANCY REPORT DRAFT

S/O No:	Pattern:	Heat No:	Description:
Customer:			

Discrepancy:

Date & Time Noted:	Location:	Operator:	Noted By:

Form No: 48-03324-72

QUALITY ASSURANCE
IN-PROCESS RECORD

HT. NO. _____

SERIAL. NO. _____

NDE – PT ☐ MT ☐ PROCEDURE:

PROCEDURAL STANDARD:

ACCEPTANCE STANDARD:

SURFACE FINISH:

CHARTING INSTRUCTIONS:

EXAMINATION	DATE	BY	EXAMINATION	DATE	BY
_____	_____	_____	_____	_____	_____
_____	_____	_____	_____	_____	_____
_____	_____	_____	_____	_____	_____

The recording of false, fictitious or fraudulent information on this document may be punished as a felony under Federal Statutes including Federal Law, Title 18, Chapter 47.

Form No. 48-03160-84

 CORPORATION   2141 N.W. 25th Ave., Portland, Oregon 97210

QUALITY ASSURANCE DEPARTMENT

MAGNETIC PARTICLE CERTIFICATION

CUSTOMER: P.O.:

MANUFACTURING ORDER: HEAT NO.:

ITEM: SERIAL NO.:

ALLOY: PATTERN NO.:

It is hereby certified that the above described material was examined in accordance with Procedural Standard:

ACCEPTANCE STANDARD:

PROCEDURE: EXTENT:

Material was found to be acceptable.

The above examination was performed by_____date_____
a qualified   ☐ SNT-TC-1A LEVEL II

                      ☐ NAVSHIPS 250-1500-1 Inspector.

ESCO Corporation   Attested to by Witness:

By:_____   _____

                                             _____

The recording of false, fictitious or fraudulent infor-   _____
mation on this document may be punished as a felony
under Federal Statutes including Federal Law, Title 18,
Chapter 47.   _____

48-03884-84

ELCO **CORPORATION**
MATERIAL TEST REPORT

48-03547-84

CUSTOMER:		ITEM		HT. NO.
M.O.	P.O.	PATTERN		SERIAL NO.
MTL. SPEC.				

MECHANICAL

PROPERTIES

TENSILE STR.-MIN. PSI		
YIELD STR. 0.2% OFFSET PSI		
ELONG. IN 2 INCHES – PERCENT		
REDUCTION OF AREA – PERCENT		
HARDNESS – BRINELL		
HARDNESS – ROCKWELL		
IMPACT FT. LBS. – CHARPY		

CHEMICAL ANALYSIS

CARBON	MANGA-NESE	SILICON	CHROMIUM	NICKEL	MOLYB-DENUM	COPPER	SULPHUR	PHOS-PHORUS	COBALT	FERRITE*	

Acidified copper sulfate test for intergranular corrosion (Strauss)

No. specimens tested   Degree of bend

          Results: Satisfactory (no cracking)   Unsatisfactory (cracking)

Boiling nitric acid test (Huey)

Corrosion loss: I.P.M.   I.P.Y.

Weldability bend test: Degree   Results

REMARKS: *Ferrite calculated by Schoefer modification of the Schaeffler diagram.

REVIEWED BY:	The recording of false, fictitious or fraudulent information on this document may be punished as a felony under Federal Statutes including Federal Law, Title 18, Chapter 47.	We certify that the foregoing is a true and correct report of the values obtained and that they comply with the requirements of the specification unless noted otherwise.
		QUALITY ASSURANCE REP. DATE

CORP. 2141 N.W. 25th PORTLAND, ORE. 97210	**RADIOGRAPHIC REPORT**		Area	Source				Interpretation				
				Ir192	Co60	BETA	LINA	Acceptable	Surface	Inclusion	Shrink	Gas

Page _____ of _____

Customer _____

ESCO S.O. _____

Customer P.O. _____

Drawing _____

Material _____

_____

Item _____

Pattern _____

Heat No.

Film

Type	Size	No. Each	Total

Procedure: QA Review

Inspector: ☐ SNT-TC-1A Level II
                  ☐ NAVSHIPS 250-1500-1
                  ☐ MIL-STD-271-NTR-1

Notes:

Form No. 47-0-3157-2-77

CORPORATION

NDE/WELDING RECORD

| Q.A. REVIEW |
| DATE: |

Form No. 48-03159-84

CUSTOMER:			ITEM	
M.O.		P.O.	PATTERN	
ALLOY		S.N.	HEAT NUMBER	

WELDING PROCEDURES	① SMAW	② GMAW	③ GMAW (HORZ.)	④ SMAW (V.O.H.)	⑤ GTAW
ELECTRODES					
WELDING PROCEDURES	⑥ ESW	⑦ SAW	⑧ ESW	⑨	⑩
ELECTRODES					

CHART

	BY	DATE		BY	DATE		BY	DATE		BY	DATE
DEFECT REMOVAL INSPECTED											
CHARTED											
O.K. TO WELD											

HT. NO

The recording of false, fictitious or fraudulent information on this document may be punished as a felony under Federal Statutes including Federal Law, Title 18, Chapter 47.

MIL-STD-248   PQR # _____   WP- _____

                                                              DATE: _____

                        WELDING PROCEDURE QUALIFICATION DATA

WELDING PROCESS:_____ ___PLATE ___PIPE ___CASTING ___OTHER

                                              NOTE: SPECIFY OTHER _____

BASE MET'L: (1) SPEC._____ FILLER METAL: (1) GOVT SPEC. _____

              (2) GRADE OR CLASS _____   (2) MIL-TYPE _____

              (3) THICKNESS _____   (3) DIAMETER_____

              (4) GROUP NO. (S-NO.) _____   (MAX. SIZES TO BE USED

_____   IN PRODUCTION)

                        JOINT DESIGN: _____ (REF. NO. OR SKETCH) _____

                        METHOD OF EDGE PREPARATION _____

                        WELDING POSITION:_____

_____ POWER SOURCE (FOR INFO ONLY) _____

     SKETCH OF JOINT   WELDING CURRENT: _____

                        ARCH VOLTAGE RANGE:_____ RANGE: _____

ELECTRODE SIZE:_____   (SEE NOTE 1)   (SEE NOTE 1)

TRAVEL SPEED RANGE (IPM): _____   POLARITY: _____

TORCH GAS: _____   FLUX: (1) GOVT SPEC: _____

TORCH TIP SIZE (OXY-FUEL): _____   (2) MIL TYPE: _____

CUP SIZE:_____   (3) SIZE:_____

SHIELDING GAS: (1) COMPOSITION_____

                  (2) FLOW RATE RANGE _____

PURGE GAS: (1) COMPOSITION_____

                  (2) FLOW RATE RANGE _____

MINIMUM PREHEAT TEMPERATURE: _____ MAXIMUM INTERPASS TEMPERATURE_____

POST-WELD HEAT TREATMENT/TEMPERATURE: _____

WELDER/WELDING OPERATOR: _____ MAN. NO. _____ STAMP_____

NONDESTRUCTIVE TEST RESULTS: _____   DESTRUCTIVE TEXTS:

APPLICABLE ACCEPTANCE STANDARD   BEND

                                                    U.T.S.   Y.S.   EL.   TEST

RT _____   _____ ____ ____ _____

PT _____   _____ ____ ____ _____

MT _____   _____ ____ ____ _____

UT _____   _____ ____ ____ _____

VT _____

*CHARPY IMPACT TEST SHALL BE PERFORMED ON WELD AND RECORDED WHEN REQUIRED BY TABLE VII,
FOOTNOTE 2.

TEST APPROVED BY: _____ AT LABORATORY ESCO CORPORATION
                         (NAME)

DATE OF CERTIFICATION:_____   VERIFIED BY:_____

                                                               (QUALIFYING ACTIVITY)

                                                    APPROVED BY: _____

                                                              (AUTHORIZED AGENT OF
Notes to Figure 12:   NAVSHIPS)

1. In processes where amperage controls, arc voltages will be recorded for information only; and where voltage controls, amperage will be recorded for information only.

2. Any of the above items not applicable should be so indicated by ™N/AʃÌ.

Figure 12 - Suggested format for reporting qualification data.

ESCO CORPORATION

WELDING QUALIFICATION TEST RECORD

WELDING STANDARD: (·) NAVSHIPS 250-1500-1   ( ) MIL STD-248

    ( ) Sec. IX of ASME B. & P.V.C.   ( ) _____

( ) QUALIFICATION   ( ) REQUALIFICATION   ( ) PROCEDURE   ( ) WELDER

PROCESS: ( ) SMAW _____   ( ) GMAW   ( ) ESW _____   ( ) SAW _____   ( ) GTAW _____

WELDER: _____ SYMBOL _____ TEST # _____

DATE ISSUED: _____ PROCEDURE NO.: _____

FILLER MATERIAL: _____ HEAT NO.: _____

BASE METAL: _____

WELD TEST PLATE: SIZE _____ JOINT _____

FIGURE: _____ OF: _____

POST WELD HEAT TREATMENT: _____

NDE REQUIRED:	SATISFACTORY	UNSATISFACTORY
( ) PT Per _____	( )	( )
( ) RT Per _____	( )	( )
( ) MT Per _____	( )	( )
( ) UT Per _____	( )	( )

MECHANICAL PROPERTIES PER: _____

	SATISFACTORY	UNSATISFACTORY
( ) .505 TENSILE NO. _____	( )	( )
( ) REDUCED-SECTION TENSILE NO. _____	( )	( )
( ) IMPACT-TYPE: _____ NO. _____ TEMP.: _____	( )	( )
( ) BEND:		
( ) SIDE, NO. _____	( )	( )
( ) FACE, NO. _____	( )	( )
( ) ROOT, NO. _____	( )	( )

_____   _____

        DATE   WELDING SUPERVISOR

Section 2
The following quality records have been provided with the courtesy of EG&G Instruments Chandler, Tulsa, Oklahoma. They are reprinted with permission.

EG&G CHANDLER

ENGINEERING
DOCUMENT ISSUE NOTICE

ORIGINATOR: DATE ISSUED:

PRODUCT(S):

PROJECT NO. (When Applicable)   ECN NO. (When Applicable)

SPR NO. (When Applicable)   SALES ORDER NO. (When Applicable)

DOCUMENT NO.	REVISION LEVEL	DOCUMENT TITLE	ISSUED TO

FORM INSTRUCTIONS:

1. This form is to be used by the Engineering Department for the initial issue of controlled documents. (See EN-2004 "Controlled Document Approval and Issue" procedure for details.)

2. Completed forms are to be fowarded to the R&D/Engineering Assistant for filing.

EN-2004.FRM

EG&G CHANDLER ENGINEERING	CAR No.

CORRECTIVE ACTION REQUEST

CUSTOMER:	ORIGINATING DEPARTMENT:
SALES ORDER NUMBER:	ORIGINATOR:
PRODUCT:	DEPARTMENT ISSUED TO:
DATE ISSUED:	RECEIVER OF CAR:

REQUIRED COMPLIANCE DATE IS WITHIN TWO WEEKS OF DATE ISSUED

DESCRIPTION OF PROBLEM:

CORRECTIVE ACTION PROPOSED BY ORIGINATOR:

CORRECTIVE ACTION TAKEN BY RECEIVER OF CAR FORM: ECN ISSUED ☐   ECN #

OTHER ☐ (DESCRIBE)

RECEIVER:	DATE:
DEPARTMENT MANAGER:	DATE:

DISTRIBUTION: WHITE - ACTION COPY   YELLOW - TRACKING   PINK - ORIGINATOR

EG&G CHANDLER ENGINEERING

SUPPLIER CORRECTIVE ACTION REQUEST

NO. _____

DATE _____ / _____ / _____

TO _____

We Have ☐ scrapped ☐ used as is ☐ returned
Other ☐ _____

_____

Quant. _____ Our P/N _____

_____

Dwg # _____ Desc _____

_____

P.O.N _____ R.M.A _____

_____

Please provide EG&G Chandler with the appropriate corrective action which will be taken to eliminate further recurrence of this situation.   **Please reply by** _____ / _____ / _____

Reason for Request:

BUYER _____

Corrective action taken as follows
(include root cause if applicable):

VENDOR REPLY

By: Name _____ Dept. _____ Date _____ / _____ / _____

Title _____

(TO BE COMPLETED BY EG&G BELOW THIS LINE)

Purch. Reviewed & Accepted   By _____ Date _____ / _____ / _____

____ Requires further action (see below)   By _____ Date _____ / _____ / _____

WHITE - PURCHASING   YELLOW - INSPECTION   PINK - VENDOR   SCAR FILE - GOLD

EG&G INSTRUMENTS
CHANDLER

No.

ENGINEERING CHANGE NOTICE

PART NUMBER(s)	PART NAME:		REF. CAR #
			DATE:
			APPROVED BY:
			RESPONSIBLE ENGINEER:
	PART(s) USED ON:		SALES/MARKETING:
			PRODUCTION CONTROL:

ACTION REQUIRED:

REASON FOR CHANGE: ☐ COST REDUCTION   ☐ QUALITY   ☐ SAFETY   ☐ OTHER (DETAIL)

RECORD CHANGES	NEW	CHG	REV LEVEL	DATE	INITIALS	DOCUMENT PART NUMBER OR ACAD DRAWING FILENAME
DRAWINGS						
PROCEDURE						
BILL OF MATERIAL						
PART SPEC						
MANUAL						
ROUTING						
SOFTWARE						

ROUTE TO: DRIVE K:\ ☐ _____   PROD CONTROL ☐   SALES/MKTG ☐

SERVICE ☐   OTHER ☐ _____

DISPOSITION OF PARTS: ☐ USE   ☐ REWORK   ☐ SCRAP   ☐ OTHER

EFFECTIVE DATE: _____ REMARKS:

MICROFILM   SENT ☐   RETURNED ☐

PRODUCTION ACTION TAKEN:

ACTION PERFORMED BY: _____ DATE:

ECN COMPLETION DATE: _____ BY:

DISTRIBUTION: WHITE - ENGINEERING/R&D   CANARY - PRODUCTION CONTROL   PINK - CAR ORIGINATOR

EG&G INSTRUMENTS
CHANDLER

DEVIATION AUTHORIZATION
(LIMITED DESIGN VARIATION)   EN-3002

PART NUMBER:	SERIAL NUMBER(S) AFFECTED:
QUANTITY OF PARTS AFFECTED:	REQUESTOR:
PRODUCT MODEL(S) AFFECTED:	DEVIATION TYPE: ☐ NON-CONFORMING MATERIAL ☐ DOCUMENTATION
DATE OF REQUEST:	RESPONSIBLE ENGINEER:

DESCRIPTION OF DEVIATION:

DOES THE PROPOSED DEVIATION REQUIRE CHANGES TO THE PRODUCT SPECIFICATION ? ☐ YES ☐ NO

NOTE: PRODUCT SALES MANAGER AND CUSTOMER APPROVALS ARE REQUIRED IF THE DEVIATION CHANGES THE PRODUCT SPECIFICATION

APPROVAL(S):   RESPONSIBLE ENGINEER   DATE:
                                 PRODUCT SALES MANAGER   DATE:

Has the customer approved the deviation ? ☐ YES ☐ NO ☐ N/A   COMPANY:
Name of customer contact authorizing deviation: DATE OF CONTACT:

IF DISAPPROVED, LIST REASON(S): ☐ Performance ☐ Longevity ☐ Interchangeability ☐ Other (Detail Below)

CORRECTIVE ACTION REQUEST WRITTEN ? : ☐ NO ☐ YES   CAR NO.

ADDITIONAL COMMENTS:

DISTRIBUTION: WHITE - ORIGINAL (FILE)   YELLOW - RESPONSIBLE PRODUCT ENGINEER   PINK -ORIGINATOR

Section 3
The following quality records have been provided with the courtesy of The Dee Howard Company, San Antonio, Texas. They are reprinted with permission.

THE DEE HOWARD CO.
An Alenia Company

Design Quality
Audit Deficiency Notice

Org Audited:	Person Contacted:	Assigned Mgr:
System/Element Audited:	Audit Project:	DQ/ADN No.:

Deficiency/Noncompliance:

Auditor:	Dept:	Phone:	Date:

DQ/ADN To Be Returned To The Design Quality Office By:

Immediate Action Taken to Correct Noted Deficiency:

Corrective Action Initiated To Prevent Future Recurrence:

Signature of Next Level Mgr:	Dept:	Phone:	Date:
Accepted by Project Engineer:	Signature:	Date:	

To Be Completed By The Auditor

Review and Comments:

Auditor's Signature:	Date:
Accepted by Design Quality Manager:	Date:

EF402

THE DEE HOWARD CO.
An Alenia Company

Design Quality
Audit Work Sheet

Org Audited:	Person Contacted	Assigned Mgr:	
System/Element Audited:	Audit Project:		
Auditor:		Dept:	Phone:	Date:

Requirement:

Deficiency/Noncompliance:

Comments:

Requirement:

Deficiency/Noncompliance:

Comments:

Requirement:

Deficiency/Noncompliance:

Comments:

Requirement:

Deficiency/Noncompliance:

Comments:

Requirement:

Deficiency/Noncompliance:

Comments:

EF403

THE DEE HOWARD CO.
An Alenia Company

DQ Document Name

IDENTIFIER - NUMBER	DATE: XX/XX/XX	PAGE i

CURRENT REVISION:	IR													

PROJECT NAME

DQ Document Name

These technical data and the designs disclosed herein are the exclusive property of Alenia and The Dee Howard Co., or contain proprietary rights of others, and are not to be disclosed to others without the written consent of Alenia or The Dee Howard Co. The recipient of this document, by its retention and use, agrees to hold in confidence the technical data and designs contained herein. The foregoing shall not apply to persons having proprietary rights to such technical data or such designs to the extent that such rights exist.

PREPARED BY:			CHECKED BY:		
GROUP	NAME	DATE	GROUP	NAME	DATE

APPROVED BY:

GROUP	NAME	DATE	GROUP	NAME	DATE
GROUP	NAME	DATE	GROUP	NAME	DATE
GROUP	NAME	DATE	GROUP	NAME	DATE
GROUP	NAME	DATE	GROUP	NAME	DATE
GROUP	NAME	DATE	GROUP	NAME	DATE
GROUP	NAME	DATE	GROUP	NAME	DATE

AUTHORIZED BY:

		DATE
ENGINEERING VICE PRESIDENT	NAME	

EF404

THE DEE HOWARD CO.
An Alenia Company

DQ DOCUMENT NAME

PROJECT NAME								
LIST OF ACTIVE PAGES								
Page	Rev.	Date	Page	Rev.	Date	Page	Rev.	Date
i	IR							
ii	IR							
iii	IR							
1	IR							
2	IR							

IDENTIFIER - NUMBER	REV.: IR	DATE: XX/XX/XX	PAGE: ii

EF405

THE DEE HOWARD CO.
An Alenia Company

DQ DOCUMENT NAME

PROJECT NAME		
REVISION LOG		
Rev.	Description	Date
IR	Initial Release, consisting of pages i, ii, iii and 1 through	XX/XX/XX

IDENTIFIER - NUMBER	REV.: IR	DATE: XX/XX/XX	PAGE: iii

EF406

THE DEE HOWARD CO.
An Alenia Company

DQ Document Name

PROJECT NAME

Identifier - Number	Rev.: IR	Date: XX/XX/XX	Page: 1

EF407

THE DEE HOWARD CO.
An Alenia Company

ENGINEERING PROCEDURE

ENGINEERING PROCEDURE NUMBER XXX	DATE: XX/XX/XX	PAGE i

CURRENT REVISION:	IR												

TITLE

These technical data and the designs disclosed herein are the exclusive property of Alenia and The Dee Howard Co. or contain proprietary rights of others and are not to be disclosed to others without the written consent of Alenia or The Dee Howard Co. The recipient of this document, by its retention and use, agrees to hold in confidence the technical data and designs contained herein. The foregoing shall not apply to persons having proprietary rights to such technical data or such designs to the extent that such rights exist.

PREPARED BY:

GROUP	NAME	DATE	GROUP	NAME	DATE

APPROVED BY:

GROUP	NAME	DATE	GROUP	NAME	DATE
GROUP	NAME	DATE	GROUP	NAME	DATE
GROUP	NAME	DATE	GROUP	NAME	DATE
GROUP	NAME	DATE	GROUP	NAME	DATE
GROUP	NAME	DATE	GROUP	NAME	DATE
GROUP	NAME	DATE	GROUP	NAME	DATE
GROUP	NAME	DATE	GROUP	NAME	DATE
GROUP	NAME	DATE	GROUP	NAME	DATE
GROUP	NAME	DATE	GROUP	NAME	DATE

AUTHORIZED BY:

ENGINEERING VICE PRESIDENT	NAME	DATE

EF338-1B

THE DEE HOWARD CO.
An Alenia Company

ENGINEERING PROCEDURE

TITLE

REVISION LOG

Rev.	Description	Date

ENG/PROC-XXX	REV.: X	DATE: XX/XX/XX	PAGE: ii

EF338-13A

THE DEE HOWARD CO.
An Alenia Company

ENGINEERING PROCEDURE

TITLE

ENG/PROC-XXX	REV.: X	DATE: XX/XX/XX	PAGE: 6

EF338-3B

Section 4

The following quality records have been provided with the courtesy of FSSL, Inc., Sugar Land, Texas. They are reprinted with permission.

The Contract Authorization form authorizes the creation and approval of a contract between FSSL, Inc. and another company.

		PAGE OF	
CONTRACT AUTHORIZATION		SALES NO.	JOB NO.
		ISSUE DATE	QUOTE NO.

CUSTOMER	CONTRACT NUMBER(S)

CONTRACT TITLE

CONTRACT EFFECTIVE DATE	THRU	CONTRACT SHIP DATE

PROGRAM MANAGER	PROJECT ENGINEER	MARKETING CONTACT

TYPE OF CONTRACT: ☐ FIXED PRICE   ☐ TIME & MATERIAL   ☐ FIELD SERVICE

DISTRIBUTION:

NAME   NAME

MARKETING

PROJECTS

FORM 1040   REV. C

The Contract Change Authorization is a form that documents mutually-agreed changes to a contract.

	PAGE OF
CONTRACT CHANGE AUTHORIZATION ████*Inc.*	REVISION NUMBER
	SALES NO. / JOB NO.
	ISSUE DATE / QUOTE NO.
CONTRACT TITLE	CONTRACT NO.

DISTRIBUTION:

NAME   NAME

MARKETING

PROJECTS

FSSI FORM 1041   REV. B

The Production Release Authorization form indicates the release of items for production so that the purchase of parts and assembly may begin.

Inc.

PRA NO. _____

DATE _____

PRODUCTION RELEASE AUTHORIZATION

PROJECT TITLE _____ MJO_____

RELEASE STATUS INFORMATION	REQUIRED DISTRIBUTION

RELEASE STATUS INFORMATION

Partial ___

Complete ___

Previous Release Made ___ Yes ___ No

REQUIRED DISTRIBUTION
Released Documents Received

Q.A. _____

Mfg./Plng. _____

REFERENCE

Top Assembly _____

IDL (if used)_____

Other _____

OTHER DISTRIBUTION (CHECK)

☐ Cognizant Engineer

☐ Project Engineer

☐ Program Management

☐ _____

☐ _____

DOCUMENT RELEASED

SIZE	SHEETS	DOCUMENT NUMBER	DOCUMENT TITLE
___	___	_____	_____
___	___	_____	_____
___	___	_____	_____
___	___	_____	_____
___	___	_____	_____
___	___	_____	_____
___	___	_____	_____
___	___	_____	_____

AUTHORIZATION

Immediate Supvr. _____ Date _____

Cognizant Engr. _____ Date _____

Documentation Cntrl. _____ Date _____

Sheet ____ of ____

The Engineering Change Notice Form is used to document changes to a drawing or specification and to ensure that all interested parties are informed of these changes.

ECN

DATE _____/_____/_____ ORIGINATOR _____ ECN NO. _____

DOCUMENT NO. _____-_____-_____ REV. _____ SIZE _____

DOC TITLE _____

PROJECT(S) _____ MJO _____

REASON FOR CHANGE:	[] DESIGN REVIEW	[] CLIENT COMMENTS	[] PRODUCTION/AS BUILT	[] TRAVELING ECN

APPROVALS	DATE	ITEMS AFFECTED	RECOMMENDED DISPOSITION
COGNIZANT ENG.		[] IN PURCHASING/VENDOR [] IN MANUFACTURE	
ENG. APPROVAL		[] IN INVENTORY [] IN FIELD	
		[] OTHER _____	(USE, SCRAP, REWORK, ETC. IDENTIFY PROCEDURE)

DESCRIPTION OF CHANGE: (DESCRIBE IN TERMS OF "WAS" AND "IS") SHEET _____ OF _____

- -
- -
- -
- -
- -
- -
- -
- -
- -
- -
- -
- -
- -
- -
- -
- -
- -
- -

DOCUMENTS AFFECTED (LOM, FDS, INTERFACE, CALCULATIONS, FAT, MANUALS, PROCEDURES, DRAWINGS, ASSEMBLIES, ENG. STANDARDS)

-	-	REV	-	-	REV	-	-	REV	-	-	REV
-	-	REV	-	-	REV	-	-	REV	-	-	REV

ECN INCORPORATION RECORD FOR DRAWING / DOCUMENT (INITIAL AND DATE)

				INITIAL ROUTING	FINAL ROUTING
DESIGNER	CHECKER	NEW REV.	CAD	Q.A. (1)	Q.A. (1)
				MANF. (1)	MANF. (1)
COGN. ENG.	DFT. SUP.	DOC. CLK.	NETWORK	OTHER	OTHER

FORM # 1007(PAGE 1) REV. E

The Purchase Order form lists items FSSL wishes to purchase, and quality requirements for the parts.

FSSL, Inc.
525 JULIE RIVERS DRIVE ΣSUGAR LAND, TEXAS 77478-2835
713/240-1122 ΣTELEX 774-248 ΣFAX 713/240-0951

PURCHASE ORDER

BUYER	DISPOSITION	PURCHASE ORDER NO.	AMENDMENT NUMBER	PAGE

ISSUED TO

SHIP TO

CONFIRMED TO: PHONE:

DATE	SHIP VIA	TERMS	F.O.B.	TEXAS SALES TAX EXEMPTION #1-76-0138001 ☐ TAXABLE ☐ EXEMPT

ITEM	QUANTITY	FSSL PART NO.	DESCRIPTION	QUALITY CODE	ACCOUNT CODE	UNIT COST	TOTAL COST	DATE REQ AT PLAN

BY ACCEPTANCE OF THIS PURCHASE ORDER AND PERFORMANCE UNDER, YOU

AGREE TO COMPLY FULLY WITH THE CONDITIONS OF PURCHASE STATED ON

THE REVERSE SIDE HEREOF AND HEREBY MADE PART OF THIS ORDER.

BUYER_____

PURCHASING MANAGER _____

_____   _____
SIGNATURE   DATE

Production Work Orders are master documents for controlling and documenting manufacturing processes.

PRODUCTION WORK ORDER

SHT. 1 OF

DESCRIPTION						M.J.O.		SUB	WORK ORDER NO.	ISSUE	RUN	RUN	RUN	RUN
SIZE	DRAWING NO.	REV.	SIZE	DRAWING NO.	REV.	SALES NO.			PART NO.		QTY	QTY	QTY	QTY
						ACCT			INVEN. PROD. AUTH		DUE	DUE	DUE	DUE
						SERIALIZATION		MFG. RELEASE		DELIVER TO:			PRIORITY	

SHOP	OPER. NO.	INSTRUCTIONS	STD HRS	DUE	QTY MOVED	DATE MOVED	QA-SA STAMP

WORK ORDER OPENING		WORK ORDER CLOSING		WORK ORDER CHANGE RECORD			
PLANNER	DATE	PLANNER	DATE	W/O ISSUE	DATE	ECN NO.	CHANGED BY
		DATE					
MANUFACTURING APPROVAL _____ ___							
QUALITY ASSURANCE APPROVAL _____ ___							

FORM 1038 1/94 REV.C

ECN. 8260

OPERATION	D I S C R E P A N C Y	TESTER OR INSPECTOR	REWORKED BY	APPROVED BY INSP/TEST

The As Shipped Configuration Verification Record (ASCVR) form is used to record traceability and configuration control for traceable items.

The form is an "AS SHIPPED CONFIGURATION VERIFICATION RECORD (ASCVR)" which contains the following fields:

- ASSY No.: _____ REV.: _____ SERIAL No.: _____ Page _____ of _____
- PROJECT: _____ INSPECTOR: _____ DATE: _____
- CUSTOMER P.O. No.: _____ JOB No.: _____ SHIPPER No.: _____

ITEM No.	PART No.	DESCRIPTION	REV.	QTY	SERIAL or HEAT No.	MATL CERT	REC. VERIFY	WAIVE

A Discrepancy Report form is used to process nonconformances discovered during incoming inspection.

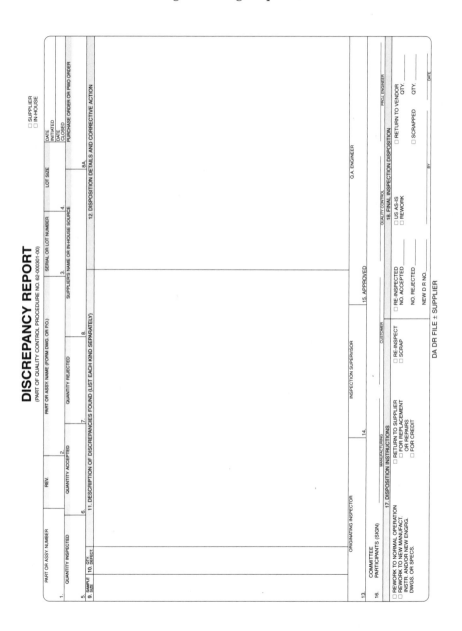

The Corrective Action Request form is used to document problems that affect the quality of FSSL's products. It is used for problems that are not easily handled with a discrepancy report.

CORRECTIVE ACTION REQUEST

CAR No:_____
DATE:_____

Directed to: _____ Answer Due: _____

Originator: _____

Description of Problem:

Probable Cause:

Corrective Action:

Completion Date: _____ Signature: _____ Date: _____

Corrective Action Approved By:_____ Date: _____

Corrective Action Close Out Verified By: _____ Date: _____

Design Review forms are used to document all items that must be acted upon and indicate who is responsible for said actions.

DESIGN REVIEW MINUTES

DATE _____		SHEET_____ OF _____	

PROJECT _____ ITEM _____

TYPE: ATTENDEES:
_____ Concept   Chairman: _____
_____ Development   Eng. Supervisor (Proj. Engr.) _____
_____ Interface   Cognizant Engr.: _____
_____ Final   Other:_____
                                            _____
                                            _____
                                            _____

ITEM	DETAIL	ACTION	COMMENTS

File:F:/APP/WP51/DSNMIN.

Design Review Checklist enumerates certain items that all designs need to fulfill.

DESIGN REVIEW CHECKLIST

ARE DESIGN CRITERIA DOCUMENTED?
Standards, regulations
Functional requirements
Functional and dimensional interface
Loads - functional and environmental
Material requirements
Reliability requirements
Safety requirements
Type approval requirements/certification
IS THE DESIGN SATISFACTORY REGARDING?
Meeting design criteria (contract or FDS)
Calculations (Stress, pressure, etc.)
Consideration of standards and regulations
Drawings conforming to Company standards
Appropriate tolerances and dimensions
Purchasing considerations
Inspection considerations (Quality notes)
Packaging Requirements
Transport Requirements
Installation Requirements
Welding Details
Testing considerations
Coating requirements
Cost effectiveness

File: F:\app\wp51\dsncklst

The Purchase Part Number Request form is filled out every time a new part is ordered. The form contains all of the information required to purchase the part.

PART NO: _____

PART NO: _____

PURCHASED PART NUMBER REQUEST

FSSL NO: _____
MILITARY: _____
VETCO NO: _____

DESC: _____
_____
_____
_____

PREF. MFG: _____ NO: _____
ALT MFG: _____ NO: _____
ALT MFG: _____ NO: _____

UNIT OF MEASURE: _____ PROJECT: _____

REQUESTER: _____ ADDED INFO: _____
DATE REQ.: _____ _____
LAST UPDATE: _____

NEW PART APPROVALS	DRAWING INFORMATION
DOC CLERK: _____	SIZE: _____
REL DATE: _____	DRAWER: _____
	LAST ECN: _____
	OLD REV: _____ NEW REV: _____

FORM NO 1112 DATED 5/19/93.   FILE: PPNRLDWG

USE "SAME AS" FUNCTION FOR P/N _____

Examples of Records from a Commercial Records Storage Facility

The following records have been provided with the courtesy of The File Box, Austin, Texas. They are reprinted with permission.

FILE BOX
RECORDS MANAGEMENT FACILITY

☐ BILL OF LADING

☐ INVOICE

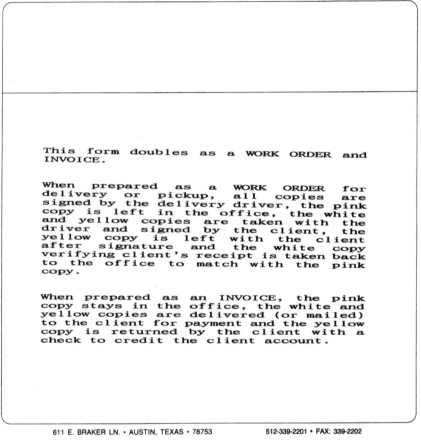

This form doubles as a WORK ORDER and INVOICE.

When prepared as a WORK ORDER for delivery or pickup, all copies are signed by the delivery driver, the pink copy is left in the office, the white and yellow copies are taken with the driver and signed by the client, the yellow copy is left with the client after signature and the white copy verifying client's receipt is taken back to the office to match with the pink copy.

When prepared as an INVOICE, the pink copy stays in the office, the white and yellow copies are delivered (or mailed) to the client for payment and the yellow copy is returned by the client with a check to credit the client account.

611 E. BRAKER LN. • AUSTIN, TEXAS • 78753   512-339-2201 • FAX: 339-2202

☐ SECURITY   ☐ 24 HOUR SERVICE   ☐ FIRE PROTECTION   ☐ PICK-UP & DELIVERY SERVICE

☐ COMPUTERIZED BARCODE SYSTEM   ☐ VAULT STORAGE AVAILABLE—CLIMATE CONTROLLED

☐ MONTHLY REPORTS AVAILABLE   ☐ ON-SITE DESTRUCTION   ☐ SUPPLIES   ☐ CLEAN-MODERN FACILITY

FILE BOX
RECORD MANAGEMENT FACILITY

611 E. BRAKER LN.
AUSTIN, TX 78753
PH. (512) 339-2201
FAX (512) 339-2202

Inventory Transmittal

ACCOUNT #:   **DEPT #:**   **ACCOUNT NAME:**

BARCODE #	CUSTOMER'S #	DESTROY DATE	MEDIA TYPE	DATE RANGE FROM	TO	SEQUENCE RANGE FROM	TO
(6)	(12)		(8)			(15)	(15)

Description: _____

The Client prepares this form with

all pertinent information keeping

Description: _____

the yellow copy for their record

Description: _____

and sending the white copy to the

storage facility with the

Description: _____

containers to be stored.

Description: _____

Description: _____

Description: _____

Description: _____

THIS INVENTORY IS TO BE STORED IN ☐ **WAREHOUSE** ☐ **VAULT**

Inventory Transmittal

FILE BOX
RECORD MANAGEMENT FACILITY

611 E. BRAKER LN.
AUSTIN, TX 78753
PH. (512) 339-2201
FAX (512) 339-2202

ACCOUNT #: **DEPT #:** **ACCOUNT NAME:**

BARCODE #	CUSTOMER'S #	DESTROY DATE	MEDIA TYPE	DATE RANGE FROM	TO	SEQUENCE RANGE FROM	TO
(6)	(12)		(8)			(15)	(15)

Description:

Description:

Description:

Description:

Description:

Description:

Description:

THIS INVENTORY IS TO BE STORED IN ☐ **WAREHOUSE** ☐ **VAULT**

FILE BOX

|||||||||

RECORD MANAGEMENT FACILITY
611 E. Braker Ln   Austin, TX 78753   Ph. (512) 339-2201   Fax (512) 339-2202

MEMORANDUM:

To facilitate your requests and to keep our information current, please fill in as indicated and return this form to our office. The signatures of the persons authorized must appear opposite their names. Please have an officer of the firm sign at the bottom.

The form is sent to you in duplicate but we require the original only. Please keep the copy for your own files.

Thank you.

AUTHORIZATION FOR ACCESS

THIS SHALL BE CONSIDERED AUTHORIZATION FOR THE FOLLOWING NAMED INDIVIDUALS TO HAVE ACCESS TO THE CONTENTS HELD IN THE ACCOUNT OF

ACCOUNT NAME	ACCOUNT NUMBER	
PRINTED NAME	**SIGNATURE**	

This form is delivered to the Client before any containers are stored in the storage facility. The Client lists all people in their office who may have access to the files or containers and has each sign. The white copy is returned to the storage facility and the yellow copy is kept by the client. If any changes are necessary, the Client requests the original Authorization for Access be returned to their office to be updated. No one can request a file or container unless listed on the Authorization for Access. The delivery drivers will not leave a file or container unless someone on the Authorization for Access signs the work order.

ADDITION TO PREVIOUS AUTHORIZATION ☐	VOIDS ALL PREVIOUS AUTHORIZATION ☐	
SIGNATURE OF COMPANY OFFICER	**POSITION**	**DATE**

Exhibit B   NA 500

FILE BOX

RECORD MANAGEMENT FACILITY
611 E. Braker Ln   Austin, TX 78753   Ph. (512) 339-2201   Fax (512) 339-2202

MEMORANDUM:

To facilitate your requests and to keep our information current, please fill in as indicated and return this form to our office. The signatures of the persons authorized must appear opposite their names. Please have an officer of the firm sign at the bottom.

The form is sent to you in duplicate but we require the original only. Please keep the copy for your own files.

Thank you.

AUTHORIZATION FOR ACCESS

THIS SHALL BE CONSIDERED AUTHORIZATION FOR THE FOLLOWING NAMED INDIVIDUALS TO HAVE ACCESS TO THE CONTENTS HELD IN THE ACCOUNT OF

ACCOUNT NAME	ACCOUNT NUMBER
PRINTED NAME	**SIGNATURE**
ADDITION TO PREVIOUS AUTHORIZATION ☐	VOIDS ALL PREVIOUS AUTHORIZATION ☐

SIGNATURE OF COMPANY OFFICER	POSITION	DATE

Additional Sources:
Useful Addresses and Periodicals

Addresses

American National Standards Institute (ANSI)
11 West 42nd Street
New York, New York 10036
212-642-4900

American Society for Quality Control (ASQC)
611 East Wisconsin Avenue
P.O. Box 3005
Milwaukee, Wisconsin 53201-3005
800-248-1946 or 414-272-8575

Association for Information and Image Management (AIIM)
1100 Wayne Avenue
Suite 1100
Silver Spring, Maryland 20910-5699
301-587-8202

Association of Records Managers and Administrators (ARMA)
4200 Somerset Drive

Suite 215
Prairie Village, Kansas 66208
800-422-2762 or 913-341-3808

CEEM Information Services
10521 Braddock Road
Fairfax, Virginia 22032
800-669-1567

Information Handling Services (IHS)
15 Inverness Way East
P.O. Box 1154
Englewood, Colorado 80150-1154
303-790-0600

Information Requirements Clearinghouse
5600 South Quebec Street
Suite 250-C
Englewood, Colorado 80111
303-721-7500

Periodicals

ARMA Records Management Quarterly
published by Association of Records Managers and
    Administrators
4200 Somerset Drive
Suite 215
Prairie Village, Kansas 66208
800-422-2762 or 913-341-3808

Disaster Recovery Journal
published by Systems Support, Inc.
P.O. Box 510110
St. Louis, Missouri 63151
314-894-0276

Document Management & Windows Imaging
published by Pinnacle Peak Publishing, Ltd.

3910 E. McDowell Road
Phoenix, Arizona 85008
602-224-9777

Imaging magazine
published by Telecom Library, Inc.
12 West 21st Street
New York, New York 10010
212-691-8215

IMC Journal
published by International Information Management Congress
1650 West 38th Street
Suite 205W
Boulder, Colorado 80301
303-440-7085

Inform
published by Association for Information and Image Management
1100 Wayne Avenue
Suite 1100
Silver Spring, Maryland 20910-5699
301-587-8202

Managing Office Technology
published by Penton Publications
1100 Superior Avenue
Cleveland, Ohio 44114-2543
216-696-7000

Records & Retrieval Report
published by The Greenwood Publishing Group, Inc.
88 Post Road West
P.O. Box 5007
Westport, Connecticut 06881
203-226-3571

Glossary

Excerpted and modified from *Glossary of Records Management Terms* (Prairie Village, Kans.: Association of Records Managers and Administrators, 1989).

Active record   Record needed to carry out an organization's day-to-day business; record subject to frequent use.

Administrative value   In appraisal, the usefulness of a record to the originating or succeeding agency in the conduct of its business.

Aperture card (modified ARMA definition)   An electronic data processing card with a rectangular hole, specifically designed as a carrier for a film image or images. Frequently used for engineering designs and drawings.

Archival value   The determination in appraisal that records are worthy of indefinite or permanent preservation.

Archives   The facilities where records of an organization are preserved because of their continuing or historical value.

Backup copy   A duplicate of a record kept for reference in case the original is lost or destroyed.

Central records   The files of several offices or organizational units physically and/or functionally centralized and managed.

411

Commercial records center   A records center, operated by an independent firm, that houses the records of several organizations on a fee basis.

Compact disc—read-only memory (CD-ROM)   An optical disk which can be read only; it cannot be written on. Used in applications where multiple copies are made from a master disk.

Computer output microfilm (COM)   1. An electronic method of converting computer-stored data to a human-readable language on microfilm. 2. Microforms containing data produced, either on- or off-line, from computer-generated signals.

Decentralized records   Records that are not centrally located. These records are often located at the point of origin or usage.

Disposition   The final action for records—normally occurring at the end of their retention period.

Document control (not an ARMA term)   A system of managing documents, distributing documents, and keeping records about the documents that have been created by an organization as part of its overall quality system.

Documentation (not an ARMA term)   As it is used in the ISO 9000 standards, encompasses both records and documents.

Documents (not an ARMA definition)   Procedures, policies, instructions, or other written or graphically depicted methods or ways of conducting either oneself or the operations in a given organization.

File management   The creating, retrieving, and updating of records within a file, and the housekeeping involving the contents of the file.

Forms management   The function that establishes standards for the creation, design, analysis, and revision of all forms within an organization.

Hard copy   The paper copy of a record.

Inactive record   A record that does not have to be readily available, but which must be kept for legal, fiscal, or historical purposes.

Lateral file cabinet Storage equipment that is wider than it is deep. Files can be arranged front to back or side by side.

Life cycle (of a record) The span of time of a record from its creation or receipt through its useful life to its final disposition or retention as a historical record.

Nonrecord material Records not usually included within the scope of official records (for example, convenience file, day file, reference material, and so on).

Official record (modified ARMA definition) A record that is legally recognized as establishing some fact.

Optical disk A high-density information storage medium where digitally encoded information is both written and read by means of a laser.

Permanent record Information that is required by law to be retained indefinitely or that has been designated for continuous preservation because of reference, historical, or administrative significance to the organization.

Record Recorded information, regardless of medium or characteristics, made or received by an organization and that is useful in the operation of the organization.

Record series A group of similar or related records that are normally used and filed as a unit and can be evaluated as a unit for determining the records retention period.

Records center A centralized area for housing and servicing inactive or semiactive records whose reference rate does not warrant their retention in the prime office area. This is usually a lower-cost facility.

Records inventory (modified ARMA definition) A detailed listing of the volume, type, function, and organization of records in order to evaluate, appraise, and organize the collection.

Records management (modified ARMA definition) The scientific and systematic control of all records that are required for conducting the business of an organization—from their creation or receipt, through their processing, distribution, organization, storage, and retrieval to their ultimate disposition.

Records manager   The individual within an organization who is assigned the responsibility of systematically managing the recorded information generated and received by the organization.

Records retention schedule   A comprehensive list of records series, indicating for each series the length of time it is to be maintained, and when such series may be reviewed for destruction or archival retention. It often indicates retention in active and inactive storage areas.

Records value   The usefulness of records for administrative, legal, fiscal, and historical purposes.

Retention period   The time records must be kept according to legal and/or organizational requirements.

Tickler file   A date-sequenced file by which matters pending are brought forward for attention on the proper date.

Vertical file cabinet   Storage equipment that is deeper than it is wide. Files can be arranged front to back or side by side.

Vital record   A record containing information essential for emergency operations during a disaster; the resumption and/or continuation of operations; the re-establishment of the legal, financial and/or functional status of the organization; the determination of the rights and obligations of individuals and corporate bodies with respect to the organization.

The author gratefully acknowledges permission from the Association of Records Managers and Administrators to use or modify glossary terms from its *Glossary of Records Management Terms.* Those interested in purchasing the entire publication can contact the publisher at 800-422-2762 (United States) or 800-433-2762 (Canada).

Selected Bibliography

In addition to the works presented here, readers are referred to the list of professional associations and periodicals presented in appendix I. Publications pertaining to various aspects of records management are too numerous to be cited here. The professional associations all have publications catalogs that can be requested.

ANSI/ASQC Q9000-1-1994. *Quality Management and Quality Assurance Standards—Guidelines for Selection and Use.* Milwaukee, Wis.: American Society for Quality Control, 1994.

ANSI/ASQC Q9001-1994. *Quality Systems—Model for Quality Assurance in Design, Development, Production, Installation, and Servicing.* Milwaukee, Wis.: American Society for Quality Control, 1994.

ANSI/ASQC Q9002-1994. *Quality Systems—Model for Quality Assurance in Production, Installation, and Servicing.* Milwaukee, Wis.: American Society for Quality Control, 1994.

ANSI/ASQC Q9003-1994. *Quality Systems—Model for Quality Assurance in Final Inspection and Test.* Milwaukee, Wis.: American Society for Quality Control, 1994.

ANSI/ASQC Q9004-1-1994. *Quality Management and Quality System Elements—Guidelines.* Milwaukee, Wis.: American Society for Quality Control, 1994.

Association of Records Managers and Administrators. *Developing and Operating a Records Retention Program: A Guideline.* Prairie Village, Kans.: Association of Records Managers and Administrators, 1986.

————. *Magnetic Diskette Recovery Procedures.* Prairie Village, Kans.: Association of Records Managers and Administrators, 1987.

————. *Records Center Operations*, 3rd ed. Prairie Village, Kans.: Association of Records Managers and Administrators, 1986.

————. *Vital Records: A Guideline*, 2nd ed. Prairie Village, Kans.: Association of Records Managers and Administrators, 1993.

Black, David B. *Document Capture for Document Imaging Systems.* Silver Spring, Md.: Association for Information and Image Management, 1992.

Bulgawicz, Susan L., CRM, and Dr. Charles E. Nolan, CRM. *Disaster Prevention and Recovery: A Planned Approach.* Prairie Village, Kans.: Association of Records Managers and Administrators, 1988.

D'Alleyrand, Marc R. *Image Storage and Retrieval Systems.* New York: McGraw-Hill, 1989.

Gorelick, Jamie S., Stephen Marzen, and Lawrence Solum. *Destruction of Evidence.* New York: John Wiley & Sons, 1989.

Green, Marj, ed. *The Business Forms Handbook*, 4th ed. Alexandria, Va.: National Business Forms Association, 1990.

Griffiths, Jose-Marie and Donald W. King, *Cost Indicators for Selected Records Management Activities: A Guide to Unit Costing for the Records Manager*, Vol. 1. ed. Elizabeth Atwood-Gailey. Prairie Village, Kans.: Association of Records Managers and Administrators, 1993.

Jacobs, Marvin. *Forms Design: The Basic Course—Plus!* Cleveland, Ohio: Marvin Jacobs, 1980.

Langemo, Mark, CRM, and Daniel A. Brathal. *Managing Business Forms.* Prairie Village, Kans.: Association of Records Managers and Administrators, 1988.

Lundgren, Terry D. and Carol A. Lundgren. *Records Management in the Computer Age.* Boston, Mass.: PWS–Kent, 1989.

Penn, Ira A., Gail Pennix, and Jim Coulson. *Records Management Handbook,* 2nd ed. Brookfield, Vt.: Gower Publishing Co., 1994.

Phillips, John T., Jr., CRM, and Paul Tarrant. *Software Directory for Automated Records Management Systems.* Prairie Village, Kans.: Association of Records Managers and Administrators, 1993.

Ricks, Betty R., Ann J. Swafford, and Kay F. Gow. *Information and Image Management: A Records System Approach,* 3rd ed. Cincinnati, Ohio: Southwestern, 1992.

Robek, Mary F., CRM, Gerald F. Brown, CRM, and Wilmer O. Maedke, CRM. *Information and Records Management,* 3rd ed. Mission Hills, Calif.: Glencoe Publishing Co., 1987.

Saffady, William. *Electronic Document Imaging Systems: Design, Evaluation, and Implementation.* Westport, Conn.: Meckler, 1993.

———. *Managing Electronic Records.* Prairie Village, Kans.: Association of Records Managers and Administrators, 1992.

———. *Micrographic Systems,* 3rd ed. Silver Spring, Md.: Association for Information and Image Management, 1990.

———. *Micrographics,* 2nd ed. Littleton, Col.: Libraries Unlimited, Inc., 1985.

———. *Optical Disk Systems for Records Management.* Prairie Village, Kans.: Association of Records Managers and Administrators, 1988.

———. *Optical Disks vs. Magnetic Storage.* Westport, Conn.: Meckler, 1990.

———. *Optical Disks vs. Micrographics.* Westport, Conn.: Meckler, 1993.

Skupsky, Donald S., JD, CRM. *Legal Requirements for Business Records: Federal Requirements.* Denver, Col.: Information Requirements Clearinghouse. (Binder, subscription service, and continual updates available.)

————. *Legal Requirements for Business Records: State Requirements.* Denver, Col.: Information Requirements Clearinghouse. (Binder, subscription service, continual updates available.)

————. *Legal Requirements for Microfilm, Computer and Optical Disk Records.* Denver, Col.: Information Requirements Clearinghouse, 1991.

————. *Recordkeeping Requirements.* Denver, Col.: Information Requirements Clearinghouse, 1991.

————. *Records Retention Procedures.* Denver, Col.: Information Requirements Clearinghouse, 1991.

Williams, Robert F., ed. *Legality of Microfilm.* Chicago, Ill.: Cohasset Associates. (Binder, subscription service, continual updates available.)

————. *Legality of Optical Storage.* Chicago, Ill.: Cohasset Associates. (Binder, subscription service, continual updates available.)

Wallace, Dr. Patricia E., CRM, JoAnn Lee, Ed.D., and Dexter R. Schubert. *Records Management: Integrated Information Systems*, 3rd ed. Englewood Cliffs, N.J.: Prentice Hall, 1992.

Index